What is the real value of excellence in architecture?

Victoria Thornton Hon FRIBA
Founding Director, Open House

The way we plan, design and build our citie
the better in many ways: good architecture
change the way we relate to our neighbour
create new employment and revitalise negl
health and well-being. The impact of good c
environment, stronger communities with a .... pride
in their local area, and new financial investment. Well-designed buildings
and public spaces are, therefore, vital in creating and sustaining a vibrant
city, from Westminster to Waltham Forest and from Camden to Croydon.
Contemporary architecture that is aspirational, innovative and visionary
can help to create a society with the same characteristics.

However, architecture is not a subject taught in the formal
education system. From school to later life, we often have no formal way
of learning how to express our ideas, needs and aspirations for the quality
of the buildings and public spaces in which we live, work, play and learn.
Open House believes everyone should have the opportunity to articulate
their views and concerns by having the right tools and language.

Open House is a respected and trusted organisation that responds
to the demands of its ever-growing audience of decision-makers, young
people and the wider community. The organisation plays a unique role
in the capital through campaigning for the independent voice, through
its London-wide remit, and through the number and diversity of people
it reaches. Its coherent approach to people and place focuses on action
research, experiential learning, exploring inspirational exemplars and
sharing good practice. Through this, Open House encourages everyone in
London to invest in good contemporary design by seeing its value.

Open House continues to make a real and practical impact by
connecting professionals, practitioners, decision-makers and Londoners
across all 33 boroughs, encouraging their mutual understanding to make
the capital a better place. We look forward to continuing to develop our
research and initiatives to focus strategically London-wide and on places
of change in the capital.

Victoria Thornton

How is London changing?

The Rt Hon Nick Raynsford MP
Open House Trustee and
Chair of Supporters at Large

Cities have continuously evolved through time, but their success has always been dependent on them providing a safe and attractive environment in which people can live, work and relax. In the increasingly competitive global context of the 21st century, the prosperity of each city will depend on its ability to satisfy these requirements.

London starts with many advantages, boasting 2000 years of history, a reputation as a home of world-class contemporary design, and an almost unparalleled economic and cultural infrastructure. As well as all these qualities, London's unique character reflects its astonishingly varied texture of diverse neighbourhoods linked together by a complex web of streets, rivers and transport networks. This rich urban geography is not static, but is changing all the time as the transformation of Canary Wharf, the Greenwich Peninsula and now the Olympic Park demonstrates so clearly.

The quality of our urban design is therefore vital to our city's future, and now more than ever we need to understand, value and advocate for the highest design standards in our built environment. Open House has performed an exceptional service over the past 17 years in raising the profile of London's buildings and public spaces, and raising awareness of their value. In Open House's 18th year I am happy to commend its vitally important work and to urge all those with responsibility for London's built environment to heed its message.

OpenHouse London

Celebrate the Capital's Architecture

19–20 September 2009

Your chance to explore hundreds of inspiring buildings for FREE. Discover how great buildings shape our lives.

openhouse.org.uk/london

OPEN HOUSE

Open House

London's leading architecture education organisation

Contents

About the organisation

Open House London 09

Open House is a unique, independent organisation committed to raising the standard for London's architecture and built environment by opening people's eyes and minds to good design.

How do we relate to our city?

Edwin Heathcote
Architectural Critic
Financial Times,
Open House Trustee

The city, the most complex and extraordinary result of civilisation, exists at different levels: as an idea – the skyline, the monuments, the museums; as a network – the intricate weave of streets and squares, of transport and communications; and as a backdrop – the frame against which we play out the dramas and rituals of our everyday lives. Each incarnation demands a distinct approach yet one that communicates and negotiates with each of the others.

Recent architectural debate has been dominated by the 'icon' but no city can be made of icons. In fact icons are anathema to the everyday: the city is made of the ordinary. That sounds dull but it isn't, because London's deep layers of history and memory, combined with and overlaid by the contemporary, create a subtly shifting palimpsest of endless invention and adaptation. Pieces of the city are reused and reinvented, they fall in and out of favour and fashion, and each era leaves its traces on a compelling background.

Each section of the city has embedded within it a story and is itself a part of the larger urban narrative. Those who have stewardship of the city must become conscious of that story and work with the fabric, not against it, to elaborate the story and make it clearer while adding a layer that brings new life. Every intervention has the potential to be a complex, endlessly fascinating template for a new chapter, but equally could become a dead end, an appendix.

London, possibly more than any other city, has proved able to reinvent itself whilst building on its own mythology and an awareness of the beauty in the subtlest patterns of its fabric rather than in the quest for the theatrical and the formal. Its narrative will develop best when those who are responsible for shaping it dig down into the layers of change, to discern what it is about the areas and buildings that have been and are able to accommodate industry and commerce but also luxury and consumption, that have made the city what it is.

It is less about the iconic than about the fabric, the pavements on which we walk, the blend of old and new, of how the city speaks to us through the parks, streets and alleys, of how the ground and the buildings rising from it become the set against which we can live our lives as best we can, and as we can only in London.

Outside In: London's public spaces

Focusing on buildings is only one part of Open House's work. Just as much as buildings, our streets, squares and parks define the experience of the city and of the neighbourhoods where we live. Thinking more holistically about these places with all involved – from those initiating the projects, such as developers or public sector clients, to those creating and designing them – is part of Open House's remit.

Cultural meaning and identity affects the experience of public spaces as much as design. Current projects such as the Mayor's Great Spaces and the Olympic Park and its legacy underline this emphasis. Open House's research programmes and professional forums examine our spaces from the outside in, looking at how they affect our behaviour and the city's cultural identity, to influence policy and raise debate for new developments and places of change.

Working with young people across London, our My City Too! programme has evidenced what they want from the places they inhabit: from their function, design and quality to the role of public art. Bringing together artists, architects, developers, policy-makers and others, our Art in the Open initiative advocates a more inspirational environment for London. As London's independent advisor on art in the public realm, it focuses on themes of common interest such as light, commemoration and celebration, and urban change.

Together our initiatives reflect our belief that public space only benefits from more inclusive creative thinking across professional disciplines, generations and perspectives. At a time of financial uncertainty Open House's aim is to show the continued value of our public spaces and the importance of creativity in these diverse dialogues to affect London's everyday experience.

Corina, 15, My City Too! Young Ambassador
"It's true that changes in London's spaces need to be for the good of everyone, so everyone's views need to be taken into account, including young people. One day we will be the ones living and working in the city!"

Elliot Lipton, Managing Director, First Base Ltd, Chair of Art in the Open Advisory Board
"Good public space has the ability to transform new developments by influencing how we relate to our homes, surrounding communities and the city. It is just as important as the design of the buildings themselves and we need to ensure that we support its quality and experience. Art in the Open, as part of Open House, plays a fundamental role for London in the development of exceptional public spaces by encouraging greater collaboration between the built environment and the visual arts sectors including clients, commissioners, artists and architects."

Learning about architecture

Against the backdrop of one of the largest-ever programmes of school building and refurbishment, we must create opportunities for young people in particular to learn how they can influence the quality of the capital's contemporary architecture for the better.

Learning about architecture can open up new ways of expressing ideas, reinvigorate perceptions of the world around us, and deepen an understanding of the individual's role and responsibility in wider society. To break down the social and cultural barriers that prevent people from becoming involved in the shaping of their environment, we must enable them to engage effectively with design ideas. Open House believes this is possible through a unique model of experience, exploration and – most importantly – creative interactive learning.

Open House year-round programmes of seminars, workshops and masterclasses for architects, teachers, governors, local authority officers and councillors and others involved in educational transformation develop participants' ability to evaluate and argue for design quality. Our network across the property, planning and policy-making worlds also enables them to share new ideas and exchange knowledge with their peers.

Open House's formal learning programmes such as Junior Open House and Open Up enable thousands of students across the capital to interact with spaces and professionals that they might never have previously encountered, involves and respects their views as potential clients, and in so doing enables them to develop a sense of value and ownership of their environment. Our model of stakeholder engagement generates new thinking that can add great value to the process of planning and designing a new school build or refurbishment.

Our new initiative, the Open House Education Fund, has been developed to enable those who are – or who seek to be – involved in educational transformation to draw on this expertise in engagement and action research. It offers opportunities for staff at all levels to build their skills: from learning how to best engage with school clients (from pupils to headteachers and governors) to developing contacts with contractors, local authorities and other decision-makers. Ultimately the Fund will create a catalyst for new thinking and research that will continue to push the boundaries of innovation in architecture education.

We would like to thank the founding supporters of the
Open House Education Fund:

- Aedas – www.aedas.com
- Allford Hall Monaghan Morris – www.ahmm.co.uk
- Allies and Morrison – www.alliesandmorrison.co.uk
- Arup – www.arup.com
- BAM Construct UK – www.bam.co.uk
- BDP – www.bdp.com
- Bouygues UK – www.bouygues-uk.com
- Charles Barclay Architects – www.cbarchitects.co.uk
- Curl la Tourelle Architects – www.cltarchitects.co.uk
- Cox Bulleid Architects – www.cbarchitects.net
- DLA Architecture – www. dla-design.co.uk
- Duggan Morris Architects – www.dugganmorrisarchitects.com
- Greenhill Jenner Architects – www.greenhilljenner.co.uk
- The Manser Practice Architects – www.manser.co.uk
- Marks Barfield Architects – www.marksbarfield.com
- Metropolitan Workshop – www.metwork.co.uk
- MSA – www.msalimited.com
- Pollard Thomas Edwards (PTEa) – www.ptea.co.uk
- Shepheard Epstein Hunter Architecture – www.seh.co.uk
- Sheppard Robson – www.sheppardrobson.com
- Studio E Architects – www.studioe.co.uk
- Studio Egret West – www.egretwest.com
- Wilmotte UK Ltd – www.wilmotte.com

Vernon Coaker MP, Minister of State for Schools and Learners
"The DCSF supports the work that Open House is doing in raising awareness of the importance of good design through its events and through the publication of the 'Learning by Design' resources showcasing recently completed schools and early years facilities. We welcome its engagement with schools through the Junior Open House week, and wish the organisation every success in the future."

How Open House works

Open House is London's leading independent architecture education organisation and charity. Our vision is to open eyes, minds and doors to the power of architecture to transform our lives. Our year-round initiatives inspire and inform decision-makers, young people and the wider community by...

Challenging:
We challenge Londoners to re-assess their ideas about architecture through Open House London every September: for one weekend in the year, 200,000 Londoners come together to explore great architecture at first hand in all corners of the capital

Inspiring:
We inspire young people to see how architecture affects their daily lives: the My City Too programme has enabled over 1000 young Londoners to share their aspirations and solutions for the future city through community projects, surveys and a manifesto

Innovating:
We unlock the potential of architecture as a learning tool: the Junior Open House and Open Up programmes for primary and secondary schools have inspired thousands of students through explorations of buildings and participation in creative workshops

Campaigning:
We campaign to promote sustainability as an integral part of design excellence. Our integrated programme of debates, explorations, exhibitions and displays, talks, tours and resources focuses on the question 'Is good design, green design?'

Investigating:
We undertake extensive research among Londoners: a recent poll, for example, found that 45% of them felt strongly that they don't have a say in the design of new public spaces and buildings in their local area

Championing:
We develop people's skills to champion the value of good design: more than 200 planning councillors are better equipped to assess the quality of design proposals thanks to the Open House Exemplar programme, now in its 4th year

Collaborating:
We create a platform for dialogue between the property sector, local authorities, teachers and architects who are brought together every year to discover what makes great places through seminars, training sessions and programmes

Influencing:
We help design professionals create successful places and spaces: our advocacy initiative **Art in the Open**, looking at the role of art in the public realm, seeks to influence key developments through research and guidance such as the resource **artintheopen.org.uk**

Support Open House

Open House is a charity that needs to raise every penny it spends in creating Open House London and our core education programmes and activities. We can only continue to fund and deliver this vital work with the support of our generous donors and sponsors. Please help our projects to continue and grow by making a contribution in one of the following ways:

Text the word **OPEN** to **84424** and make a **£3** donation*

Make a **secure donation** online at **justgiving.com/openhouse**

Send a **cheque** or **credit/debit card** details, using the form on **p71**

To support our advocacy programmes contact our **Development** team on **development@openhouse.org.uk**

*Open House will receive £1.87 after network charges and VAT. You may also be charged your standard network rate for sending the text.

Open House London 09 starts here

openhouse.org.uk/london

My London

Victoria Thornton Hon FRIBA, Founding Director, Open House

Welcome to Open House London 2009: the capital's biggest architecture festival is again throwing open the doors of hundreds of buildings giving you the chance to explore the best of the city's architecture. Great buildings and the city's public spaces shape our daily lives as we live, learn, work and play. Get out on 19 & 20 September and get inside what makes London great. Here, some Londoners share their thoughts on London and recommendations for the event...

Boris Johnson, Mayor of London

"I'm delighted to support Open House London 2009. London's architecture really does tell the story of this magnificent city. Experiencing a building in the flesh can help to understand, appreciate and critique it. Open House London hopes to inspire everyone to explore the Capital and take an interest in good design for generations today and into the future."

Peter Bishop, Director, Design Development & Environment, London Development Agency

"London's unique architecture – from the domestic to cultural and civic landmarks – forms a vital part of London's identity and history. Open House provides the opportunity to explore some of our greatest buildings and to stumble across the unusual, the new and the quirky; such as 85 Swains Lane, a new house set in Highgate Cemetery by Eldridge Smerin."

Robert Noel, Chairman, Westminster Property Association and Supporter of Open House

"Open House gives us the excuse to feast on our architectural heritage and learn about an individual building's place in our national history and life today. Walk from Apsley House through St James's Park to Westminster Hall then move onto the Royal Courts of Justice."

Richard Rogers, Lord Rogers of Riverside CH

"Open House is a wonderful concept trying to help break down the barrier between the architectural profession and the public by explaining what architects do and how buildings are designed and built. It is very hard to recommend one building in a city where there are so many good architects and buildings."

Sean Griffiths, Practice Director, FAT

"London is a mess interspersed with monuments that are never positioned monumentally which is what is good about it. It's not a city of objects, but one which unfolds as you move through it. Not withstanding that its monuments are marvellous and eccentric from Hawksmoor's churches to Trellick Tower. Most of the churches are open all year round, so for Open House I'd recommend Trellick which isn't."

Tony Chambers, *wallpaper** editor-in-chief

"Classics like the Royal College of Physicians, Highpoint and Trellick Tower are an obvious must-see during Open House London, but there is a wealth of contemporary architecture too, like the Siobhan Davies Studios by Sarah Wigglesworth Architects, 85 Swains Lane by Eldridge Smerin or the Sunken House by Adjaye Associates."

John Alker, Head of Advocacy, UK Green Building Council

"Where do you start with the architecture on offer in London? There is such quality and diversity, both new and old. It's also heartening to see the growth of sustainability – green building – not as some optional extra, but as integral to the overall concept of good design. It's almost unfair to single buildings out, but I'm looking forward to taking in the new LSE building – a major renovation, which has created a fantastic new space while retaining original features. I'll also take in one or two of the exemplar green homes, which offer such a positive vision of the future – low impact, but high quality of life."

Andrew Whiting, Practice Director, HÛT

"It's the dynamism of London that I love – the way that architecture, sometimes subtle, sometimes conspicuous, can transform existing spaces, buildings and areas. Go and have a look at the adjacent Village Underground and Rivington Place projects as an example."

Paul Finch OBE, Editor emeritus of the *Architectural Review* and Director, World Architecture Festival

"London is full of architectural marvels both old and new. I would strongly recommend a visit to Hopkins & Partners' Portcullis House, the MPs' building opposite Big Ben. It has real gravitas and a marvellous central space. Best of all, you can use the Westminster Underground Station below, designed by the same architect as part of the Jubilee Line programme. The station is magnificent - no interior space in London comes near it. A wonderful example of architecture applied to engineering."

Margaret Howell, Fashion Designer

"Grand, famous, small, obscure, London's buildings open for us this weekend; a privilege not to be missed. What I find really exciting though is insight into sometimes extraordinary personal spaces, such as Richard Wilson's studio on the river Thames, Slice of Reality. One's spirit is totally lifted by the experience."

Agnieszka Glowacka, Practice Director, Glowacka Rennie

"Variety is the spice of life, and the diversity of architecture and spatial experiences on offer in London makes it a great city. In this spirit of variety I recommend two very different and distinctive Open House experiences: Churchill's underground bunker in Neasden (37 bomb-proof rooms steeped in history, buried 40 feet below ground) and Centre Point (32 glazed floors of beautiful capital views, soaring 385 feet above Tottenham Court Road station)."

Ken Allinson, Architect and Author

"Open House has to be the finest, largest and most lively and stimulating architectural event in London's cultural calendar. Here is culture and Culture in a unique intermix of the everyday and the self-consciously aspirational, all of it cut through by a shared concern for quality in such a manner that it is difficult to say if Open House is about architecture or simply London life. It's there for you to construct your own agenda, with sufficient content to enable you to determine your own content. And, while some of the event's content remains among recurring favourites, some 30-40% changes each year, especially among the group of smaller and private properties. Make the most of it in 2009!"

Jim McClelland, Founder & Editor, *sustain'* magazine

"Sustainability in the built environment calls not for single-issue politics, but for a spirit of pluralism in design. It is not about 'either/or', it is about 'and'. Take the example of Rye Oak Children's Centre in Southwark, by Eger Architects: zero-carbon-rated construction, with up to 20% energy from renewables AND water recycling AND natural ventilation AND a living 'brown' roof for biodiversity. All elements combine to deliver significant local-community benefit, integrated into the urban fabric alongside existing Victorian architecture. Joined-up. Smart. Sustainable."

Charlie Luxton, Architect and Broadcaster

"London may not have the Grand Beauty of Paris or the visual power of New York. Its magic lies in the fact it's a city of such density of stories and richness of history, like an attic full of treasures waiting to be discovered by the curious explorer..."

**Robert Elms Show 12noon – 3pm
BBC London 94.9FM**

"When Open House throws open the portals of so many otherwise inaccessible London buildings, it also opens our eyes to the surprising variety of architectural wonders in our midst and our minds to infinite possibilities of the built environment.

For years now we have covered this staggeringly successful cultural event with relish on my daily show on BBC London 94.9. Every year we receive an avalanche of calls and e-mails from people eager to know more about the opportunities afforded by this unique extravaganza of the edifice. They are hungry to see behind the façades, to learn the tales and the techniques that all buildings have to tell. Which is why queues form round the iconic sites and tens of thousands attend the big ticket tours.

But it isn't just City Hall, Foreign Office & India Office or Lloyd's of London which attract attention. It's countless, usually unnoticed buildings out in the suburban boroughs or tucked down unsung side-streets. The true architectural stamp of London is its variety, the clash and the juxtaposition, the old and new, grand and humble jostling for attention and all are available to us during Open House London.

So yet again from Barking to Bromley, Havering to Hillingdon, volunteers will prepare to open their doors to the inquisitive crowds, aficionados will plan their weekends for maximum exposure and Londoners in general will learn a little more about the city we share. BBC London 94.9 will of course be with them."

BBC LONDON 94.9 FM

By design

Explore and debate design issues at openhouse.org.uk/designmatters

Open House London enables everyone to explore and debate what makes excellent architecture and design. We think that the best way to do this is to experience architecture up close, and to join the debate about the current design issues facing the capital. Here are some of the issues on our agenda this year...

Art and Places

Across London various initiatives are underway that connect people, place and art as part of the longer-term redevelopment of areas, helping to humanise their current and future experiences. This year Open House London is highlighting some of these approaches, showing how new forms of more local engagement are inspiring the capital's places. Look out for the **red dots** in the main section.

In Hackney, at 20, Dalston Lane (p34) find out more about changes to the area reflecting its creative identity. At Greenwich Peninsula (p32) there are tours of the area including the public realm and artists' commissions. In South East London find out more about the planned Peckham Space, (p56 and pictured right) and how it's responding to its surroundings.

If you have a favourite artwork outside in London's public spaces, then take part in our survey (p72) and help Open House's year-round work influencing London's public art.

Also take a look at the greatest regeneration project currently taking place, with tours of the London 2012 Olympic Park (p50).

How we live

It's estimated that the population of London will increase to over 8 million by 2016. The need for well-designed housing is great. Look for the **yellow dots** throughout the listings for past and present housing exemplars to compare and contrast how we are living now. Projects include Adelaide Wharf (p33 and pictured above right), and Laycock Street (p43). Also head out to Stratford to the new East Thames building (p50) for the exhibition **'Homework: Design in Social Housing 1979-2009'**, exploring the history of social housing and how vibrant communities are created and greener objectives met. It includes a section on the Open House My City Too! youth engagement programme and the **Inside Out initiative for East Potential** exploring through an interactive game the relationship between young people and the built environment, and their right to 'be safe, enjoy and achieve'.

Exemplars

Also, look out for the blue and purple dots which represent school and office exemplars. Civic Trust and RIBA Award Winners such as the King's Cross Construction Skills Centre (pictured below) are also identified in the building descriptions.

Have your say

Tell us what you think about London and its architecture on p72, or go to our website openhouse.org.uk to join the debate!

Coming in September...
Join the 'Opening up London' great debate.
See openhouse.org.uk/designmatters

Coolly, madly, greenly

See openhouse.org.uk/green for more info on all things green in the event this year

This year, Open House London helps to look at innovation in green design by showcasing new and renovated eco buildings. Nearly half of the UK's energy consumption comes from the ways in which our buildings are lit, heated and used. Creating sustainable design solutions are among the most urgent issues for architects and designers. Find out how we can build in a greener way whilst integrating design, whether through new build or retro-fitting existing buildings.

Visit offices, school and community buildings like the City Academy (p34), Brookhill Children's Centre (p31) and Roots and Shoots (p47), as well as new build homes Eds Shed (p33), the development at 188 Portland Road (p44) and many retro-fitted eco-homes such as Sherland Road (p52), 89 Culford Road (p33) and Retro-eco house (p55). Also check out the Sponge eco-tour (see p67) for what is happening in West London. Look out for the green dot against building listings for Eco Exemplars or the G for Green Features at buildings.

Open House also works in partnership with a number of organisations to help embed green design and thinking into our everyday lives:

Camden walking mapguide – showing how to walk the borough year-round, get healthy, see some great buildings and lead the way in making a greener, cleaner, well-designed city. Launched as part of Car Free Day in Camden on 11 September and created by **LB Camden** in association with Open House and **Legible London**. For details on how to obtain a copy of this pamphlet see **openhouse.org.uk/green**

Green Building Guide – looking at how to plan, design and live sustainably in the 21st Century by exploring all the different aspects of what makes a building 'green'. In association with *sustain'* magazine and the **UK Green Building Council**. For details on how to obtain a copy of this pamphlet see **openhouse.org.uk/green**

The Mayor of London's **Skyride** also takes place on Sunday 20 September – why not get on your bike and experience central London car-free, and then cycle to some Open House buildings. See **goskyride.com/london**

Also new this year is our **cycling route competition**. Devise a bike-friendly route between Open House buildings, submit to us before the event, and the winning routes will be published on our website and win a fantastic prize! See **openhouse.org.uk/green** for details and how to enter.

Display energy certificates – look out for the certificates – which give an A to G energy efficiency rating – in large public buildings opening their doors for Open House London this year.

and.....
Love London – we are a partner for the capital's greenest annual festival, providing Londoners with the opportunity to explore what makes a cleaner, greener and healthier London. Takes place in June every year. See **http://lovelondon.london21.org** Don't miss it in 2010!

Our **Lives of Buildings programme** for the Mayor's Story of London festival in June this year in partnership with English Heritage explored the importance of reusing existing building stock. Research carried out during the event found that **68% of people think that it is important that old buildings are updated to be more eco friendly**.

Lastly, we want you to tell us what you think about green design through our Green Design poll! **Please help us by logging on to openhouse.org.uk/poll**

Kids corner

Events for children and families are taking place throughout the weekend. Some highlights are given below. See openhouse.org.uk/kidscorner for more

City of a Thousand Architects: Building Challenge – for kids aged 5- 10
Saturday 19 and Sunday 20 September
City Hall (top floor), The Queens Walk, SE1 2AA
10am – 1pm
Kids and parents can express their creativity and take on the building challenge to create exciting and fun architectural structures and designs for an alternative London skyline.

Architectives Treasure Hunt: Exploring London's architectural gems – for kids aged 7-13
Saturday 19 and Sunday 20 September
Various locations around London's riverside – see openhouse.org.uk/kidscorner for full details
Collect your Architectives passport, activity book and map and follow the trail to discover, explore and investigate London's exciting architectural gems.
Supported by The London String of Pearls.

Eco London: Re-modelling the city – all ages
Saturday 19 and Sunday 20 September
Blue Fin Building, Blue Sky Space, 110 Southwark Street, London, SE1 0SU
12noon – 3pm
Come and create your own vision of London's riverside architecture – using modelling materials to make your own 3D eco designs for the city adding to our huge 3D floor plan.

School's Out! – Junior Open House exhibition of primary students' work
Saturday 19 and Sunday 20 September
City Hall (top floor), The Queens Walk, SE1 2AA
10am – 1pm
Be inspired by the exciting school designs created by primary students during this year's Junior Open House architecture education programme.
All welcome.
Supported by the John Lyons Charity

Also...
Many buildings are hosting childrens' activities, such as the family events at Imperial War Museum (p55) and Westminster Academy (p67), creating your own wearable building at Trinity Buoy Wharf (p59), and modelmaking at Stanton Williams' Offices (p43). Look for the **C** against listings in the index and in the main programme to find all activities.

This year we are also holding a **kids photography competition**. Photograph Open House London 2009 buildings and enter to win a prize. To find out more and how to enter go to openhouse.org.uk/kidscorner

ArchiKids Club
Be an Architective!
Are you aged between 7 and 12?
Do you like exploring architecture and the city?
Then you need to join the ArchiKids club!

ArchiKids Club is a virtual club. It's online, interactive and full of activities to help explore the world of architecture. Visit archikids.org.uk for more details.

Spotlight

Several buildings are hosting special events over the weekend, highlighted with pink dots in the main programme. More are spotlighted here and further details of these can be found on openhouse.org.uk/spotlight

Join the London Night Hike...

Friday 18 September

Join 2000 people to walk through late night London, discover Open House architecture by night and support people living with, through and beyond cancer. Open House and Maggie's present the fifth annual London Night Hike taking on a 20 mile route across the capital. Join this overnight festival on foot which includes City Hall, London Eye, Channel 4, Fulham Palace, The Royal Geographical Society, Horse Guards and Maggie's London. Designed by Lord Rogers, the charity's first cancer caring centre in London opened last year to support people in the capital affected by cancer.

Register at **maggiescentres.org/nighthike** or call 0845 602 6427

maggie's
cancer caring centres

Find out what *The Architect's Journal* is highlighting in this year's programme, see openhouse.org.uk/ajchoice

Open House London and Wallpaper*

Leading global design destination Wallpaper* magazine takes its pick of the numerous Open House offerings all around London and flags up its favourite architecture to visit during the 2009 event. A bespoke detailed clickable map on wallpaper.com will guide you through the magazine's recommended star architecture trail, providing information for its chosen must-see locations.
See wallpaper.com

Celebrating the Modern Swimming Pool

Thursday 17 September, 6:30pm – 8:30pm
Margaret Howell, 34 Wigmore Street W1U 2RS
Refreshments from 6:30pm; Talk at 7.15pm

Margaret Howell will be celebrating the architecture of swimming pools and lidos with talks by Keith Ashton from S&P Architects, specialists in swimming pool design and Ken Worpole, writer on architecture, landscape and public policy. A selection of photographs of swimming pools and lidos from the RIBA archive library will be exhibited 12-17 September. Continues 23 September-7 October.
Tickets for the talk are free but pre-booking is required, go to openhouse.org.uk/spotlight

MARGARET
HOWELL

Reimagining Buildings:
Talk at Wilton's Music Hall

Monday 14 September, 6:30pm-8:15pm
Wilton's Music Hall, Graces Alley, Ensign Street E1 8BJ
Refreshments from 6:30pm; Talk at 7.15pm

Buildings, like people, undergo an ageing process. With their accumulation of scars and wrinkles, buildings can very often gain a quality that they lack upon completion, when shiny and new. In this talk at the oldest music hall in London to survive in its original form, author David Littlefield explores how elderly buildings can live so powerfully in the imagination.
Tickets are free but pre-booking is required, go to openhouse.org.uk/spotlight

Attend Open House London in style...

Friday 18 or Saturday 19 September

Competition to enjoy an overnight stay for two in a deluxe room at Grosvenor House, a JW Marriott Hotel. Champagne Rose Tea for two served in the Park Room on your arrival day. After a relaxing night in the hotel and a delicious breakfast enjoy a full day exploring Open House London. To enter, answer this question: In what year did Grosvenor House first open to the public? Answers to competition@openhouse.org.uk by 6pm Thursday 3 September. The winner will be the first correct answer drawn at random and will be informed by Friday 4 September. See openhouse.org.uk/spotlight for terms and conditions. Grosvenor House will also be giving Open House tours during the event, see p63.

Rose Afternoon Tea Offer

To celebrate the 80th Birthday of Grosvenor House, mention Open House London on booking before 31st October 2009 and enjoy a 10% discount on the Rose Afternoon Tea. **Call 020 7499 6363 or visit londongrosvenorhouse.co.uk to find out more and book.**

GROSVENOR HOUSE
A JW MARRIOTT. HOTEL
LONDON

Photography competition: 'Juxtaposition'

Open House invites you to photograph a building or an aspect of a building you have visited during Open House London 2009. Capture the essence of this year's theme 'Juxtaposition' and be in with a chance of winning your image as a large, mounted print. Submitted photos may also be used in future Open House publicity. Entries will be judged by our expert panel – renowned architectural photographers Grant Smith and Morley von Sternberg and *Guardian* picture editor Marissa Keating. Our website openhouse.org.uk/competition has full details of all categories, criteria, terms and how to enter.

Essential information

Admission is free for all Open House London events on 19 – 20 September 2009. This section tells you all you need to know about the event, the information you will need and how to get it, and what to expect on the day.

Buildings by Area – Contents

Here's a map to help you find your way around London, and as a reference to the following borough sections. Also see contents, left.

What will I find when I get to the buildings?

At many of the 700 sites, there will be someone to show you around and answer your questions. These are the Open House guides and stewards, and there are thousands of them – some professional, some amateur enthusiast, all volunteering their time and knowledge. In recognition of their role their badge enables them to gain priority access to buildings apart from those that are pre-booking only. For information about volunteering in 2010, please email volunteers@openhouse.org.uk.

Open House London Volunteer 2009 Please allow priority entry

Will I get to meet any of the architects?

Look out for the entries marked with a code A throughout this guide and in the index; it means that architects will be giving talks and tours of some of the buildings they've designed. There are a staggering **1600 tours being given by architects** this year in total. Where there is a bright green **A** flagged up in the guide you will also find the **practice director on site**. Also, some of their studios/offices will be open, so that you can see the projects they're working on. Sometimes you can also meet the property owner who will also appreciate your positive feedback!

Don't forget to look out for the factsheets too which will be available at most buildings.

How do I find out more about the buildings and how to get around?

See openhouse.org.uk/london

The website is your other resource for your planning. It builds on the information you see in this programme. There are interactive searches for period of architecture, type of building, name of architect or geographical location. You can see where buildings are located and plan your route between them, using the handy map-based interface. All pre-bookings taken through Open House operate on here. There are images and factsheets for most entries. A link to live travel news from TfL will let you know about planned engineering works. The website also gives you further information on many of our other programmes, and allows you to order copies of this guide and other Open House publications.

What info can I find in this programme?

Each building and walk entry contains address, opening days and hours, access to visitors, pre-booking details where relevant, amenities and transport, with bus numbers listed at the end. A brief description and the name of the architect, plus any special events or themes are also given. See key listing below right. All main areas are open to the public unless otherwise stated.
Also note the colour-coded arrows indicating opening days! Blue means open Saturday only, pink means Sunday only, purple means both days! See key below right.

Stop Press
Please do try to check this! From 16 September amendments, additions and withdrawals to the list of participating buildings will be available by visiting the Open House website. Online listings will be kept up to date throughout.

Do I need to book?

Entry to a few of the properties will require you to book in advance. Where this is through the building contact details are given. Bookings administered by Open House are indicated. These have to be made via our website, and **openhouse.org.uk/generalinfo** has full details of the booking process, how to place your booking (which is through our online search listings) and how to release bookings. Spaces are limited and are on a strictly first come, first served basis. Open House regrets that we cannot guarantee availability of places. As places on these tours are restricted please ensure that you attend.
NOTE: online pre-booking is only open from 10 August – 16 September unless otherwise stated.

How can I get another copy of the programme?

Copies can be bought from:
- openhouse.org.uk/shop
- Britain & London Visitor Centre, 1 Lower Regent Street SW1
- Tate Modern, Bankside SE1
- The Building Centre, Store Street WC1
- RIBA bookshop, 66 Portland Place W1
- Copies can be picked up **free from participating local London libraries**, subject to availability.

Can you tell me about access for visitors with disabilities?

This year Open House is again working in partnership with **Artsline**, the disability information service, to provide **online access information** for the event. Where buildings have supplied this information, it can be seen on **artsline.org.uk/openhouse** so that visitors can prepare for a successful and enjoyable visit. Please note, the Artsline office is not able to provide other general information.

This Guide is also available in large print formats by emailing admin@openhouse.org.uk

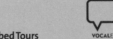

VocalEyes Audio Described Tours
This year **blind and partially sighted people** will have the rare opportunity to go on VocalEyes audio described tours of Haberdashers Hall, BBC Bush House, Foreign Office and Johnson Building. Each tour will be led by one of their describers with a representative from the building or the building's designers. Contact VocalEyes on 020 7375 1043, email toby@vocaleyes.co.uk or visit vocaleyes.co.uk to find out more and book. VocalEyes is a national charity providing access to the arts through audio description.
Supported by The Greater London Fund for the Blind

What are the terms of entry?

Open House London is a free event in which all sections of the community are invited to participate. Please note that each building's opening, security arrangements and refusal of entry are controlled by individual owners, and entry to each building is on terms and at times specified, over 19 & 20 September 2009. Participation in events and activities is at your own risk. Information in this guide is provided by contributors. Open House has taken all reasonable care to verify the information provided and cannot accept responsibility for any variation from the details published here. Please do respect building owners and their privacy, and be mindful of photo-taking.

Disclaimer: Neither Open House nor the leader or organiser of any event, activity or walk advertised here or on the Open House website nor any other programme listing, print or electronic, shall be held liable for the death or injury, accident or damage to the person or property (including theft or loss) of any event participant or any guest or any person occurring during or arising from participation in any of the events advertised in the Open House London programme.

Where else in the world can I find Open House events?

Open House cities also now include New York, Dublin and Galway.
openhousenewyork is 10-11 October
Open House Dublin is 8-11 October
Open House Galway is 16-18 October

Open House London is London's independent contribution to the European Heritage Days initiative which takes place across 48 countries. **For details of events across the UK in September for Heritage Open Days visit www.heritageopendays.org.uk**

The dates for Open House London in 2010 are 18 & 19 September

What do the icons and abbreviations in the listings mean?

A = Architect on site
B = Bookshop
C = Children's activities
d = Partial access for people with disabilities
D = Full wheelchair access
G = Green Features
N = Open to the public every or most days and free of charge
P = Parking
Q = Long queues envisaged
R = Refreshments
T = Toilets

A Architect practice director on site
● Art in the Public Realm
● Green Exemplar
○ Housing
● Office Exemplar
● School Exemplar
● Spotlight Event

→ Open Saturday
→ Open Sunday
→ Open Saturday and Sunday

We hope you enjoy Open House London 2009!

Barking & Dagenham

Eastbury Manor House

Northbury Junior School Extension

Barking Abbey with St Margaret's Church
The Broadway, North Street, Barking IG11 8AS
→ Sat 10am-4pm. Tours of Abbey ruins and church; Curfew tower (max 15 at one time) and St Margaret's bell tower (max 10 at one time). Tower tours not suitable for infirm. Bell ringing demonstrations. Last entry 3.30pm. B d N P R T
Grade I listed St Margaret's Church (1215) has interesting monuments, art and stained glass and includes Arts and Crafts work by George Jack. Captain Cook married here. Abbey dates from 666AD and includes ruins, Curfew Tower and Chapel of Holy Rood restored 2005 by Ronald Wylde Associates.
Tube/Rail: Barking; 5,62,179,287,366,169,369

Barking Town Hall
Clockhouse Avenue, Barking IG11 7LU
→ Sat 9am-5pm. Tours every hour on the hour. Last entry 4.30pm. Max 10 at one time. D N T
Designed in the 1930s but not built until the 1950s, the lower part of the building retains a strong Thirties influence. Despite a regular arrangement of windows in the Georgian style, the imposing clock tower has unexpectedly Baroque tendencies. Herbert Jackson & Reginald Edmonds 1930s/1950s.
Entry: foyer, council chamber, main staircase, Mayor's parlour.
Tube/Rail: Barking; 5,62,169,179,238,287,366,368,369,387

Castle Green ●
Gale Street, Castle Green, Dagenham RM9 4UN
→ Sat 8.30am-1pm. Pre-book tours ONLY on 020 8724 1500. Last entry 12.30pm. Max 20 at one time. C D P R T
An extended PFI school and community facility in the heart of the borough. Design encourages imaginative teaching methods. State of the art facilities have been developed in line with new pedagogy focusing on importance of communication. Architecture plb with Bouygues UK 2005.
Entry: school, community theatre, sports and arts areas.
Tube: Becontree; Rail: Barking; 145,62,173,287

Civic Centre
Wood Lane, Dagenham RM10 7BN
→ Sun 9am-5pm. Regular tours. Last entry 4.30pm. D N P T
Grade II listed Art Deco style building in mulberry stock brick with imposing Portland stone entrance and portico. Recently refurbished interior has excellent Art Deco ceilings and botticino marble stairs and foyer. E Berry Webber 1936. Entry: main foyers, staircase, Mayor's parlour, council chamber.
Tube: Dagenham East; Rail: Romford; 5,103,128,150,175

Eastbury Manor House
Eastbury Square, Barking IG11 9SN
→ Sat/Sun 10am-4pm. Half-hourly tours. Last tour 3pm. B D P R T
Architecturally distinguished and well-preserved, brick-built, 16C Grade I listed Manor House, originally the residence of a wealthy Tudor Essex gentleman. It contains notable wall-paintings, and a fine original turret staircase. Many of the original features have been restored. Charming walled garden. Restoration by Richard Griffiths Architects 2008-09. Entry: house and gardens.
Tube: Upney; Rail: Barking; 62,287,368

Northbury Junior School Extension ●
North Street, Barking IG11 8JA
→ Sat 10am-5pm. Regular tours, first come basis. D R T G
This expansion to a Victorian school takes the form of a giant timber classroom box, raised up on wooden legs to the level of the upper teaching areas. The box is clad in a curtain wall giving every classroom an eight metre-wide, three metre-high window to the world outside. Sustainable features include stack-effect natural ventilation, solar-reflective glass, green roof, full-heat recovery and ventilation. Greenhill Jenner 2009.
Tube/Rail: Barking; 5,368,62,179,366

Nursery Building – 'Children's House'
Kingsley Hall, Parsloes Avenue, Dagenham RM9 5NB
→ Sun 10am-4.30pm. Last entry 4pm. Other buildings on site open, exhibition running. B D P R T
Designed in 1925/6, the 'Children's House' has been in continuous use for children's work since it was opened by Ishbel MacDonald in 1932. The first recognised nursery school on any new housing estate. Charles Cowles Voysey 1931.
Tube: Becontree; Rail: Chadwell Heath; 5,62,145,364

St Patrick's Church
Blake Avenue, Barking IG11 9SQ
→ Sat 1pm-5pm. Regular tours, last tour 4.30pm. Max 15 per tour. D R T
Built thanks to a generous gift from local benefactress, Mrs Lavinia Keene. Unscathed by the war it has undergone significant refurbishment in 2008. An unusual and striking building in a Moderne style with concrete, brick interior contrasting vividly with the dramatic, colourful and cinematic reredos (the architect is known for his cinema designs). Recently Grade II listed. A E Wiseman 1940. Entry: chancel, nave, lady chapel, vestry, choir vestry, garden.
Tube: Upney; Tube/Rail: Barking; 287,368,62

The Broadway
Broadway, Barking IG11 7LS
→ Sat 11am-5pm. Regular tours, pre-book ONLY on 020 8507 5607. Opportunity to observe/participate in workshops.
Original theatre recently modernised with striking but sympathetic new double-height foyer space, preserving the original façade which now forms part of interior. Herbert Jackson and Reginald Edmonds/Tim Foster Architects (refurb) 1930/2004. Entry: foyers, auditorium, studios, offices.
Tube/Rail: Barking; 5,238,387,366,369

The Millennium Centre
The Chase, Dagenham Road, Rush Green, Romford RM7 0SS
→ Sat/Sun 1pm-5pm. D N P T G
Steel structure, timber-clad exterior and interior, and a sweeping south-facing roof designed to house solar panels. Eco-friendly building using recycled materials throughout, including car windscreens and newspapers. Penoyre and Prasad 1997.
Tube: Dagenham East; Rail: Romford; 174

WALKS/TOURS

Becontree Estate Bus Tour, Dagenham
→ Meet: Sun 10am for bus departure at Civic Centre, Dagenham RM10 7BW
First come basis. Guided tour, duration approx 3-4 hours. Max 45 on tour. P T
Built by the LCC during the 1920s and early 1930s, the estate was once the largest of its kind in Europe, with over 25,000 houses. Later building programmes extended the estate to house an estimated population of 90,000. Entry: all parts of Becontree Estate including entry to Kingsley Hall and three vacant homes.
Tube: Dagenham East; Rail: Romford; 5,87

Supported by

London Borough of
Barking & Dagenham

Bexley

All Saints, Foots Cray
Rectory Lane, Foots Cray DA14 5BP
→ Sat 10am-5pm/Sun 1pm-5pm. Max 50 at one time. D P T
Medieval church (c1330) amended 1863 by Hakewill and
retaining original elements such as windows and an arch to
the north aisle, and altar tomb of Sir Simon de Vaughan.
Entry: nave, chapel, chancel.
Rail: Sidcup; 321,51,492,233

Christ Church, Erith
Victoria Road, Erith DA8 3AN
→ Sat 11am-5pm/Sun 10am-5pm. C D P R T
Grade II* listed with unique wall paintings and stained glass,
including two windows commemorating the coronation of
King Edward VII. James Piers St Aubyn 1874. Entry: church,
church hall, grounds.
Rail: Erith; 99,229,428,469,B12

Danson House
Danson Road, Welling DA6 8HL
→ Sun 11am-5pm. Last entry 4.15pm. D P R T
Fine Palladian villa of Oxford stone built as a weekend retreat
for Sir John Boyd, a rich City merchant. Four rooms on the
principal floor surround a central elliptical staircase in a
top-lit well with eight Ionic columns below a dome. Closed
for 30 years, long term restoration work by English Heritage
has restored it to its former glory. Robert Taylor 1762/Purcell
Miller Tritton (restoration). Entry: terrace level, principal floor,
bedrooms, gardens.
Rail: Bexleyheath; 89,96,B13,B14

Erith Playhouse
38-40 High Street, Erith DA8 1QY
→ Sat/Sun 1pm-5pm. Half hourly backstage tours. Last tour
4.30pm. Max 8 per tour. Special 60th anniversary activities.
C d R T
195 seat repertory theatre, rebuilt in 1973 retaining the heart of
the theatre – the original 'Oxford Cinema' auditorium dating
from 1913. Still operating carbon arc follow spots c1956. Entry:
foyer, auditorium, backstage, props, lighting.
Rail: Erith; 99,229,428,B12,469

Gothic Bath House
112 North Cray Road, Bexley DA5 3NA
→ Sun 1pm-5pm. Regular tours, first come basis. C d R T
Grade II* listed 18C Gothic-style bath house in grounds of
the now vanished Vale Mascal estate beside the River Cray.
Perhaps designed by Capability Brown or a disciple. Flint
walled with brick edging, pairs of cinquefoiled windows and
cruciform gabled roof with chimney stack. Restored in 1990 to
its original appearance. Entry: garden, island.
Rail: Bexley; 492

Townley Grammar School for Girls

Hall Place
Bourne Road, Bexley DA5 1PQ
→ Sat 10am-4.30pm/Sun 11am-4.30pm. Tours Sun at 11.30am,
1.30pm, pre-book ONLY on 01322 621 235. B D N P R T
Grade I listed early Tudor three-sided mansion built for a Lord
Mayor of London c1540 with later (c1650) extensions. Now
reopened after major restoration and development. One of
the first opportunities to see the newly restored Great Hall
and Tudor kitchen. Set in formal gardens on the banks of the
River Cray with splendid 18C gates.
Rail: Bexley; 132,229,492,B15

St James, North Cray
North Cray Road, North Cray DA14 5LT
→ Sat 10am-5pm/Sun 1pm-5pm. Max 50 at one time. D P T
A pretty church in decorated English Gothic style with
interesting memorials, good 17C pulpit and fine carvings,
some dating to 15C and 16C. Edwin Nash 1852. Entry: all areas.
Rail: Bexley; 492 from Sidcup or Bexley

St John the Evangelist
Church Road, Sidcup DA14 6BX
→ Sat 10am-5pm. Tours at 11am, 12noon, 3pm. Max 20 per
tour. D N R T
A large high-Victorian nave, high church chancel and choir.
Stained glass, much by Comper. 17C pulpit and reredos with
many wall tablets. George Fellowes-Prynne.
Rail: Sidcup then 51,233,492

Danson House

St Mary The Virgin, Bexley
Manor Road, Bexley DA5 3LX
→ Sat 10am-5pm/Sun 1pm-5pm. Bell-tower open at times
posted on the day. D P T
Fine flint-built 12C Anglo-Norman church with Medieval
timber roof. Restored 1883 by Basil Champneys to Medieval
design. Memorials in church link it to great houses in Bexley.
Grade II* listed. Entry: nave, north aisle, chancel, vestry.
Rail: Bexley; B12,132,229

Townley Grammar School for Girls ●
Townley Road, Bexleyheath DA6 7AB
→ Sat 10am-1pm. Regular tours, first come basis. d T G
New additions to the campus to provide facilities for
performing arts, science and indoor sports have added colour
and a little quirkiness to the original austere school buildings
of the 1930s. Sustainable features include an underground
labyrinth for natural summer cooling. Described as 'truly
inspirational' by one parent. Studio E Architects 2007.
Rail: Bexleyheath, Bexley

WALKS/TOURS

Erith Town Walk
**Self-guided walk – Guide notes to be collected from Christ
Church Erith, Victoria Road, Erith DA8 3AN**
→ Sat 11am-5pm/Sun 10am-5pm.
Erith has existed for over 1000 years. Its development and
growth has been closely linked to the River Thames and this
influence can be traced in the buildings and spaces of the
modern town.
Rail: Erith; 99,229,428,469,B12

Supported by

LONDON BOROUGH OF BEXLEY

St Mary Magdalen's Catholic Junior School

Sattavis Patidar Centre

Alperton Cemetery Chapel & Columbarium
Clifford Road, Alperton HA0 1AF
→ Sat 10am-4pm. Last entry 4pm. D P R T
Alperton features a simple brick chapel with a Welsh slate roof and beautiful stained glass windows. Burial registers for Alperton, Carpenders Park, Paddington, Willesden Old & New Cemeteries and Wembley Old Burial Ground open for searching. Cemetery of the year 2007. Borough Surveyor 1942. Entry: cemetery, chapel, columbarium, registry.
Tube: Alperton; 79,83,224,245,297,487

BAPS Shri Swaminarayan Mandir
105-119 Brentfield Road, Neasden NW10 8LD
→ Sat/Sun 10am-4pm. Tours on the hour. Last entry 3.30pm. Max 30 per tour. B D N P R T
First traditional Hindu Mandir outside India. 2,000 tonnes of Italian marble and 2,828 tonnes of Bulgarian limestone first shipped to India to be shaped by 1,500 craftsmen. Completed with the vision and inspiration of Pramukh Swami Maharaj, the fifth spiritual successor of Lord Swaminarayan. Entry: all areas except monks' quarters, admin block, kitchen, gym. NB. Respectful dress please—no shorts, short skirts, sleeveless blouses.
Tube: Neasden, Harlesden then 206; Rail: Stonebridge then PR2

Brent Museum Collection Store
Willesden Green Library Centre, 95 High Road NW10 2SF
→ Sat/Sun 10am-5pm. Tours at 11am, 2pm, pre-book ONLY on joe.carr@brent.gov.uk. Duration 1 hour. Max 8 per tour. Sat only Brent Archive Open Day. D T
Housed in the modernised Library, Brent Museum pioneered community involvement in building the collection and holds hundreds of objects relating to the history of Brent since around 1800. Entry: museum collection store on tours only.
Tube: Willesden Green; 52,98,260,266,302

Brent Town Hall
Forty Lane, Wembley HA9 9HD
→ Sat/Sun 9am-1pm. Max 6 at one time. D P R T
'The best of the pre-war modern Town Halls around London' (Pevsner). Serene composition of overlapping brick planes with design links to Dutch modernism of the 1920s. Classic 1930s council chamber. Clifford Strange 1937-40.
Tube: Wembley Park; Rail: Wembley Central; 297,182,83,245

Capital City Academy ●
Doyle Gardens NW10 3ST
→ Sat 10am-2pm. Regular tours. Max 80 at one time. D P T
First new build City Academy. Glass and stainless steel, slightly curved following the slope of the grounds. Beautiful lines reflect the sky and the surrounding green. Foster and Partners & BAM 2003. Entry: theatre, main reception, arts areas.
Tube: Willesden Green; Rail: Kensal Rise, Kensal Green; 206,266

Old St Andrews Church, Kingsbury
Church Lane NW9 8SX
→ Sat 11am-4pm. D
Small, recently conserved Grade I listed church. Probably the oldest building in Brent. Fine 17C & 19C memorials to local families.
Tube: Wembley Park; Rail: Wembley Hill; 83,302

Ruach Ministries Christian Centre (former Gaumont State Cinema)
197-199 Kilburn High Road NW6 7HY
→ Sat 11am-4pm. D T
Once the largest cine-variety theatre in England (over 4,000 seats). Italian Renaissance-style interior and original Wurlitzer theatre pipe organ. Grade II* listed. George Coles 1937. Entry: main hall only.
Tube: Kilburn, Kilburn Park; Rail: Kilburn High Road, Brondesbury Park; 16,16A,32,98,31,28

Sattavis Patidar Centre
Forty Avenue, Wembley HA9 9PE
→ Sun 9am-11am. Tours on the hour. Max 20 per tour. D P T G
New facility of distinctive design on a landmark site, by award-winning architects, funded by Gujarati Trust. Wave-formed roof is supported by cigar-shaped inclined columns along main façade. Interiors are transformed with coloured lights. Facilities include halls, theatre auditorium, classrooms and library and are used by all communities. Agenda 21 Architects 2005. Entry: all areas except offices.
Tube: Wembley Park; Rail: North Wembley; 245,223,83,182,297

St Mary Magdalen's Catholic Junior School ● ●
Linacre Road NW2 5DD
→ Sat 10am-5pm. First come basis, queuing outside if necessary. Last entry 4.45pm. Max 30 at one time. D G T A
New build junior school replacing existing school on the same extremely confined urban site in tight residential context. Many environmental features including high levels of daylight and natural ventilation, wind catchers, sun pipes and green roofs. Curl la Tourelle Architects 2009. Entry: school, grounds.
Tube: Willesden Green; 260,266,98,302,52

Stonebridge Hillside Hub
6 Hillside NW10 8BN
→ Sat 10am-5pm. First come basis, queuing outside if necessary. D T G A
The Stonebridge Hillside Hub has a pivotal role in the masterplan for the Stonebridge Estate, now in its final phase. Two 'wings', one accommodating a Primary Care Trust and the other a retail unit, are fused together by a central community facility. Each wing is topped with mixed tenure residential units clad in larch timber. Remainder of the estate, accessible for viewing, includes an Alsop nursery, sports centre, new social housing, open space and a few last remaining 60s tower blocks. Edward Cullinan Architects 2009. Entry: community centre and garden, possible entry to residential unit, health centre atrium.
Tube/Rail: Harlesden, Stonebridge Park; 18,PR2,206,266,260

The Stables Gallery & Art Centre
Gladstone Park, Dollis Hill Lane NW2 6HT
→ Sat/Sun 11am-5pm. Last entry 4.45pm. Max 100 at one time. D N P R T
Original stables block, c1820, probably used by visitors and owners of nearby Dollis Hill House. Only dedicated contemporary art gallery in borough with walled garden and courtyard. Entry: gallery, hayloft, nosebag.
Tube: Dollis Hill, Neasden; 232

Underground Bunker, Neasden
Brook Road NW2 7DZ
→ Sat 8.30am-5pm. Pre-book ONLY Mon-Fri 9am-5pm on 020 8782 4239 or email katy.bajina@stadiumha.org.uk. Comprehensive tour given. Sensible footwear and clothing should be worn. Last entry 5pm. Max 25 at one time. P T
Underground 1940s bunker used during WWII by Winston Churchill and the Cabinet. Purpose-built of reinforced concrete, totally bomb-proof subterranean war citadel 40 feet below ground, with Map Room, Cabinet Room and offices, housed within a sub-basement protected by a 5ft thick concrete roof.
Tube: Neasden, Dollis Hill; 245,182,332,232

BRENT COUNCIL

Bromley

Biggin Hill Airfield
Scout Aviation Ctr, 518 Churchill Road, Biggin Way TN16 3BN
→ Sun tours at 10.30am, 11.30am, 1pm, 2pm, 3pm, 4pm. Max 30 per tour. d P T
Surviving installations from the Battle of Britain on the eastern edge of the airfield adjoining West Kent Golf Course (also accessible by footpath). Air Ministry 1940. Entry: pillbox, aircraft blast shelter, bomb-proof sleeping quarters, exhibition.
Rail: Bromley South then 246 or 320 bus then approx 1 mile walk

Bromley and Sheppard's College
London Road (entrance via Wren Gates, no cars), BR1 1PE
→ Sat tours at 1.45pm, 2.30pm, 3.15pm, 4pm, pre-bookable on 020 8464 3558 or 020 8460 4712. Max 20 per tour.
Founded to house the widows of clergymen, the original building consisted of 20 houses built around a classically-styled quadrangle. Captain Richard Ryder – one of Sir Christopher Wren's surveyors – was in charge of design and construction (1666). Entry: grounds, quadrangle, chapel.
Rail: Bromley North & South; 208,358

Bullers Wood School
St Nicolas Lane, Logs Hill, Chislehurst BR7 5LJ
→ Sat 10am-1pm. Last entry 12.30pm. Max 30 at a time. D P R T
Typical mid-Victorian stucco-fronted house built on a grassy hillside, extended in 1888 by Ernest Newton whilst William Morris simultaneously redesigned the interiors. The library, formerly the drawing room, is famous for its unique William Morris hand-painted ceiling. Ernest Newton c1850. Entry: Bullers Wood House library, 2 classrooms.
Rail: Chislehurst, Elmstead Woods, Bickley; 314

Camden Place (Chislehurst Golf Club)
Camden Park Road, Chislehurst BR7 5HJ
→ Sat/Sun tours 10am and 11am, pre-book ONLY on 020 8467 2782. Max 8 at one time. D P R T
Early 18C mansion and home of Napoleon III 1870-80. Brick façade, remarkable Egyptian chimneypiece of polished pink granite and breakfast room with exquisite plaster ceiling. Golf Club from 1894. George Dance the Younger (remodelled) 1717-19C. Entry: ground floor.
Rail: Chislehurst

Crofton Roman Villa
Crofton Road, Orpington BR6 8AF
→ Sun 10am-5pm. Tours at 11am, 2.30pm, 3.30pm. B C D P
Remains of ten rooms of a masonry Roman villa-house from AD 140 with evidence of opus signinum and tessellated floors. Details of channelled and pillared hypocaust systems.
Rail: Orpington (adjacent); 61,208,353

Eltham College
Grove Park Road SE9 4QF
→ Sat/Sun 12noon-4pm. Regular tours. Last tour 3.30pm. P T
Nine-bay mansion of 1700, much reworked, with remains of Adam-style decorations put in by the second Earl Bathurst (whose town house was Apsley House, Piccadilly). Part of Eltham College since 1912. Entry: main house, chapel.
Rail: Mottingham, Grove Park; 126,124,161

St George's RAF Chapel of Remembrance
Main Road, Biggin Hill TN16 3EJ
→ Sat 10.30am-4.30pm/Sun 12.30pm-4.30pm. Last entry 4pm. Max 20 at one time. D N P T
Chapel building in shape of an aircraft hangar, with plain brick interior and stained glass windows commemorating the spirit of WWII air and ground crew. Messrs Beasley/Harper/Williams 1951.
Rail: Bromley South; 320

Sundridge Park
Plaistow Lane, Bromley BR1 3TP
→ Sun 11am-4pm. B D R T
Beautiful mansion building by Nash with landscaping by Humphry Repton. Completed by Samuel Wyatt who designed the fine interiors, roofs and domes. John Nash 1797. Entry: ground floor and gardens.
Rail: Sundridge Park, Bromley South

The Berresford House
Brooklyn, Lodge Road, Bromley BR1 3ND
→ Sun 10am-5pm. Tours every half hour, except 1pm. Pre-book ONLY through Open House, see p15 for details. Last tour 4.30pm. Max 6 per tour. P T A
Set in woodland on a sloping site its cedar-clad timber-framed construction was ahead of its time. Resisting radical change, the house is often used for photo-shoots and has recently been listed. 'Perfect house' – Grand Designs, April 2008. Ivor Berresford 1957-58.
Transport: car necessary

The Churchill
High Street, Bromley BR1 1HA
→ Sat 10am-12noon. Regular tours, pre-book ONLY on 0870 060 6620. Max 20 per tour. d T
Wonderful example of a repertory theatre in style of European opera houses, with vast stage, sub-stage workshops and auditorium seating 785. Ken Wilson 1977. Entry: auditorium, stage, wings, dressing rooms, rehearsal spaces.
Rail: Bromley South, Bromley North; 119,138,208,227,726

The Keston Windmill
Heathfield Road, Keston BR2 6BF
→ Sat/Sun 10.30am-4pm. Last entry 4pm. Regular tours, max 10 at one time. d P Q R
A 1716 post mill and Kent's oldest surviving windmill, black and weatherboarded, on a brick roundhouse. Entry: windmill only. NB. Steep stairs.
Rail: Bromley South, Hayes; 246,146

The Odeon, Beckenham
High Street, Beckenham BR3 1DY
→ Sat/Sun tours at 10am, pre-book ONLY through Open House, see p15 for details. Max 8 at one time. D R T
Art Deco cinema with proscenium arch, stained glass windows and typically Deco mouldings. Robert Cromie 1930. Entry: main foyer, auditorium.
Rail: Beckenham Junction; 227,194,358,367,726,352,351

The Priory
Church Hill, Orpington BR6 0HH
→ Sat/Sun 10am-5pm. Tours 11am, 12.30pm, 2pm of building and art store. Last entry 4.30pm. Max 20 per tour. d N T
Medieval/Post-Medieval Grade II* listed building (13C-19C) set in attractive Italianate gardens. Originally a rectory and then manor house attached to the Priory of Christ Church Canterbury. Entry: main hall, galleries.
Rail: Orpington; 51,61,208,353

Sundridge Park

The Berresford House

WALKS/TOURS

Self-guided trail of Chislehurst
→ Sat/Sun. Organised by the Chislehurst Society. Collect trail brochures from chislehurst-society.org.uk, or by post from PO Box 82, Chislehurst, BR7 5TT (please enclose stamped addressed C5 envelope)
Self-guided walk round the best examples of local architects' work, including E.J.May, Ernest Newman, Somers Clarke, etc.
Rail: Chislehurst; 61,269,162

Supported by

Bromley
THE LONDON BOROUGH

Camden

12 Regent's Park Road ●
12 Regent's Park Road NW1 7TX
→ Sat/Sun 1pm-5pm. First come basis. Max 5 at one time. G T
Eco-refurbishment of Victorian terrace combining unique
art deco interiors with maximum energy efficiency including
sustainable materials, green roof and green technologies.
Tube: Chalk Farm, Camden

19 North End
19 North End NW3 7HR
→ Sat 1pm-5pm. Tours every half hour, pre-book ONLY
through Open House, see p15 for details. Max 4 per tour. P A
Modernist house of yellow stock brick built as a private
residence for family use by architect, academic and decipherer
of Minoan script Linear B. Iconic fitted interior, designed
to house furniture (no longer there) designed by Bauhaus
architect Marcel Breuer for architect's parents. Original
finishes still intact. Michael Ventris and Lois Ventris 1953.
Tube: Golders Green, Hampstead; 210,268

2 Willow Road
2 Willow Road NW3 1TH
→ Sun 10am-4pm. Tours on the hour, pre-book ONLY through
Open House, see p15 for details. Max 10 per tour. d
Unique Modernist home largely in original condition. The
house, which has 3 floors at the front and 4 at the back, is
designed for flexibility, efficient use of space and good day-
lighting. It also contains fittings and furniture designed by
Goldfinger and his modern art collection including works by
Riley, Ernst and Moore. Ernö Goldfinger 1939.
Tube: Hampstead; Rail: Hampstead Heath; 24,46,268,603,C11

39 Frognal – Kate Greenaway Studio
39 Frognal NW3 6YD
→ Sun 10am-1pm. First come basis. Max 12 at one time. T
A substantial studio-house originally built for illustrator Kate
Greenaway; the painting studio is at 45 degrees to catch the
north light. Norman Shaw 1885. Entry: studio, room, terrace.
Tube: Hampstead; Tube/Rail: Finchley Road; 268,46

56 Camden Mews
56 Camden Mews NW1 9BX
→ Sat 1pm-5pm. First come basis, queuing outside if necessary. A
This historic mews house was completely remodelled
internally, incorporating glass screens and folded steel plate
stairs leading to open plan living/kitchen on the first floor.
Knott Architects 2009. Entry: ground, 1st floor.
Tube: Camden Town; Rail: Camden Road; 29,253,390,274

73 Chester Road ●
73 Chester Road N19 5DH
→ Sat 10am-5pm. Tours on the hour, first come basis. Last tour
5pm. Max 6 per tour. NB. only 2 volunteers per group. G
Semi-detached late Victorian house, carefully transformed
in 2006 to make it fit for 21C, reducing its carbon footprint by
70%. Sustainable features include walls internally insulated;
high performance windows; solar panels; light pipe; wood
burning stove, water saving techniques.
Tube: Archway; C2,C11,214,134,390

Lumen United Reformed Church and Community Centre

79 Stoneleigh Terrace
79 Stoneleigh Terrace N19 5TZ
→ Sun 10.30am-4.30pm. NB. Closed 1pm-2pm. Tours every 30
mins, first come basis. Last tour 4pm. Max 6 per tour. R T A
Light-filled 1970s Brutalist terraced house, recently
remodelled. Peter Tábori, Camden Architect's Department
1972-9/David Kohn Architects refurb 2007. Entry: house.
Tube: Archway; 4,C11

8 Kendalls Hall
8 Kendalls Hall, New End NW3 1DE
→ Sun 1pm-5pm. Pre-book ONLY on info@serranoevans.com.
Last entry 4.45pm. Max 12 at one time. d A
Private house conversion displaying a holistic approach
to architecture, interior, furniture and movement design.
Includes a new site specific installation based on various
stages of the site's life. Serrano Evans Partnership 2009.
Tube: Hampstead; Rail: Hampstead Heath; 46,268,168,C11

8 Stoneleigh Terrace
8 Stoneleigh Terrace N19 5TY
→ Sun 10am-5pm. NB. Closed 1pm-2pm. Tours on the hour.
Last tour 4pm. Max 15 per tour. T
Built during the golden era of Camden public housing by an
architect who studied with Ernö Goldfinger and worked with
Lasdun. Peter Tábori, Camden Architect's Department 1972-9.
Tube: Archway; 4,C11

85 Swains Lane

85 Judd Street
85 Judd Street WC1H 9NE
→ Sat 10am-5pm. First come basis. Max 7 at one time. Q A
New-build residence with concrete ceilings and unpainted
render, remodelled in 2002/07 using materials in unusual
contexts such as black resin floors, pink terrazzo worktops,
bronze cupboards, plastic walls. Fred Manson 1988/Project
Orange 2002. Entry: entrance, main room, roof garden.
Tube: Russell Square; Tube/Rail: King's Cross St Pancras; 10,30,73

85 Swains Lane ●
85 Swains Lane N6 6PJ
→ Sat 10am-5pm. First come basis, queuing outside if
necessary. Max 10 at one time. G Q T A
Built on a unique site overlooking Highgate Cemetery, this
new house is set over four floors. The façade echoes the
monumental masonry of the cemetery in contrast to the
largely glazed cemetery elevations that wash the fairfaced
concrete interior with natural light. RIBA Award Winner 2009.
Eldridge Smerin 2007.
Tube: Archway; C2,C11,146,210,271

Alexandra Road ●
13(b) Rowley Way, Abbey Road NW8 0SF
→ Sat 10am-5pm. Regular tours. Last entry 4.30pm. Max 4 at a time.
The last large social housing complex in London – a low-rise,
high-density enclave. Terraced housing reinterpreted. Listed
Grade II* in 1993. Flat virtually as originally designed. Neave
Brown 1968-79. Entry: whole flat.
Tube: Swiss Cottage; Rail: South Hampstead; 159,139

British Library
96 Euston Road NW1 2DB
→ Sun 11am-5pm. Caring for Your Family Archive: 11am-4pm,
pre-book on 01937 546 546. Talk on Asian and African
collections 11.30am & 2pm. Tickets available on day. BDNRT
Highly acclaimed building of red brick with colourful window
details and roof, this is the ultimate in post-modernity. RIBA
Award Winner. Colin St John Wilson & Associates 1998. Entry:
all public areas, Asian & African Studies reading room.
Tube/Rail: King's Cross St Pancras, Euston; 10,30,73,91

Burgh House
New End Square NW3 1LT
→ Sat/Sun 12noon-5pm. Last entry 4.30pm. B d N R T
Grade I listed Queen Anne house (1704) retaining original
panelling and 'barley sugar' balusters with a modern gallery
set in a small award-winning Gertrude Jekyll terrace garden.
Entry: basement café, period rooms, art gallery, shop, Museum.
Tube: Hampstead; Rail: Hampstead Heath; 46,24,268,168,C11

Café Caponata & Forge Arts Venue
3-7 Delancey Street NW1 7NL
→ Sat 10am-6pm. Tours 10am-1pm. Max 20 per tour. D N R T A
A new mixed use building with recital hall, café and restaurant and apartments above, on the site of former Café Delancey, linked by a double-height glazed courtyard with vertically planted 'living' wall. Burd Haward Architects 2009. Entry: café, restaurant, courtyard, recital hall, possible entry to 1 flat.
Tube: Camden Town; Rail: Camden Road; C2,253,24,88,168,29

Cecil Sharp House
2 Regent's Park Road NW1 7AY
→ Sat 12.30pm-5.30pm. Hourly tours. Max 20 per tour. d T
Purpose built in 1930 to house the (now) English Folk Dance and Song Society, this Grade II listed building includes a 60ft mural by Ivon Hitchens (1954) and was designed by members of the Art Workers Guild. Martineau & Fletcher 1930. Entry: Kennedy Hall, gardens, Vaughan Williams Memorial Library.
Tube: Camden Town; Rail: Camden Road; 274,C2,29,253,168

Centre Point
103 New Oxford Street WC1A 1DU
→ Sat 9am-5pm. Tours on the hour, pre-book ONLY through Open House, see p15 for details. All bags, coats to be checked in, metal detectors operating. Max 20 per tour. D T
34 storey, 121m Grade II listed London landmark. The structure is claimed to be the first in London to be erected not requiring scaffolding, with prefabricated precast-concrete H-shaped units lifted into place by crane. Richard Seifert 1967. Entry: reception, CBI podium level, 18th, 31st, 32nd and 33rd floors.
Tube: Tottenham Court Road; Tube/Rail: Euston; 134,24,390,29

Congress Centre
23-28 Great Russell Street WC1B 3LS
→ Sat 10am-5pm. Regular tours. Max 25 per tour. B D T A
TUC HQ, excellent representation of the 1950s period and one of the most significant post-war listed buildings in London. High quality finishes and sculptures by Epstein and Meadows. Recently refurbished. Grade II* listed. David Aberdeen 1957/ Hugh Broughton Architects (refurb) 2003. Entry: reception, marble hall, conference hall, foyers.
Tube: Tottenham Court Road; Tube/Rail: Euston; 10,24,29,73,134

Dominion Theatre
268-269 Tottenham Court Road W1
→ Sun 10am-5pm. Max 12 at one time. T
Large and stylish, originally conceived to serve either as theatre or cinema. Grade II listed. William & TR Milburn 1929. Entry: foyer, auditorium, circle bar. NB. brief church services.
Tube: Tottenham Court Road; 1,7,8,10,14,19,24,25

Freemasons' Hall
60 Great Queen Street WC2B 5AZ
→ Sat 10am-5pm. Last entry 4.30pm. B D N
Monumental classical exterior belying elaborate and varied interior decoration: extensive use of mosaic, stained glass, decorated ceilings and lighting. Ashley and Newman 1927-33. Entry: Grand Temple and ceremonial areas.
Tube: Holborn, Covent Garden; 1,59,68,91,168,171,188

Friends House
173-177 Euston Road NW1 2BJ
→ Sun 1pm-5pm. Regular tours. Max 10 per tour. B D N T
Described by the Architectural Review in 1927 as '...eminently Quakerly, or, in other words, unites common sense with just so much relief from absolute plainness as gives pleasure.' Winner of RIBA bronze medal in 1927. Hubert Lidbetter 1926. Entry: meeting house, meeting rooms, library, bookshop, café.
Tube: Euston Square; Tube/Rail: Euston; 10,18,30,73,91,68,205,253

Garden Court Chambers ●
57-60 Lincoln's Inn Fields WC2A 3LS
→ Sat 10am-4pm/Sun 10am-1pm. Hourly tours. Last tour Sat 4pm, Sun 1pm. Max 20 per tour. Display of historical photography and architectural drawings in reception. d Q T
Inigo Jones' 1630s design at no.59-60 intended as model for Lincoln's Inn Fields development, copied by no.57-58 with portico and elliptical staircase added by Soane in 1700s. Sympathetically refurbished by current occupiers, a barristers' chambers. Retains many original features. Entry: reception, staircases, meeting & conference rooms.
Tube: Holborn; Tube/Rail: Charing Cross; 1,59,68,91,168,171,188

German Gymnasium – King's Cross Central Visitor Ctr
26 Pancras Road N1C 4TB
→ Sat/Sun 10am-5pm.
Home of the German Gymnastics Society established in London c1861. Arguably the first purpose-built gymnasium in Britain. Building hosted the indoor events of National Olympian Games in 1866. Original bolt-laminated timber arch roof believed to be a prototype of King's Cross station roof. Now contains exhibitions of Argent's regeneration of the 67 acre King's Cross development and neighbouring projects. E A Gruning 1864-5. Entry: exhibition.
Tube/Rail: King's Cross St Pancras; 46,214,73,390

Goodenough College, London House
Mecklenburgh Square WC1N 2AB
→ Sat 2pm-5pm. Tours every 20 mins. Last tour 4.40pm. D P T
Neo-Georgian Grade II listed postgraduate college. Unique brick and flint exterior, impressive Empire-era public rooms, and quadrangle with arcaded cloister. Sir Herbert Baker 1933. Entry: Great Hall, library, chapel, Churchill room.
Tube: Russell Square; Tube/Rail: King's Cross St Pancras; 17,45,55,38

Government Art Collection
Near Tottenham Court Road W1 (full details given at time of booking)
→ Sat/Sun 10am-5pm. 45 min tours on the hour. Pre-book ONLY on 020 7580 9120 or gac@culture.gsi.gov.uk. Last entry 4pm. Max 25 per tour. T
Guided tour of premises and behind-the-scenes look at how this major collection of British art operates. Entry: all areas except office accommodation.
Tube: Goodge Street, Warren Street; Tube/Rail: Euston; 10,14,24,29

Gray's Inn
Gray's Inn WC1R 5ET
→ Sun tours at 10.30am, 12noon, 2pm. Duration 1 hour. Must enter via entrance in High Holborn next to Cittie of York. Pre-book ONLY through Open House, see p15 for details. Max 30 per tour. D T
700 year old legal collegiate institution. Hall includes 16C screen. Much of Inn redesigned in neo-Georgian style by Sir Edward Maufe after 1941 bombing. Entry: hall, large pension room, small pension room, chapel and the walks.
Tube: Chancery Lane, Holborn, Blackfriars; Tube/Rail: King's Cross St Pancras; 8,19,25,38,45,55,242,341

Hampstead Friends Meeting House
120 Heath Street NW3 1DR
→ Sat 2pm-6pm/Sun 1pm-5pm. Regular tours. D T
Listed Arts and Crafts freestyle building with plain interior and many charming original features, sympathetically modernised in 1991. Entrance via listed gateway. Fred Rowntree 1907. Entry: ground floor, 1st floor library.
Tube: Hampstead; Rail: Hampstead Heath; 268

Hampstead Theatre
Eton Avenue NW3 3EU
→ Sat 10am-1pm. Behind-the-scenes tours at 10.30am, 11.15am, 12noon, 12.45pm. First come basis. Max 15 per tour. D
RIBA award-winning glass building with environmentally-sound auditorium. Bennetts Associates 2003. Entry: front of house. Entry on tours: front of house, stage area, dressing rooms, green room, wardrobe, auditorium, box office, workshop.
Tube: Swiss Cottage; 31,187

Highgate Literary & Scientific Institution
11 South Grove N6 6BS
→ Sun 12noon-4pm. Unrestricted entry to Victoria Hall, guided tours to other rooms. Last entry 3.15pm. Max 12 per tour. d T
Fine stuccoed building overlooking Pond Square, and home to Institution since 1840. Formed from 1790 coach house, stables and yard, with final additions c1880. Entry: Victoria hall, members' room, library, Coleridge room.
Tube: Highgate, Archway; 214,210,271,143

Jestico + Whiles
1 Cobourg Street NW1 2HP
→ Sat 10am-5pm. R T G A
Conversion of former Victorian stable block to provide radical mix of lofts and workspace. Exhibition of current architecture and interior design. Sustainable features include natural ventilation, fast-reacting warm air and ventilation system. Jestico + Whiles 1998. Entry: studio, exhibition space.
Tube: Euston Square; Tube/Rail: Euston; 10,18,24,27,29,30,73,88

John McAslan + Partners
7 William Road NW1 3ER
→ Sat 10.30am-5pm. Regular architect-led tours, first come basis, queuing outside if necessary. D T A
John McAslan + Partners' new office, recently converted by the interiors team, with an opportunity to see models of King's Cross Station, Cheapside and Olympic Energy Centres. John McAslan + Partners 2009. Entry: studios, model-shop.
Tube: Warren Street; Rail: Euston; 10,14,24,29,73

Johnson Building ● ●
77 Hatton Garden EC1N 8JP
→ Sat 1pm-5pm. Regular tours. Max 40 at one time. Sun 3.30pm VocalEyes tour for blind and partially sighted people, contact Toby Davey toby@vocaleyes.co.uk/020 7375 1043 for more info and how to book. D T G A
One of Derwent London's flagship developments in London's midtown, a part-refurbishment and part new-build centred around stunning central atrium. Sustainable features include displacement air-conditioning and 'DALI' lighting technology. RIBA Award Winner 2008. Allford Hall Monaghan Morris 2006. Entry: atrium, Faber Maunsell's upper office floors.
Tube: Chancery Lane; Tube/Rail: Farringdon; 55,38,521,25,8

Kentish Town Community Centre ●
17 Busby Place NW5 2SP
→ Sun 12noon-7pm. First come basis. Max 80 at one time. Model and drawings of proposed developments; local history exhibition; photographic exhibition 'Rome by car' by Megan Williams and Hoppy Hopkins and Sue Hall ishowing their restored historic videos at 6pm. D P T G A
Small flagship project nestled at the centre of a Kentish Town suburban block to form a new heart for the local community. Sustainable features include solar heat reflecting film on glass roof. EnterArchitecture with Ian Haywood Partnership 2004.
Tube/Rail: Kentish Town; Rail: Camden Road; 29,253,134,214,390

Kentish Town Health Centre
2 Bartholomew Road NW5 2AJ
→ Sat 10am-4pm. First come basis. Max 40 at one time. D T A
A compact building which covers the majority of its triple-frontage site and encourages interaction with the community through an internal streetscape. A volumetric concept of 'sliding blocks' facilitates an interplay between departments. RIBA Award Winner 2009. Allford Hall Monaghan Morris 2008.
Tube/Rail: Kentish Town; C2,134,214,46

Kenwood House
Hampstead Lane NW3 7JR
→ Sat/Sun 11.30am-4pm. 'Behind the Scenes' guided tours 12noon, 2pm, 3pm including to lecture theatre and library, max 20 per tour. 'Repton Talk and Tour' on Repton's views across Kenwood, 2pm, max 20 per group. Lord Iveagh's Coach and the Buckland Caravan 12noon-3pm. B d N R T
Outstanding Neo-classical villa in beautiful grounds on Hampstead Heath. The decorated library is one of Adam's masterpieces. Robert Adam 1764-79. Entry: house, grounds.
Tube: Archway, Golders Green then 210; Rail: Hampstead Heath

King's Cross Construction Skills Centre ●
180 York Way N1 0AZ
→ Sat 10am-1pm. Max 15 at one time. D G T
One of the first buildings to be erected at King's Cross Central is LB Camden's conservation skills and recruitment centre. The building detailing is used as a 'lesson in construction' for the students. Externally, the roof features photovoltaic panels and a sedum roof to support biodiversity. RIBA Award Winner 2009. Camden Building Quality Award Winner 2009. David Morley Architects 2009.
Tube/Rail: King's Cross St Pancras; 46,214,73,390,91,17

Lissenden Gardens Estate
91-100 Parliament Hill Mansions, Lissenden Gds NW5 1NB
→ Sun 10am-5pm. First come basis. Max 10 at one time. P
Turn of 20C 'labour-saving' arts and crafts mansion flats overlooking Parliament Hill Fields, with successful layout and balconies. Bought at tenants' instigation by Camden Council in 1973 and still providing much loved homes. Boehmer & Gibbs 1898. Entry to two specified flats, exterior of estate.
Tube: Kentish Town, Tufnell Park; Rail: Gospel Oak; 214,C2,C11

Little Green Street ●
Little Green Street NW5 1BL
→ Sat 10am-5pm. Regular tours, first come basis, to various houses including nos 1-2,3,4,5,10 and The Greenhouse on Little Green Street. Last entry 4.30pm. Max 5 on tours to houses. Extensive display of interpretive material. R A
One of the few intact cobbled Georgian streets in London, former shops and small works now all residential. Many original features in houses on north of street. Extensive conversion to The Greenhouse emphasising light and views, retaining a sense of cohesion with the remainder of the street. Partially rebuilt 20C extension to no.3 (both by 51% Studios).
Tube/Rail: Kentish Town; Rail: Gospel Oak; C2,214

Llowarch Llowarch Offices – Brunswick Centre
147 O'Donnell Court WC1N 1NX
→ Sat 12noon-4pm. First come basis. Max 5 at one time. T A
Example of purpose designed studio/workshop on concourse level above the retail units within the recently refurbished Grade II listed Brunswick Centre. Chance to see inside the normally inaccessible 'A-framed' streets. Patrick Hodgkinson 1972. NB. Architects' projects, models and drawings on display.
Tube: Russell Square; Tube/Rail: King's Cross; 7,59,68,168,91,188

London School of Economics: New Academic Building
54 Lincoln's Inn Fields WC2A 3LJ
→ Sun 1pm-5pm. Regular half-hourly tours, first come basis. Last tour 4.30pm. Max 20 per tour. D T G A
Originally constructed in 1915 this Beaux Arts building was dramatically transformed in 2008, retaining the original façade. Highlights include a soaring central atrium with art installation by Joy Gerrard, a set piece lecture theatre and roof top terrace. Camden Building Quality Award Winner 2009. Nicholas Grimshaw and Partners 2008. Entry: ground, lower ground, 1st, 5th, 7th, 8th floors and balcony.
Tube: Holborn; Tube/Rail: Charing Cross; 1,168,521,15,26

London School of Hygiene & Tropical Medicine
Keppel Street WC1E 7HT
→ Sat 10am-5pm. Tours on the hour, first come basis. Last tour 4pm. Max 20 per tour. Exhibition on history of building. D T
Beautiful Grade II listed Art Deco building with highly decorated façade, period library, north courtyard extension and new south courtyard building. P Morley Horder & Verner O Rees 1929/Devereux Architects 2003/2009. Entry: entrance hall, library, north and south courtyard buildings.
Tube: Goodge Street, Russell Square; Tube/Rail: Euston; 10,24,29

Low Energy Victorian House towards zero carbon dwellings ●
17 St Augustine's Road NW1 9RL
→ Sun 11am-5pm. Regular tours, first come basis, queuing outside if necessary. Max 15 at one time. T G
A rare example of a solid-walled Victorian house which has been refurbished in 2008 with the aim of reducing emissions by 80%. A Camden Council property, the challenge was to show how Victorian and other period housing can be bequeathed to future generations.
Tube: Camden Town; Rail: Camden Road; 390,274

Lumen United Reformed Church and Community Ctr
88 Tavistock Place WC1H 9RS
→ Sat 10am-5pm. Hourly tours except 1pm, first come basis. Last tour 4pm. Max 10 per tour. D N R T
Created within the shell of an existing 1960s United Reformed church. There are three main elements to the redesign: a dramatic 8m high window, a new extension housing community spaces, and new sacred space the 'Shaft of Light': a white-rendered spectacular conical intervention which reaches through the full 11m height of the building to a single roof-light. RIBA Award Winner 2009. Theis and Kahn 2009.
Tube: Russell Square; Tube/Rail: King's Cross St Pancras; 91,168,59

Mary Ward House
5-7 Tavistock Place WC1H 9SN
→ Sat/Sun 10am-5pm. Regular tours every 45 minutes. Last tour 4pm. Max 20 per tour. C d R T E
One of London's finest expressions of the Arts and Crafts Movement, very much in the spirit of Voysey, and an excellent example of late Victorian philanthropy. Grade I listed. First purpose-designed settlement. Dunbar Smith & Cecil Brewer 1898. Entry: Mary Ward Hall, ground floor, lower ground floor.
Tube: Russell Square; Tube/Rail: Euston, King's Cross; 59,68,91,168

Pushkin House
5A Bloomsbury Square WC1A 2TA
→ Sat/Sun 11am-4pm.
A centre of Russian culture in London, this Grade II* listed house has a fine staircase which has been meticulously restored. Henry Flitcroft 1744. Entry: basement, ground, 1st floors.
Tube: Holborn 1,8,19,25,38

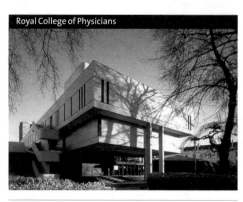
Royal College of Physicians

Qube ●
90 Whitfield Street W1T 4EW
→ Sat 10am-1pm. Last entry 12.30pm. Max 40 at a time. T G A
The scheme includes 9,290sqm of office space on five floors set around an internal atrium, as well as shops and seven 2-bedroom apartments occupying a prominent position in the West End. The building has solar control glazing and energy efficient high frequency luminaires. EPR 2007. Entry: lobby, 1st/4th/5th floors.
Tube: Warren Street, Goodge Street; Tube/Rail: Euston; 10,14,24,29

Roundhouse
Chalk Farm Road NW1 8EH
→ Sat/Sun 10am-3pm. Tours on the hour. Last tour 3pm. Max 40 at one time. D N R T
Originally constructed to turn steam engines, designed by Robert Dockray under the principal engineer Robert Stevenson, it reopened after a £30m refurbishment in June 2006 and has re-established its place as a cultural landmark. Includes state-of-the-art creative studios for young people to participate in projects and courses. RIBA Award Winner 2007. Robert Dockray 1846/John McAslan & Partners (refurb) 2006. Entry: main performance space.
Tube: Chalk Farm; Rail: Kentish Town West; 31,168,26,27,46

Royal Academy of Dramatic Art
62-64 Gower Street WC1E 6ED
→ Sat tours at 11.30am and 1pm. Pre-book ONLY on 020 7908 4800. Max 15 at one time. D R T
Theatres, public bar and first class teaching facilities with large glass curving bay and terracotta grid of cleverly disguised flytower, and shaft of daylight from roof through glass floor to workshops in basement. RIBA Award Winner. Avery Associates Architects 2001. Entry: 3 theatres, workshops, rehearsal rooms, public spaces. Student productions will be running.
Tube: Euston Square, Goodge Street; Tube/Rail: Euston; 10,24,29,30

Royal College of Physicians
11 St Andrew's Place, Regents Park NW1 4LE
→ Sun 10am-4pm. Regular tours bookable on the day. Last entry 3.30pm. D P R T
Dramatic interior spaces and white mosaic exterior elevated on piloti. Grade I listed and one of London's most important post-war buildings. Sir Denys Lasdun 1964/1996. Entry: main hall, theatres, library, Osler Room, Censors' Room, council chamber, Silver Room.
Tube: Great Portland Street, Regents Park; Rail/Tube: Euston, King's Cross St Pancras; C2,18,27,30,88,205,453

Roundhouse

London School of Economics: New Academic Building

Sir John Soane's Museum & 14 Lincolns Inn Fields
13 & 14 Lincoln's Inn Fields WC2A 3BP
→ Sat 10am-5pm. Last entry 4.30pm. Restricted access. C Q T A
Soane's house, gallery, library and art collection surviving as
built, with some of London's most spectacular room settings.
Also open will be No.14 Lincoln's Inn Fields, built by Soane in
1824 and let out in his lifetime as a private house. The building
restored in 2006-7 will house a new education centre and
research facility. A beautiful and rare example of Soane's late
work with a number of fine interiors. RIBA Award Winner
2009. Sir John Soane 1812 & 1824. Entry: main museum and
No.14 Lincoln's Inn Fields.
Tube: Holborn; 1,8,19,25,38

St George's Bloomsbury ●
Bloomsbury Way WC1A 2HR
→ Sat 10am-7pm/Sun 12noon-5pm. Tours on the hour, first
come basis. Last tour Sat 5pm, Sun 3pm. Sun 4pm Lecture
on Hawksmoor's Freemasonry and Esoteric Symbolism.
Hawksmoor and Bloomsbury exhibition. C d T A
Last of Hawksmoor's six London churches and consecrated in
1730, it is instantly recognisable by its majestic large columned
portico and stepped tower with newly carved lions and
unicorns. Reopened in 2006 following a five-year restoration.
First chance to see the 2009 restoration of the beautiful North
Gallery. Nicholas Hawksmoor 1720s.
*Tube: Tottenham Court Road, Holborn, Russell Square; Tube/Rail:
Euston; 38,8,19,25,55*

St Giles-in-the-Fields
60 St Giles High Street WC2H 8LG
→ Sat 10am-6pm/Sun 12noon-5pm. D T
Grade I listed Palladian church by architect of Woburn Abbey,
with one of London's best preserved early Georgian interiors
with Grade II* listed panelled Vestry room with period
furniture. Recently restored 17C/18C historic organ. Henry
Flitcroft 1730-34. Entry: church, vestry room, ringing chamber.
Tube: Tottenham Court Road; 1,7,8,10,14,19,24

St Martin's, Gospel Oak
Vicars Road NW5 4NL
→ Sat 10am-4pm/Sun 12noon-2pm. D P R T
Grade I listed and (according to Pevsner) London's craziest
Victorian church; exceptional roof, soaring tower, unusual
detail and supporting interior with alabaster pulpit. Major
restoration and refurbishment now complete. Edward
Buckton Lamb 1865. Entry: church, hall, gardens.
Tube: Chalk Farm; Rail: Gospel Oak; 24,46,C11

St Pancras International
Pancras Road NW1 2QP
→ Sat/Sun 10am-5pm. Regular half-hourly tours, meet at
The German Gymnasium, 26 Pancras Road, NW1 2TB, first
come basis. Last entry 4pm. Max 20 per tour. D N T
A unique Grade I listed Victorian landmark which has
undergone a £800 million transformation into a world-
class destination station and acted as a catalyst for the
regeneration of the King's Cross area. Foster + Partners,
Union Railways, Chapman Taylor 1868 & 2007. Entry: upper
concourse, arcade, circle.
Tube/Rail: King's Cross St Pancras, Euston; 205,73,214,390,46

St Pancras Old Church
Pancras Road NW1 1UH
→ Sat 9am-5pm/Sun 10.30am-5pm. Regular tours.
Introductory talks Sat/Sun at 11am & 3pm. Presentation
about church and history Sun 5pm. D N R T
Dating from 11/12C and standing on oldest site of Christian
worship in London (3C). Inside is much 17C ornamentation
and outstanding 6C Altar Stone, reputed to have belonged
to St Augustine. Surrounding Churchyard, containing tombs
of Sir John Soane, Mary Wollstonecraft and others, has been
extensively restored and recently refurbished.
NB. Sun 9.30am service.
*Tube: Mornington Crescent, Camden Town; Tube/Rail: King's
Cross St Pancras; 46,214*

The Art Workers Guild
6 Queen Square WC1N 3AT
→ Sat 10am-6pm/Sun 12noon-5pm. Regular tours. d R T
1713 terraced house with hall at rear (F W Troup 1914). Notable
renovated Arts and Crafts interior. Portraits of Guild Masters
since 1884. Entry: hall, committee room and library. NB.
Exhibition of current members' work.
*Tube: Russell Square, Holborn; Tube/Rail: King's Cross St Pancras;
59,68,91,168,188*

The Swedenborg Society
20-21 Bloomsbury Way WC1A 2TH
→ Sat 10am-4pm. Half hourly tours. Last tour and entry
3.45pm. Max 20 at one time. B d T
Grade II listed Georgian domestic building c1760, formerly part
of Bedford Estate. Interior refurbished 1925-6 to form lecture
hall, library and bookshop. Oak woodwork and green Doulton
tiles line the staircase. Entry: hall, Wynter room, Gardiner
room, bookshop.
Tube: Holborn; Tube/Rail: King's Cross St Pancras; 8,19,25,38,55

UCL (University College London)
Gower Street WC1E 6BT
→ Sat 10am-4pm. Regular tours from information point
(Front Quad, Gower Street), taking in Front Quad, Cloisters,
Flaxman Gallery and Jeremy Bentham. General access to
Strang Print Room, Grant Museum and Petrie Museum
(both accessed via Malet Place). Max 30 on tours. C D T
The third oldest university in England, having been founded
as the University of London in 1826. UCL's neo-Grecian central
portico is its famous landmark, and is generally recognised
as William Wilkins' greatest work (1827-9). Main campus
includes Strang Print room, with over 10,000 fine art objects,
Grant Museum contains all aspects of the animal kingdom
and Petrie Museum of Egyptian and Sudanese archaeology
(both museums have children's activities and the Grant has
drop-in family activities).
Tube: Euston Square, Goodge Street; Tube/Rail: Euston; 10,18,24

UCL – Cruciform Building
Gower Street WC1E 6BT
→ Sat 10am-4pm. Regular tours departing from building
foyer. R T
Building was opened in 1906 as the new home for University
College Hospital, it now houses the UCL Wolfson Institute
for Biomedical Research Research and the UCL Medical
School. Many of the original unusual features retained
including the Royal Dalton collection of tiled children's stories,
especially commissioned for the then Children's Ward. Alfred
Waterhouse 1896. Entry: areas on tours.
Tube: Euston Square, Goodge Street; Tube/Rail: Euston; 18,24,29

Supported by

Camden Building Quality Awards 2009
This is Camden's 4th bi-annual Building Quality Awards
which celebrates the building and construction industry
in the borough and beyond through Camden's Partner
Authority Scheme arrangement (PAS). These awards
compliment the Camden Design Awards by focusing on the
quality of construction and the construction process rather
than just the design aspects of the built environment. The
Building Regulations are constantly changing and issues
around sustainability and inclusive design are of particular
importance.

City of London

International Headquarters of the Salvation Army

New Street Square

1 Finsbury Circus
1 Finsbury Circus EC2M 7EB
→ Sat/Sun 10am-1pm. Architect-led half-hourly tours, pre-book ONLY through Open House, see p15 for details. Last tour 12.30pm. Max 10 per tour. D A

This Lutyens Grade II listed building has been comprehensively redeveloped to provide a high quality contemporary interior, with a fully glazed spectacular atrium roof to maximize daylight and aspect. Edwin Lutyens 1925/Gaunt Francis (refurb) 2009. Entry: reception, listed staircase, atrium, 4th floor listed room, 8th floor.
Tube/Rail: Liverpool Street, Moorgate; 43,76,100,141,205

10 Queen Street Place ●
10 Queen Street Place EC4R 1BE
→ Sat/Sun 10am-5pm. Tours on the hour except 1pm. Pre-book ONLY through Open House, see p15 for details. Last entry 4pm. Max 20 per tour. D R T G A

Overlooking the Thames these new offices incorporate three atria linked by glazed bridges bringing light deep into the interior. The building is topped by a roof garden. John Robertson Architects/HOK International/Seth Stein Architects 2006. Entry: entrance hall, scenic lifts, client suite, roof terrace.
Tube/Rail: London Bridge, Liverpool Street; Tube/DLR: Bank; Rail: Blackfriars; 344,15,17,11,23

120 Fleet Street (ex Daily Express)
120 Fleet Street EC4A 2BB
→ Sat/Sun 9am-4.30pm. Last entry 4pm. Max 20 at one time. D Q

Dazzling foyer restored to its 1930s splendour; the best British example of the Art Deco style. Sir Owen Williams/Robert Atkinson 1932. Entry: ground floor only.
Rail: Blackfriars; 11,23

201 Bishopsgate and The Broadgate Tower ●
201 Bishopsgate, Primrose Street EC2M 3AB
→ Sat/Sun 9am-5pm. First come basis, queuing if necessary. Last entry 4.30pm. Tours Sat only 10am-2pm. Max 30 at one time. G Q T

The 34-storey tower and 12-storey building are now completed and form part of the two and half acre extension to the Broadgate development. Created by the A-frame structure, a galleria runs between the two buildings, opening to a major new public square. Skidmore Owings & Merrill 2008. Entry: reception areas, one shell and one upper floor.
Tube/Rail: Liverpool Street; 23,149,214,242,271

Andaz London (former Great Eastern Hotel)
Liverpool Street EC2M 7QN
→ Sat 1pm-5pm. Regular tours. D R T

Grade II listed grand Victorian railway hotel refurbished with stylish contemporary interiors. Greek Masonic Temple with magnificent Grade I listed interior of marble and mahogany, built 1912 at immense cost, also open. Charles Barry 1884/Conran & Partners and Manser Practice 2000. Entry: lobby, restaurants, bars, temple.
Tube/Rail: Liverpool Street; 8,11,26,35,42

Apothecaries' Hall
Black Friars Lane EC4V 6EJ
→ Sun 10am-3pm. First come basis. Last entry 2.45pm. Max 100 at one time. Q

A courtyard building with some of the best-preserved 17C livery hall interiors, on the site of the Blackfriars Priory on which the original hall burnt down in 1666.
Thomas Locke 1672. Entry: parlour, court room, great hall.
Rail: Blackfriars; 4,11,15,23,26,45,63,76,172

Bank of England
Threadneedle Street EC2R 8AH
→ Sat/Sun 9.30am-4pm. Regular half hour tours. Last entry 4pm. Max 20 per tour. D Q T

Soane's 18C creation internally rebuilt in imperial classical style. Soanian remnants are screen walls and reconstruction of Bank Stock Office in 1988. Sir Herbert Baker 1925-39. Entry: Parlours including Court Room (NB. many steps).
DLR/Tube: Bank; Tube/Rail: Liverpool Street; 8,11,26,43,76,133,242

Barbican Centre
Silk Street EC2Y 8DS
→ Sat 12noon-3pm. Tours by Barbican staff, pre-book ONLY on 0845 120 7500. Meet at Barbican advance ticket desk, level G. B D R T A

An exploration of the Barbican via the Highwalks, the history of the site and the history behind the original design and the ideas that inspired it. Gives an overview of the £14.1million refurbishment by AHMM making one of Britain's most notoriously difficult buildings accessible. RIBA Award Winner 2007. Chamberlin Powell & Bon 1963/Allford Hall Monaghan Morris (refurb) 2006.
Tube: Barbican; Tube/Rail: Moorgate, Liverpool Street; 4,243,47,78,11

Bart's Hospital Great Hall
St Bartholomew's Hospital, West Smithfield EC1A 7BE
→ Sun 11am-4pm. Last entry 3.45pm. Max 40 at one time. Q R T

Founded in 1123 and rebuilt by Gibbs as the Hospital's showpiece. Grade I listed, the staircase to the Great Hall is decorated by spectacular canvases by William Hogarth. Church of St Bartholomew the Less also open (services 11am & 4pm, visitors welcome). James Gibbs 1730-32. Entry: Great Hall, Hogarth staircase, Guild Room, Museum.
Tube: Barbican, St Pauls; Tube/Rail: Farringdon; Rail: City Thameslink; 4,8,25,56,172,242

Bells and Belfries at St Botolph Aldgate
Aldgate High Street EC3N 1AB
→ Sat 10am-12noon & 2pm-4pm bell ringing demonstrations and belfry tours, last entry 3.30pm; Sun, no ringing, open all day. Max 20 in belfry. Access otherwise unrestricted. Refreshments all day.

Rare opportunity to see the bells and belfry of this church by the architect of Mansion House, with demonstrations taking place. Inside is Rubens' East window and London's oldest organ. George Dance the Elder 1744.
Tube: Aldgate; Tube/Rail: Liverpool Street; Rail: Fenchurch Street; 42,78,100,67,15

Broadgate (self-guided tour) ●
→ Sat/Sun 7am-4.30pm collect self-guided notes from 10 Exchange Square EC2M 2QA

One of the City's most vibrant areas includes the 10 Exchange Square and 155 Bishopsgate office buildings with interesting public art. RIBA Award Winner. Arup Associates and SOM 1984-90. Entry: receptions and public art areas of buildings on trail.
Tube/Rail: Liverpool Street; 8,11,26,35,42,47

Butchers' Hall
87 Bartholomew Close EC1A 7EB
→ Sat 10am-5pm. First come basis. Last entry 4.30pm. D T
The sixth Butchers Hall and second on this site (1883 to present) following considerable damage from Zepplins in 1915 and bomb damage twice during WWII. Howard Kelly 1959. Entry: hall, court room, great hall.
Tube: Barbican, St Paul's; 4,8,25,56,242

Chartered Accountants' Hall
Moorgate Place EC2R 6EA
→ Sat 9am-1pm. Regular tours. Last tour 12.40pm. d
Late Victorian neo-Baroque building with modern-style 1970 extensions supporting 5 stories of offices over the Great Hall. John Belcher 1893/William Whitfield 1970. Entry: main and small reception rooms, great hall.
Tube/DLR: Bank; Tube/Rail: Liverpool Street, Moorgate; 76,100,133,153,214,271

City of London School
Queen Victoria Street (main entrance on river walkway nr Millennium Bridge) EC4V 3AL
→ Sat/Sun 10am-4pm. Last entry 3.30pm. B D R T
Founded in 1442, the new building was designed by the City architects' department on the site of the 15C Baynard Castle. Includes much Victorian art. Stuart Murphy & Tom Meddings 1986. Entry: 'Public' rooms, new and old theatre and Great Hall with Walker organ.
Tube: Mansion House, St Paul's; Rail: Blackfriars; 4,11,15,26,45,63

Clothworkers' Hall
Dunster Court, Mincing Lane EC3R 7AH
→ Sat 10am-5pm. Regular tours, pre-book ONLY by email to archivist@clothworkers.co.uk or 020 7623 7041 x 208. Max 30 per tour. Display of archives relating to the history of the Company and its home. D T
Home to The Clothworkers' Company, founded in 1528, Clothworkers' Hall is the sixth livery hall to stand upon the site. The interiors evoke the history of English Classicism from Wren to the present day and include portraits of notable Clothworkers – including Samuel Pepys – and a stunning set of 18C Brussels tapestries. Herbert Austen Hall 1955-58. Entry: all ceremonial rooms.
Tube: Bank, Monument, Tower Hill; Rail: Fenchurch Street; 15,25,40

Dr Johnson's House
17 Gough Square EC4A 3DE
→ Sat 11am-5.30pm. Short introductory talks throughout the day. Last entry 5pm. Max 100 at one time. B T
Fine example of 18C four-floor town house (c1700), with original panelling and staircase. Famous 'swinging panels' now restored to show the open-plan first floor. Johnson compiled his famous Dictionary of the English Language (1755) here. Entry: all areas. NB. The House will also be open free of charge on Friday 18 Sept, 11am-5.30pm, in honour of Samuel Johnson's 300th birthday.
Tube: Chancery Lane; Tube/Rail: Farringdon; 4,11 15,26,76

Drapers' Hall
Throgmorton Avenue EC2N 2DQ
→ Sun 10am-4pm. First come basis, queuing outside if necessary. Last entry 3.30pm. D T
Livery hall first built in the 1530s, twice destroyed by fire and rebuilt (1666 & 1772). Late 19C façade and opulent Victorian interior. H Williams and Sir T G Jackson 1868. Entry: principal function rooms.
DLR/Tube: Bank; Tube/Rail: Moorgate, Liverpool Street; Rail: Cannon Street; 21,26,76,242,388

Bart's Hospital Great Hall

Guildhall
Gresham Street EC2P 2EJ
→ Sat 10am-5pm/Sun 10am-4pm. Last entry Sat 4.30pm, Sun 3.30pm. B N
The City's seat of municipal government since 12C. Grade I listed, rare example of Medieval civic architecture with post-war extensions and rebuilding. John Croxton 1440/George Dance the Younger 1789. Entry: Great Hall.
DLR/Tube: Bank; Tube: St Paul's, Mansion House; Tube/Rail: Moorgate, Liverpool Street; 8,76,100,133,242

Guildhall Art Gallery ●
Guildhall Yard EC2V 5AE
→ Sat 10am-5pm/Sun 10am-4pm. Regular tours, first come basis. Last entry Sat 4.30pm, Sun 3.45pm. Special exhibitions 'John Gay – a Centenary Celebration' of photographic work including iconic London views, and 'Transfiguration' – paintings of the Olympic site by Raphael Pepper and Dan Llewelyn Hall. B D T
Purpose built art gallery housing City of London's art collection, built over remains of London's 2C Roman amphitheatre. Though modern, the Gallery's front façade is sympathetic to the architecture of its Grade I listed neighbour and makes use of the same traditional materials – Portland stone and Collyweston stone slates. Interior uses fine finishes of marble, American elm, damask wall coverings etc. Richard Gilbert Scott 1999. Entry: art gallery and Roman amphitheatre.
DLR/Tube: Bank; Tube: St Paul's, Mansion House; Tube/Rail: Moorgate, Liverpool Street; 8,76,100,133,242

Guildhall School of Music & Drama
Silk Street, Barbican EC2Y 8DT
→ Sun 10am-5pm. Regular tours to backstage areas, first come basis, first tour 10.15am. Some performances taking place. d R T
In 1977, the renowned Guildhall School moved into its present quarters, part of the Barbican, which include professional backstage and practice facilities and studios. Chamberlin, Powell & Bon 1977. Entry: lobby, concert hall, tours of backstage and studio areas.
Tube: Barbican; Tube/DLR: Bank; Tube/Rail: Moorgate, Liverpool Street; 4,43,64,76,100,153

Guildhall

Haberdashers' Hall ●
18 West Smithfield (opposite Bart's Hospital by traffic barrier under flagpole) EC1A 9HQ
→ Sat 10am-5pm. Last entry 4.45pm. Max 350 at one time. Sat 10.30am VocalEyes tour for blind and partially sighted people, contact Toby Davey toby@vocaleyes.co.uk/020 7375 1043 for more info and how to book. D A
Opened by the Queen in 2002 as the first new livery hall in the Square Mile for nearly 40 years, this is a brick building with traditional lime mortar and handsome lead roof, standing around a peaceful courtyard. American oak panelling and old artefacts and pictures provide internal finishes. Michael Hopkins and Partners 2002.
Tube: Barbican, St Paul's; Tube/Rail: Farringdon; 8,25,56,242,521

International Headquarters of the Salvation Army ●
101 Queen Victoria Street EC4V 4EP
→ Sat 10am-5pm. Architect-led regular half-hourly tours, first come basis. Last entry 4pm. Max 15 per tour. D R T A
A transparent and welcoming working environment with full height glazing and feature steel columns. Brief was to create a space 'modern in design, frugal in operation and evangelical in purpose. Sheppard Robson 2005. Entry: lower ground floor, ground floor, 1st floor.
Tube: Mansion House, St Paul's; Tube/Rail Cannon Street; Rail: Blackfriars; 388,4,11,15,17,26

Leadenhall Market
Gracechurch Street EC3V 1LR
→ Sat/Sun 10am-4pm. Tours 10am-3pm of Roman remains in 90 Gracechurch Street. Max 10 per tour.
Classic cast-iron Victorian covered market by the architect of Tower Bridge and Smithfield Market. Video installation running on both days. Sir Horace Jones 1881. Entry: market streets. NB. Local amenities will be open both days.
DLR/Tube: Bank; Tube: Monument; Tube/Rail: Liverpool Street; 25,40,35,48,344

Bank of England

Lloyd's of London

Tower 42

Leathersellers' Hall
15 St Helen's Place EC3A 6DQ
→ Sat 10am-5pm. Tours on the hour, except for 1pm. Pre-book
 ONLY on 020 7330 1444. Last tour 4pm. Max 25 per tour. T
Post-war building with interiors in neo-Georgian style, this is
the 6th hall in the Leathersellers' Company's history since its
foundation in the Middle Ages. Louis de Soissons Partnership
1960. Entry: Assembly room, Reception room, Livery Hall.
DLR/Tube: Bank; Tube/Rail: Liverpool Street; 35,47,48,149,344

Lloyd's of London
One Lime Street EC3M 7HA
→ Sat 10am-5pm. First come basis, queuing if necessary. Last
 entry 4pm. D R T G
Home of Lloyd's international insurance market and one
of the City's most celebrated buildings, this is – like Rogers'
Pompidou Centre in Paris – a key example of British High-
Tech architecture. RIBA Award Winner. Sustainable features
include many ahead of their time with new initiatives
introduced in recent years to further improve energy
efficiency. Richard Rogers Partnership 1986. Entry: ground
floor, lifts, 11th floor gallery, Adam room.
*DLR/Tube: Bank; Tube: Monument; Tube/Rail: Liverpool Street;
Rail: Fenchurch Street; 25,40,35,48,344*

Mansion House
Walbrook EC4N 8BH
→ Pre-book ONLY. Entry only by pre-booked tour Sat & Sun
 at 9am, 10am, 11am, 12noon, 2pm, 3pm, 4pm. Apply in
 writing by 11 September to Mansion House Tours, Public
 Relations Office, City of London Corporation, Guildhall, PO
 Box 270, EC2P 2EJ. Indicate preferred tour times in order.
 Max 4 tickets per booking. Give names of all attendees
 in application. Tickets allocated by draw; successful
 applicants notified in writing.
Residence of the City of London's Lord Mayor, retaining its
18C character, with superb plasterwork and wood carving.
George Dance the Elder 1739-52. Entry: public areas of house
on ground & 1st floors.
*DLR/Tube: Bank; Tube: Mansion House; Tube/Rail: London
Bridge, Liverpool Street; 8,11,15,25,26,76,242*

Middle Temple Hall
Middle Temple Lane EC4Y 9AT
→ Sun 1pm-5pm. Last entry 4.30pm. Max 500 at a time. D N T
London's finest surviving Elizabethan Hall (1562), 101ft long
and 41ft wide, highly atmospheric, with double hammerbeam
roof, screen and notable paintings. 17C and 20C additions.
Entry: Hall.
Tube: Temple; Rail: Blackfriars; 4,11,15,26,76,172,341

New Street Square
New Street Square EC4A 3BF
→ Sat 10am-4pm. Regular tours, first come basis. Max 10 at
 one time. D G A
New Street Square creates a new destination between High
Holborn and Fleet Street serving the 'mid-town' area of the
City, with a substantial group of new buildings set around a
new public square and hosting a programme of public art and
performance. Bennetts Associates 2007/8.
Tube: Chancery Lane; Tube/Rail: Farringdon, Blackfriars; 4,11,15,26,76

Old Turkish Baths
7-8 Bishopsgate Churchyard EC2M 3TJ
→ Sat/Sun 12noon-5pm. Last entry 4.30pm. R T
Originally a Turkish bath, this little late-Victorian curiosity
survived 20C bombs and redevelopment to become a
restaurant in the 1980s. Well-preserved interior. Harold
Elphick 1894.
Tube/Rail: Liverpool Street; 8,11,23,78

Osborne House
12 Devonshire Square EC2M 4TE
→ Sat 10am-5pm/Sun 1pm-5pm. Last entry 4.45pm. Max 20 at
 one time. B
Fine Grade II listed mid-Georgian house, well preserved
internally with beautiful ornate cornices and plasterwork.
Now HQ of National Association of Flower Arrangement
Societies. Entry: ground floor, 1st floor, lower ground floor.
NB. Free mini flower demonstrations Sat 11am, 12.30pm,
2pm, 3.30pm, max 20 per session. Pre-book ONLY in writing
enclosing SAE to Director, NAFAS, Osborne House, 12
Devonshire Square, EC2M 4TE
Tube/Rail: Liverpool Street; 8,11,48,149,23

Painters' Hall
9 Little Trinity Lane EC4V 2AD
→ Sat 10am-3pm. Max 80 at one time. Informal talks given by
 past Masters, Clerk, and Beadle. D T
Acquired in 1532 and rebuilt in 1670 after the Great Fire, the
Hall was partially destroyed in 1941 by enemy action and
rebuilt in a neo-Georgian style in 1960. The original charters
are of particular interest. H D Searles-Wood 1915/Harrington
(restoration) 1961. Entry: court rooms, livery hall, painted
chamber.
Tube: Mansion House; Rail: Blackfriars; 4,11,15,25,26,76

Pipers' City of London Model at The City Marketing Suite
**City of London's Marketing Suite, within Guildhall Complex
(entrance at 80 Basinghall Street, leading from Gresham
Street) EC2P 2EJ**
→ Sat/Sun 10am-4pm. D T
An overview of the latest developments and architecture in
the City of London via the interactive 1:500 scale Piper model
that shows the future skyline with all of the proposed new
towers.
*DLR/Tube: Bank; Tube: Mansion House, St Paul's;
Tube/Rail: Moorgate, Liverpool Street; 43,8,24,21,76,133,100,242*

St Paul's Information Centre
St Paul's Churchyard EC4M 8BX
→ Sat architect-led tours at 10am, 10.30am, 11am, 11.30am,
 first come basis. Max 20 per tour. d N G A
A significant intervention in one of London's most
important urban quarters. The structure is clad in a specially
manufactured system of 220 pre-finished stainless steel
panels. This subtly reflective surface provides a striking
counterpoint to the stonework of St Paul's. RIBA Award
Winner 2009. make architects 2007.
*Tube: Mansion House, St Paul's; Tube/Rail: Blackfriars;
4,11,15,26,45,63,76,100,172*

The City Churches

47 churches within the City of London, the vast majority of which will be open; some of the oldest buildings and the largest enclosed spaces in the Square Mile.

→ Sat/Sun, times vary.

The range of styles includes Norman, pre-fire Medieval, Sir Christopher Wren's greatest masterpieces, through to rebuilding after WWII and modern re-workings of ancient spaces. Hidden inside are famous monuments, stained glass, paintings and fittings by some of the greatest artists of their day, donated over the centuries by City figures. The three churches listed below give some idea of the range available. Full details for each church will appear on the Open House website and a list of opening times will also be available from St Paul's Information Centre, and from each church during the weekend. Regular tours will take place at most churches every half hour or similar.

St Helen Bishopsgate – Great St Helen's EC3A 6AT

Sat 10am-5pm/Sun 2pm-4pm. Regular tours, first come basis. One of the few City buildings to survive the Great Fire of London and dates from 1210 onwards. Unusual double nave with the best pre-Great Fire collection of monuments in any London parish church. Damaged by two terrorist bombs in the 1990s, then extensively and controversially reordered by Quinlan Terry.

St Mary-le-Bow – Cheapside EC2V 6AU

Sat/Sun 10am-5pm. Regular tours, first come basis. Founded by William the Conqueror's Archbishop Lanfranc in 1080 (of which the highly significant crypt largely survives) St Mary-le-Bow was rebuilt several times, most notably by Wren after the Great Fire and again by Laurence King in 1964 after WWII destruction to Wren's design. Home of the Bow Bells.

St Stephen Walbrook – Walbrook EC4N 8BN

Sat/Sun 9am-6pm. Informal tours 10am-4pm. Wren's own parish church with the building personally supervised by him in 1672. Within a rectangular outline is nested a square space defined by twelve columns and covered by a huge dome. Controversial central stone altar by Henry Moore installed in 1987. Birthplace of the Samaritans
Tube: Bank; Tube/Rail: Moorgate, Liverpool Street

The Maughan Library & Information Services Centre, King's College London

Chancery Lane WC2R 1LR

→ Sat/Sun 1.30pm-5pm. Last entry 4.30pm. D R T

London's first fireproof building, built to house records of the Court of Chancery. Now renovated to house a fine university library. J Pennethorne & Sir John Taylor 1851/Gaunt Francis Associates 2001. Entry: Round room, Rolls chapel (now Weston room), some library areas.
Tube: Chancery Lane, Temple; Rail: Blackfriars; Tube/Rail: Charing Cross; 68,171,4,11,13,15,27,172,341

Tower 42

25 Old Broad Street EC2N 1HQ

→ Sat tours at 10am, 11.30am, 1pm, 2.30pm, pre-book ONLY through Open House, see p15 for details. Max 10 per tour. Security checks. D T

The City of London's tallest building, consisting of three hexagonal chevrons, at 601ft was the first to break previous restrictions on tall buildings in London. During a comprehensive refurbishment in 1995, a new glass and steel entrance was built on Old Broad Street and the external steel cladding was replaced. Richard Seifert & Partners 1981/GMW Partnership/Fletcher Priest 1995. Entry: foyer, levels 24 & 42.
DLR/Tube: Bank; Tube/Rail: Liverpool Street; 25,40,35,48,344

1 Finsbury Circus

Trinity House

Tower Hill EC3N 4DH

→ Sat 10am-1pm. Last entry 12.30pm. Max 60 at one time. D T

Fine late Georgian exterior with interior painstakingly reconstructed after destruction by incendiary bomb in 1940. Good fittings, statues and works of art from original building. Samuel Wyatt 1796/Albert Richardson 1953. Entry: 1st floor ceremonial rooms.
Tube: Tower Hill; Rail: Fenchurch Street; 25,15,40

Watermen's Hall

16 St Mary-at-Hill EC3R 8EF

→ Tours Sat at 9am, 10.30am, 12noon, 2pm. Pre-book ONLY in writing enclosing SAE to The Assistant Clerk giving name(s), address & tel no. Max 2 tickets per application. State tour time preferred. Tickets sent by post. Max 30 per tour. D

Only remaining Georgian Hall in the City of London, and perfect example of domestic architecture of the period. William Blackburn 1780. Entry: parlour, freemen's room, court room, silver room, hallway.
Tube: Monument; Rail: Fenchurch Street; 15,25,35,45

WALKS/TOURS

Alleyways of the City (East)

Meet: Guildhall Art Gallery, Guildhall Yard EC2P 2EJ

→ Sat/Sun frequent tours from 10.30am to 3pm. Length 1 1/2 hours approx. Last walk 3pm. Max 30 per walk. B Q T

A walk including Ye Old Butlers Head, Masons Avenue; Kings Arms Yard; Drapers Hall; St Margarets Lothbury; front of Royal Exchange; St Michael, Cornhill; St Clement, Eastcheap finishing at the Monument. Walk led by qualified City of London guide.
DLR/Tube: Bank; Tube: Barbican, St Paul's; Tube/Rail: Moorgate; 8,21,25,43,133,141,242

10 Queen Street Place

Alleyways of the City (West)

Meet: Guildhall Art Gallery, Guildhall Yard, EC2P 2EJ

→ Sat/Sun frequent tours from 10.30am to 3pm. Length 1 1/2 hours approx. Last walk 3pm. Max 30 per walk. B Q T

A walk through ancient narrow alleyways away from the traffic, passing Goldsmiths & Wax Chandlers Halls, St Anne & St Agnes Church, St Mary-le-Bow, Pancras Lane, Laurence Pountney Hill through to St Magnus finishing at the Monument. Walk led by qualified City of London guide.
DLR/Tube: Bank; Tube: Barbican, St Paul's; Tube/Rail: Moorgate 8,21,25,43,133,141,242

Behind the scenes at the Barbican

Meet: Guildhall Art Gallery, Guildhall Yard, EC2P 2EJ

→ Sat hourly tours from 10.30am to 3pm. Length 1 1/2 hours approximately. Last walk 3pm. Max 30 per walk. B Q T

A walk through the listed Barbican Centre visiting the gardens, and possibly one of the flats in a tower block. Walk led by a qualified City of London guide.
DLR/Tube: Bank; Tube: Barbican, St Paul's; Tube/Rail: Moorgate; 8,21,25,43,133,141,242

Wren Churches

Meet: Guildhall Art Gallery, Guildhall Yard, EC2P 2EJ

→ Sat/Sun frequent tours from 10.30am to 3pm. Length 1 1/2 hours approx. Last walk 3pm. Max 30 per walk. B Q T

An opportunity to pass several of Wren's churches, and visit at least two churches, learn about their history, finishing at the Monument. Walk led by qualified City of London guide.
DLR/Tube: Bank; Tube: Barbican, St Paul's; Tube/Rail: Moorgate; 8,21,25,43,133,141,242

Supported by

CITY OF LONDON

Croydon

Airport House
Purley Way, Croydon CR0 0XZ
→ Sat/Sun 11am-3.30pm. Regular tours of Croydon Airport Visitor Centre, first come basis. d P R T
Grade II listed 1928 building in classical Retardaire style. It was one of the first purpose-built airport terminal buildings in the world. Closed in 1959. Entry: former check-in area, aircraft departure point, control tower. NB. Facilities at adjacent 1928 Aerodrome Hotel also open to public.
Rail: East Croydon, then 119 bus to Croydon Colonnades

Church of St Mary the Blessed Virgin
Addington Village Road, Addington CR0 5AS
→ Sun 2.30pm-5.30pm. First come basis. Last entry 5pm. Exhibition running. T
Founded in 11C, with Jacobean memorial c1615. Burial site of 5 Archbishops of Canterbury. Entry: church, graveyard.
Tram: Addington Interchange; 130, T33

Croydon Town Hall and Clocktower Complex
Katharine Street CR9 1ET
→ Sat character-led tours at 10am, 11am, 1.30pm, 3pm, includes behind-the-scenes to usually restricted areas of the Town Hall (no access to bell tower). Pre-book ONLY for tours on 020 8253 1030. Tours last approx 1 hour. Max 25 per tour. Open access to Clocktower and Museum of Croydon. D R T
Original Town Hall built 1895 (Hemnan), Clocktower development opened in 1993 (Tibbalds) and Museum of Croydon Galleries opened in 2006 (FAT).
Rail/Tram: East Croydon, West Croydon; 1,2,3,109,119,154,197,466

Mitcham Road Cemetery & Crematorium
Mitcham Road CR9 3AT
→ Sun 10am-4pm. Regular behind-the-scenes tours of crematorium, max 15 per tour. Cemetery tours at 10am, 12noon & 2pm, departing from front of cemetery office, approx 2 hours, suitable for disabled. D P R T
Interesting memorials and monuments give an insight into Croydon's rich past. Includes talks and demonstrations.
Rail: West Croydon; 64,109,198,250,289

No. 1 Croydon (formerly NLA Tower) ●
12-16 Addiscombe Road, Croydon CR0 0XT
→ Sat/Sun 9am-5pm. Regular tours, first come basis.
Local landmark office tower block, currently undergoing refurbishment. Early opportunity to preview recent works to interior, and comment on future proposals for the area in a public exhibition of the East Croydon Masterplan by Studio Egret West. Richard Seifert 1970/AHMM (refurb) 2006. Entry: ground and other floors
Rail: East Croydon

No. 1 Croydon (formerly NLA Tower)

Old Palace, Croydon
Old Palace Road, Old Town CR0 1AX
→ Sat 2.30pm & 3.30pm tours, pre-book ONLY through Open House, see p15 for details. Last entry 4pm. Max 30 per tour. B d T
Grade I listed manor house, summer residence of Archibishops of Canterbury from 13C-18C. Elizabeth I and other monarchs regularly visited. Contains one of the finest Great Halls with its original roof from 1440s, Tudor bedroom, long gallery, great chamber, domestic chapel.
Tram: Church Street, Reeves Corner; Rail: East Croydon, West Croydon

Religious Society of Friends Adult School Hall
60 Park Lane, Croydon CR0 1JE
→ Sat 10am-4pm/Sun 2pm-4pm. Closed Sat 12noon-2pm. D
Constructed and opened in 1908, the building was designed for educational purposes. It is notable for its innovatory open roof structure and simplicity of design. William Curtis Green 1908. Entry: hall, stage.
Rail/Tram: East Croydon; 60,64,190,197,405

Shirley Windmill
Postmill Close, Upper Shirley Road, Croydon CR0 5DY
→ Sun 12noon-5pm. Regular tours, first come basis. Duration 1 hour. Last tour 4pm. d R T
The present brick tower windmill was built in the mid 1850s to replace a post mill destroyed by fire. Now renovated to near-working condition, it is the only surviving windmill in Croydon. Entry: windmill.
Rail/Tram: East Croydon; 466,130,119,194,198

St John the Evangelist
Auckland Road SE19 2DT
→ Sat 10am-5pm/Sun 11.30am-5pm. Sat 6.30pm organ recital. d P T
Grade II* listed church one of John Pearson's finest with brick vaulted interior and soaring gothic spaces; described in 1887 'as the most beautiful parish church of modern days'. Includes stained glass by Kemp and Comper and a magnificent organ by T C Lewis. J Loughborough Pearson 1887.
Rail: Crystal Palace; 410

St Michael & All Angels with St James
Poplar Walk, Croydon CR0 1UA
→ Sat 9.30am-4.30pm. Last entry 4pm. B d N P R T
Grade I listed church, one of Pearson's last and finest. Brick-vaulted magnificent interior with lavish font, pulpit and fine Father Willis organ with Bodley casing. Comper Lady chapel. J L Pearson 1871.
Tram/Rail: West Croydon; 64,198,60,455,250

Taberner House ●
Park Lane, Croydon CR9 1JT
→ Sat 10am-5pm. Last entry 4.50pm. Max 15 in viewing gallery at one time for 15 mins only. Urban Design and Planning Officers available for questions. T
19-storey tower constructed for Council administration with amazing views of London and South-East. H Thornley, with Allan Holt and Hugh Lea (borough engineers) 1964-7. Entry: 18th floor viewing gallery.
Rail/Tram: East or West Croydon; 50,109,154,194,197

Whitgift Almshouses
North End, Croydon CR9 1SS
→ Sat tours at 10am, 11.15am, 12.15pm, 2.15pm, 3.15pm. Pre-book ONLY on 020 8688 1733. Max 30 per tour. d T
Tudor almshouses dating from 1596 and founded by the Archbishop of Canterbury John Whitgift. Chapel and Courtyard with original 16C clock. Entry: courtyard, chapel, audience chamber.
Rail: East Croydon; tram/buses to central Croydon

WALKS/TOURS

Tudor Croydon Tour
→ Meet: Sat 2.30pm at Croydon Clocktower entrance, Katharine Street CR9 1ET. Pre-book ONLY on 020 8253 1030. Approx 1 1/2 hour duration. Max 40 per tour.
Croydon's importance in Tudor times was due to the influence of the Archbishops of Canterbury, who owned land locally and occupied the Old Palace. Join Borough archivist, Chris Bennett, for a tour of buildings and locations in Croydon with Tudor connections.
Rail/Tram: East Croydon, West Croydon; 1,2,3,109,119,154,197,466

Welcome to SuperCroydon
→ Meet: Sun 12noon at East Croydon Station CR0 1LF
After WWII, Croydon transformed from a market town on London's outskirts into a 20C super suburb. This tour offers a walk around England's Alphaville via its 7 hills.
Rail/Tram: East Croydon, West Croydon; 50,109,154,194,197

Supported by

CROYDON COUNCIL
www.croydon.gov.uk

Ealing

2 Castlebar Road

14 South Parade
14 South Parade W4 1JU
→ Sun 10am-5pm. First come basis, queuing if necessary. Last entry 4pm. Max 10 at one time. Q
One of Voysey's first houses, this studio house is consciously different in style to the red-brick dominance of the Bedford Park suburb. CFA Voysey 1891. NB. Bedford Park Society stall present.
Tube: Turnham Green, Chiswick Park

2 Castlebar Road
2 Castlebar Road W5 2DP
→ Sat/Sun 1pm-5pm. First come basis, queuing outside if necessary. d R T
A reworking of a painted render suburban villa retaining the 'L' shaped perimeter whilst the new volume of the house is set apart from the 'original' villa so that a distinct glazed gap is visible between the two elements. Also contains an art gallery. De Matos Storey Ryan 2005.
Tube/Rail: Ealing Broadway; E1,E2,112,65,297,226

Ealing Abbey
Charlbury Grove W5 2DY
→ Sun 1pm-5pm. Tours on the hour. Max 100 at one time. B D N R T
Building began in 1897 and has only recently been completed. Architects include F and E Walters (1897 – the nave), Stanley Kerr Bates (1960 – transepts), and Sir William Whitfield (1997 – choir and apse). Entry: church, adjacent centre.
Tube/Rail: Ealing Broadway; 297

Ealing Town Hall, Council Chamber and Mayor's Office
New Broadway W5 2BY
→ Sat 11am-4pm/Sun 11am-3pm. Tour, talk and refreshments with present and past Ealing Mayors, approx every 30mins. Last entry 30 mins before close. Max 20 per tour. D P R T
Late Victorian ragstone Gothic Town Hall with sumptuous Imperial staircase. Recently restored. Charles Jones (West Wing) 1888. Entry: may include Victoria hall, council chamber, Nelson room, Mayor's parlour.
Tube/Rail: Ealing Broadway; 65,83,112,207,297,E1,E2,E7

Holy Cross Old and New Churches
Oldfield Lane South, Greenford UB6 9JS
→ Sat/Sun 11am-5pm. Regular guided tours. B C D P R T
Small 15C parish church with flint-clad nave and wood cladding on tower. Adjacent new church of Canadian cedar red-wood construction, also open.
Tube/Rail: Greenford; 92,105,E6,E10,95

Morris House ●
Swainson Road W3 7UP
→ Sat/Sun 1pm-5pm. Half hourly tours. Max 10 per tour. Architects on site. Last entry 4.30pm. T A
This conversion of a former car parts warehouse provides 41 new apartments. The external shell is retained and the new accommodation is slotted inside creating a building within a building. Stephen Davy Peter Smith Architects 2008. Entry: public areas, corridors, 1 apartment.
Tube: Stamford Brook; Rail: Acton, Shepherd's Bush; 272,207

Pitzhanger Manor House
Walpole Park, Mattock Lane W5 5EQ
→ Sat/Sun 11am-5pm. Regular tours. Last entry 4.45pm. d N R T
Former country residence designed by Sir John Soane for his own use. Grade I listed building, expressing Soane's idiosyncratic architectural style with its stripped classical detail, radical colour schemes and inventive use of space and light. Sir John Soane 1800-10. Entry: Manor House.
Tube/Rail: Ealing Broadway; 65,83,207

South Acton Children's Centre ●
Castle Close, off Park Road North W3 8RX
→ Sat 10am-3pm. Tours at 10am, 10.45am, 11.30am, 12.15pm, 1pm, 1.45pm, 2.30pm. B D T
Reworking of two existing 1960s nursery schools creates an integrated children's centre in partnership with Sure Start, providing new playroom extensions and community facilities, centred on a new landscaped play area. Training room is an elegant blue brick box with large window revealing activity within. Llowarch Llowarch 2006. Entry: all areas except offices.
Tube: Acton Town; Rail: South Acton; 266,E3,207,607,44E

St Thomas the Apostle
Boston Road, Hanwell W7 2AD
→ Sat/Sun 10am-7.30pm. Tour/lecture Sat 11am, 2pm. D N P T
Built in the distinctive style of the architect and containing many fine works of 20C art. Edward Maufe 1934.
Tube: Boston Manor; Rail: Hanwell; E8

The Manor House (Southall)
The Green, Southall UB2 4BJ
→ Sun 10am-2pm. Regular tours. Max 25 at one time. P T
Grade II* listed Elizabethan timber framed manor house (now offices) with 18C additions, set in magnificent grounds. Richard Awsiter 1587. Entry: rented accommodation not open.
Rail: Southall; 105,120,195,E5,H32

WALKS/TOURS

Brentham Garden Suburb
→ Meet: Sat/Sun 10.30am at The Brentham Club, 38 Meadvale Road W5 1NP. Max 2 hrs duration. B P R
Britain's first co-partnership garden suburb, first houses built 1901. Parker and Unwin's plan introduced 1907, mainly Arts and Crafts style; fascinating social history. (Organised by The Brentham Society and Brentham Heritage Society).
Tube: Hanger Lane; Tube/Rail: Ealing Broadway; E2,E9

Northala Fields: A Recycled New Park

Ealing Common Walk
→ Meet: Sun 2.30pm at Hanger Lane end of Inglis Road W5 3RN. d P R
Walk across Ealing Common taking in the range of architectural styles. Highlights: the home of a Wimbledon champion, an historic Ealing Studios film director and the death mask of a prime minister.
Tube: North Ealing, Ealing Common; Tube/Rail: Ealing Broadway; 83,112,207,427

Hanwell Flight of Locks & Three Bridges
→ Meet: Sat/Sun 1pm, 2pm, 3pm, 4pm at The Fox public house, Green Lane W7 2PJ. Duration 1 hour.
Restored flight of locks at Hanwell is a scheduled ancient monument, while Three Bridges is a unique stacked intersection of road, rail and canal, and Brunel's last major railway project. Walks led by experts in local waterway history. Isambard Kingdom Brunel 1794/1859.
Tube: Boston Manor; Rail: Hanwell; E8,83,207 to Ealing Hospital

Northala Fields: A Recycled New Park
→ Meet: Sat 11am at the Northala Fields car park off A40, Kensington Road UB5 6UR. Pre-book ONLY on 020 7467 1470 or email marketing@lda-design.co.uk. Duration approx 1 hour. Max 30 per tour.
Using waste from other building work, such as the new Wembley stadium, the mounds of Northala Fields shield Ealing from the busy A40 whilst providing an impressive landmark and a brand new park. Walk led by one of the design team.
Tube: Ealing Broadway, Northolt; E10,90,120,140,282,398

Walking Through Shared Heritage
→ Meet: Sun 2.30pm at Chiswick Business Park, Building 3, 566 Chiswick High Road W4 5YA
See p39 for full details.

Supported by

www.ealing.gov.uk

Enfield

Priory Hospital North London

Gunpowder Park

Bowes Road Library
Bowes Road N11 1BD
→ Sat 9am-5pm. Regular tours. Last entry 4.30pm. N P
Part of a 1930s building combining pool, library and clinic. Now listed and retaining some original features including oriel windows. Curtis and Burchett 1935-39.
Tube: Arnos Grove; Rail: New Southgate; 232,34,184

Enfield Magistrates Court
The Court House, Lordship Lane N17 6RT
→ Sat 10am-4pm. Tours every half hour. d R T
Grade II listed building in a neo-Georgian design constructed of brown and blue brick with rubbed red brick and stone dressings and banding and symmetrical elevation. W T Curtis 1938. Entry: court rooms, cells, justices' retiring rooms.
Tube: Wood Green; Rail: Bruce Grove; 243,279,149,349,W3,123

Forty Hall
Forty Hill, Enfield EN2 9HA
→ Sat/Sun 11am-4pm. Special tours on Sat of areas not usually open to the public, pre-book ONLY on 020 8363 8196. d N P R T
Grade I listed Jacobean house built 1629-32. Home of Sir Nicholas Rainton, Lord Mayor 1632-33. Last private owners were the Parker-Bowles family. Entry: ground & 1st floors.
Rail: Enfield Town; 191 (10 mins walk)

Friends Meeting House & Burial Grounds
59 Church Hill N21 1LE
→ Sat/Sun 2pm-5pm. Last entry 4.15pm. Max 20 at a time. D P R T
Established 1688, the present Grade II listed building of yellow stock brick dates from 1790. A simple building with central double door under a bracketed cornice hood, flanked by large sash windows, with delicate glazing bars, under gauged brick arches. The curved entrance wall allowed carriages to turn in the narrow lane. Entry: ground floor.
Tube: Southgate; Rail: Winchmore Hill; 125,329,W9

King George V Pumping Station
Swan & Pike Road, Enfield
→ Sat 10am-5pm. Regular tours. Last entry 4pm. P T
Designed to pump water from the River Lee into the George V reservoir, the building houses three old disused gas Humphrey pumps, and two electric pumps currently in service.
Tube: Turnpike Lane and 121 bus; Rail: Enfield Lock; 121

Kingsmead School Theatre
Southbury Road EN1 1YQ
→ Sat 10am-1pm. First come basis, queuing outside if necessary. Max 10 at one time. D P T
A new auditorium created within the shell of a 1960s school hall. A three-sided steeply raked open-stage space, with fixed seating for 280 people. A balcony across the rear of the stage provides a raised performance area for actors, musicians or singers. Tim Foster Architects 2007.
Tube: Oakwood; Rail: Southbury, Enfield; 121,191,231,307,317

Lee Valley Athletics Centre
Lee Valley Leisure Complex, 61 Meridian Way, Picketts Lock N9 0AS
→ Sat/Sun 10am-5pm. Last entry 4.30pm. Max 300 at one time. D N T G
A world class indoor training facility, the only one of its kind in the South East, this naturally lit and ventilated building is highly sustainable. David Morley Architects 2007. Entry: all areas except offices and changing areas.
Tube/Rail: Tottenham Hale; Rail: Ponders End, Angel Road, Edmonton Green; W8

Millfield Arts Centre
Silver Street N18 1PJ
→ Sat 1pm-5pm. Half hourly tours. Max 100 at one time, 20 on tours. P R T
Grade II* listed small Georgian suburban villa (1778) with later additions. Formerly orphanage and hospital, currently a multi-use community and arts centre. Entry: house including cellars and WWII bunker.
Tube: Wood Green then 144; Rail: Silver Street; 34,102,W6,144,144a

Myddelton House
Bulls Cross, Enfield EN2 9HG
→ Sun 10am-4pm. Last entry 3.30pm. d P R T
Neo-classical yellow Suffolk stock brick villa with mid 19C extension to north and west front. Victorian conservatory to side. Adam style ceilings to ground floor. George Ferry and John Wallen 1818. Entry: ground floor only, selected rooms, gardens. NB. No entry to contemporary buildings.
Rail: Turkey Street; 217,317

Parish Church of St Andrew Enfield
Market Place, Enfield EN1 3EG
→ Sat 9.30am-3.30pm/Sun 12noon-3pm. D N R
Listed church 13C-19C with fine organ case and monuments.
Tube: Oakwood; Rail: Enfield Town, Enfield Chase; 121,191,192,231

Priory Hospital North London
Grovelands House, The Bourne N14 6RA
→ Sun 10am-12noon. Pre-book ONLY on 020 8920 5604 (Sarah Bradley Mon-Fri 9.30am-2.30pm). Last entry 12noon. Max 30 per tour. P R T
Grade I listed neo-classical villa designed for Walker Gray. Grounds laid out by Repton. Elegant trompe l'oeil breakfast room. John Nash 1797. Entry: main house, ground and 1st floors, ice house.
Tube: Southgate; Rail: Winchmore Hill; 121,125,299,W6

Royal Small Arms Factory
RSA Centre, 35 Island Centre Way, Enfield (off A1055 Mollison Avenue) EN3 6GS
→ Sat 10am-5pm. Regular tours, first come basis. Former Arms Factory employees present to answer questions. D N P
Grade II listed arms factory closed to public for 170 years, buildings on site included a church (the original font is displayed in the central courtyard at the Centre) a police station and a school. Now restored as mixed-use village and commercial centre. Clocktower c1783. Shepheard Epstein Hunter (refurb) 2000.
Rail: Enfield Lock; 121

Vincent House ●
2e Nags Head Road, Ponders End EN3 7FN
→ Sat 10am-1pm/Sun 2pm-5pm. First come basis, queuing outside if necessary. Last entry Sat 12.45pm/Sun 4.45pm. Max 100 at one time. D N R T G A
Sustainable landmark building in a regeneration area, provides homes, charity offices and a European style double-height café at a busy crossroads. The brick drum dominates the corner whilst solar panels can be glimpsed at roof level. Sustainable features include high insulation, hot water and photovoltaic solar panels, and ground source heat pump. The Tooley & Foster Partnership 2008. Entry: café, meeting room, garden.
Rail: Southbury; 313,491,191,279,121

WALKS/TOURS

Gunpowder Park: A Blast from the Past is New Green Space
→ Meet: Sun 11am at the Field Station, Sewardstone Road EN9 3GP. Tour led by one of the designers. Pre-book ONLY on 020 7467 1470 or email marketing@lda-design.co.uk. Duration approx 1 hour. Max 30 per tour.
Once a Royal Ordnance manufacturing and testing facility, Gunpowder Park is part of the Lee Valley's network of green space. Now five years old, the park offers new habitat, leisure facilities and great character of landform.
Tube: Loughton; Rail: Enfield Lock, Waltham Cross; 211,212,505

Supported by

ENFIELD Council
www.enfield.gov.uk

Greenwich

Brookhill Children's Centre ● ● ●
130 Brookhill Road SE6 6UZ
→ Sat/Sun 10am-5pm. First come basis. Last entry 4.30pm. Max 12 at one time. Sat help plant a fruit tree, see a cookery demo and celebrate the launch of a new eco-schools design project. Sat/Sun children's play activities. C D G P R T
External and internal colours are bright to create an uplifting atmosphere. Constructed from timber cassette panels and clad in a mixture of render and larch cladding. Roofs are non-PVC single ply membrane with sedum blankets. Low energy systems. Civic Trust Award 2009. Architype 2007.
Rail/DLR: Woolwich Arsenal; 53,177,422,122,161

Charlton House ●
Charlton Road SE7 8RE
→ Sun 10am-4pm. Last entry 4pm. Two contemporary artists Emily Jost and Lucy Williams exhibit their work in the Long Gallery, drawing inspiration from the house. D P R T
London's only surviving great Jacobean mansion, set in Charlton Park, red brick with white stone dressings and beautifully proportioned hall. A Newton 1607-12/Norman Shaw (restored) late 19C. Entry: Minstrel Hall, Long Gallery, Grand Salon, White Room, Newton, Prince Henry & Dutch Rooms, Old Library, grounds.
Rail: Charlton; 53,54,422

Devonport Mausoleum
National Maritime Museum, Romney Road SE10 9NF
→ Sun 11.30am-3.30pm. Visitors to follow signage placed outside National Maritime Museum main entrance. D T
Handsome mausoleum (1750) in former Royal Navy cemetery, restored 1999 by the University of Greenwich. Many interesting plaques. Entry: cemetery and mausoleum.
DLR: Cutty Sark for Maritime Greenwich; DLR/Tube: Canary Wharf; Rail: Greenwich, Maze Hill; 177,180,188,199,286

Dreadnought Library
West Gate (King William Walk), or East Gate, (Park Row), and Romney Road crossing, Maritime Greenwich Campus SE10 9LS
→ Sun 11am-4.30pm. Regular tours. Last tour 4pm. Max 10-15 per tour. D T
Formerly Dreadnought Seamen's Hospital, now library and computer centre of the University of Greenwich. Glazed corridors with fine views, and steel and glass courtyard roof. James 'Athenian' Stuart 1764-68/Dannatt Johnson (refurb) 1999. Entry: guided tour routes only.
DLR: Cutty Sark for Maritime Greenwich; DLR/Tube: Canary Wharf; Rail: Greenwich, Maze Hill; 177,180,188,199,286,386

Eltham Lodge
Royal Blackheath Golf Club, Court Road SE9 5AF
→ Sun 10am-12.30pm. Tours on the hour. Last tour 12noon. Max 25 per tour. P
Grade I listed Caroline mansion built for Sir John Shaw. Refurbished 18C with fine plaster, ceilings and staircase. Club house of Royal Blackheath Golf Club since 1923. Hugh May 1664. Entry: main hall, lounges, staircase, dining room, snooker room, O'Shea room.
Rail: Mottingham; 124,126,161

Eltham Palace Great Hall
Court Yard, Eltham SE9 5QE
→ Sun 10am-5pm. Great Hall Tour 11am, 12noon, 2pm, 3pm, first come basis. Max 30 per tour. B D P R T
Tour of the remains of the Medieval royal palace which was originally Henry VIII's boyhood home.
Rail: Eltham, Mottingham; 124,126,132,161,162

Gala Bingo Club (formerly Granada Cinema)
186 Powis Street SE18 6NL
→ Sun 10.30am-11.30am. Last entry 11.15am. Max 20 at one time. R T
Lavish and atmospheric former cinema with interior by Theodore Komisarjevsky, converted to Bingo Hall in 1960s. Grade II* listed. Cecil Masey and Reginald Uren 1937. Entry: auditorium, foyer, circle area. NB. Children under 18 not permitted.
Rail: Woolwich Arsenal; 51,53,54,96,99,122,161,177,178,180,244

Greenwich Magistrates' Court
9 Blackheath Road SE10 8PE
→ Sat 9.30am-4pm. Regular tours, first come basis. Last entry 3pm. d N P R T
Grade II listed building with imposing Portland stone frontage. A crisply detailed example of Edwardian civic design. J Dixon Butler 1909. Entry: public waiting areas, courts, cells. NB. Centenary events include costumed historical mock trials and their modern equivalents; display of documents and court records; antique fire engine and prisoner transport.
DLR: Deptford Bridge; Rail: Greenwich; 53,177

Greenwich Yacht Club
1 Peartree Way SE10 0BW
→ Sat/Sun 1pm-4.30pm. Regular tours, first come basis. Max 40 at one time. Club members available for discussion. Annual art show and members' bar. d R T A
Contemporary timber and aluminium building using existing pier, offering unique views of the river, The O2 and Thames Barrier. Frankl + Luty 2000. Entry: main club house, sail loft, boat yard. Outbuilding adapted as art show venue with panoramic river views.
Tube: North Greenwich; Rail: Westcombe Park; 161,177,180,472

Millennium Primary School ● ●
50 John Harrison Way SE10 0BG
→ Sat 10am-2pm. Regular tours. Last entry 1.30pm. D P T G A
As part of the pioneering Millennium Village on the Greenwich Peninsula, this is a new kind of facility for a sustainable urban community. Curvaceous, larch-clad building incorporating many energy saving-features. Edward Cullinan Architects 2001. Entry: hall, classrooms, Early Years Centre, playground.
DLR: Cutty Sark for Maritime Greenwich; Tube: North Greenwich; Rail: Charlton; 108,161,188,422,472,486

Old Royal Military Academy
Firepower, The Royal Artillery Museum, Royal Arsenal, Woolwich SE18 6ST
→ Sat/Sun 11am-4pm. Last entry 4pm.
Grade II* listed building (1716-20) attributed to Nicholas Hawksmoor. Birthplace of the Royal Artillery and one of first military academies of Europe. Commissioned by the Board of Ordnance. Entry: Ordnance room, Academy room.
Tube: North Greenwich; Rail: Woolwich Arsenal; 53,54,96,422,472,180,161,380

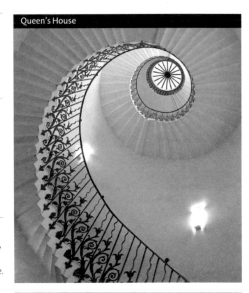
Queen's House

Old Royal Naval College
King Charles Court, King William Court, Painted Hall, Chapel & Admiral's House, Queen Anne Court, Queen Mary Court West Gate (King William Walk), or East Gate (Park Row) and Romney Road crossing. Entry from pier via Cutty Sark Gardens SE10 9LW
→ Sat/Sun 10am-5pm Painted Hall, Chapel & Admiral's House. Sun 11am-4.30pm King Charles Court, King William Court, Queen Anne Court, Queen Mary Court. Regular tours. Last tour 4.30pm. Max 20 per tour. R T
Designed by Wren in 1695, finished by Hawksmoor and Vanbrugh as the Greenwich Hospital for Seamen and later the Royal Naval College (1873-1998). Managed by the Greenwich Foundation, housing University of Greenwich (Maritime Campus) and Trinity College of Music. Grade I listed.
King Charles Court – Earliest of the buildings, designed by Wren for Charles II in 1661. Refurb by John McAslan & Partners in 2001. Entry: guided tour routes only.
King William Court – Wren-designed building completed under the direction of Hawksmoor and Vanbrugh, 1698-1712. Original wood panelling, refurbished by Dannatt Johnson in 2001 for University of Greenwich. Entry: guided tour routes.
Painted Hall, Chapel & Admiral's House – Hall ceiling painted by Sir James Thornhill 1708-27. Neo-classical chapel designed by James 'Athenian' Stuart 1789. Entry: Painted Hall and Chapel open, guided tour of Admiral's House only, every 30 mins, 10.30am-4pm, max 20 on tours. Talk Sat 2pm on 'The Baroque'.
Queen Anne Court – Wren & Hawksmoor building completed 1749 when Thomas Ripley built the pavilions facing the river. Highlights include council board room, grand staircase and restored Portland stonework. Refurbished in 2000 by Dannatt Johnson for University of Greenwich. Entry: guided tour routes.
Queen Mary Court – Last major building on the site (1751). Original layout, timber panelling, barrel vaulting and Portland stone. Refurbished in 2000 by Dannatt Johnson for University of Greenwich. Entry: guided tour routes only.
DLR: Cutty Sark for Maritime Greenwich; Rail: Greenwich, Maze Hill; 177,180,188,199,286,386

Greenwich Peninsula

Queen's House
Romney Road SE10 9NF
→ Sat/Sun 10am-5pm. Hourly tours 11am-4pm, first come basis. Last entry 4.30pm. Max 20 per tour. D N T
The opulent summer villa of Charles I's queen, Henrietta Maria, this is the first purely classical Renaissance building in Britain which reflected a turning point in English architecture. Much of the original splendour of the house is retained, including the 'grotesque-style' painted ceiling of the queen's bedchamber, the 'Tulip Stairs', original painted woodwork of the Great Hall and its finely laid 1635 marble floor. Inigo Jones 1635.
DLR: Cutty Sark for Maritime Greenwich; Rail: Greenwich, Maze Hill; Riverboat: Greenwich Pier; 129,177,180,188,199,286,386

Ranger's House
Chesterfield Walk SE10 8QX
→ Sun 11am-5pm. Regular introductory tours throughout the day, max 25 per tour, first come basis. B D P T
Handsome Grade I listed red brick villa recently refurbished. Houses Wernher Collection – nearly 700 works of art on display collected by Sir Julius Wernher (1850-1912). Captain Francis Hosier c1700.
DLR/Rail: Greenwich; Rail: Blackheath; DLR: Cutty Sark for Maritime Greenwich

River Sculpture/Studio (Slice of Reality) ●
River Thames, off Thames Path, Meridian Gardens, nr Drawdock Point, Blackwall Point, Greenwich SE10 0PH
→ Sun 10am-4pm. A T
Sliced vertical section of sea-going sand dredger. Original ship reduced in length by 85% leaving vertical portion housing the ship's habitable sections; bridge, poop, accommodation and engine room. Now studio space with models and drawings on show. Conversion by Richard Wilson 1999. Entry: interior, decks.
Tube/Rail: North Greenwich; 188,422,108

Severndroog Castle
Castle Wood, Shooters Hill SE18 3RT
→ Sat/Sun 10am-3pm. Regular tours, first come basis, queuing if necessary. Queue closes 3pm. Max 20 at one time. P Q T
Grade II* listed triangular brick Georgian tower with Gothic windows. Standing 63ft tall in woodlands it offers spectacular views across the capital. Built to commemorate the 1755 conquest of the Malabar Coast by Sir William James. Richard Jupp 1784. Entry: ground, 1st floor, roof/viewing platform.
Rail: Eltham, Woolwich, Welling; 89,122,161,244,486

St Alfege Church, Greenwich
Greenwich Church Street SE10 9BJ
→ Sat/Sun 11am-4pm. Tours of Crypt Sat 1.30pm, 3.30pm/Sun 12noon, 1pm, pre-book ONLY on 020 8853 0687. Last entry 4pm. D T
Magnificent Baroque church, Grade I listed, gutted by fire in 1941 and restored by Sir Albert Richardson to original design. Many original features. Burial site of Thomas Tallis, organist/ choirmaster (1505-85), Nicholas Hawksmoor 1714 and General Wolfe, soldier. Entry: ground floor (not tower or crypt).
DLR: Cutty Sark for Maritime Greenwich; Rail: Greenwich; 177,180,188,199,286,386

St Saviour's Church, Eltham
Corner Middle Park Avenue/Churchbury Road SE9 5JH
→ Sat 10am-4.30pm. Last entry 4.30pm. Max 20 at one time. N P T
One of London's first Modern style churches, greatly influenced by 1920s German Expressionism. N F Cachemaille-Day 1932-3. Entry: all areas except tower.
Rail: Mottingham; 160

Station Officers Mess & Ruins of Garrison Church – RA Barracks, Woolwich
Repository Road (entrance via Front Parade West Gate), Woolwich SE18 4BB
→ Sun 10am-3pm. Regular tours on the hour, first come basis. Last tour 3pm. Max 30 per tour. Security bag checks. P R T
Grade II* listed (1776-1802), commissioned by the then Board of Ordnance. Front Parade, at 1080ft, is said to be the longest Georgian frontage in Europe. Comprises both the Officers' and WOs' and Sgts' Messes of the Barracks, linked in centre by magnificent South Arch. Officers' Mess, opened in 1802, was the first communal Mess to be used by the Army. Entry: Front Parade, Officers' Mess including ante rooms and ruins of garrison church, bombed during WWII.
Tube: North Greenwich then 422 or 486 bus; Rail: Woolwich Arsenal, Woolwich Dockyard; 53,54,96,161,180

Thames Barrier & Information Centre
1 Unity Way, Woolwich SE18 5NJ
→ Sat/Sun 10.30am-4.30pm. Last entry 4pm. Max 40 at one time, subject to availability. D P R T
Information centre sited by the dramatic Thames Barrier (1984), explaining its function, construction and future. Entry: information centre only.
Tube: North Greenwich, then 161,472; Rail: Charlton, then 177,180,472,161

The Fan Museum
12 Crooms Hill SE10 8ER
→ Sat 11am-5pm/Sun 12noon-5pm. Max 50 at one time. B D R T
Carefully restored Grade II listed early Georgian town houses, retaining the original domestic scale and character and features, including elegant façades, staircase with 'barley sugar' baluster, panelled rooms, and front courtyard with wrought iron railing and gates. It now houses the only museum devoted to the art and craft of fans. John Savery 1721/ John Griffiths (conversion). Entry: museum, part of garden.
DLR: Cutty Sark for Maritime Greenwich; Rail: Greenwich, Maze Hill; 177,180,188,286,386

Tudor Barn and Gardens
Well Hall Pleasaunce, Well Hall Road SE9 6SZ
→ Sat/Sun 10am-5pm. Tours 11.30am, 2.30pm. Max 50 at one time. P R T
16C restored barn set in grounds with Medieval moat, only surviving building from 'Well Hall', home to Margaret Roper, daughter of Sir Thomas More, Lord High Chancellor of England under Henry VIII. Now a venue, restaurant and café set in beautiful gardens. Former home of children's author E Nesbit. Civic Trust award-winner. Entry: interior on tours, gardens.
Rail: Eltham; 286,161

Woolwich Town Hall
Wellington Street SE18 6PW
→ Sat 9am-4pm. D T
Florid Edwardian Baroque design with domed entrance hall, grand staircase and stained glass windows, a great example of civic architecture of the time belonging to the Classical tradition rather than the Gothic Revival favoured outside London. Alfred Brumwell Thomas 1906. Entry: Victoria hall, council chamber, committee rooms, public hall.
Rail/DLR: Woolwich Arsenal; 51,53,54,96,99,122,161,380,422

WALKS/TOURS

Greenwich Peninsula: Site and Public Art ●
→ Meet: Sat 10am, 12.30pm, 3pm at North Greenwich tube station entrance, Peninsula Square SE10 0PH. Tours led by directors of Art in the Public Realm. First come basis, approximately 2 hours. Max 30 per tour. G N
The site is being transformed into a new urban district for London with sustainable design and landmark architecture with a strong focus on public realm. Includes permanent and temporary public art including 'Slice of Reality' (see separate entry) and Antony Gormley's 'Quantum Cloud', helping to create a sense of place and identity.
Tube: North Greenwich; Thames Clipper Riverboats; 129,161,188,422

Supported by

Hackney

The Bridge Academy

120 Mapledene Road
120 Mapledene Road E8 3LL
→ Sat 1pm-5pm. First come basis, queuing outside if
necessary. Last entry 4.40pm. Max 10 at one time P Q T G A
Victorian terrace house with interior spaces opened up and
glass extension to rear. Modernisation includes Sun space and
upgraded insulation throughout. Platform 5 Architects 2007.
Tube: Bethnal Green; Rail: London Fields, Dalston Kingsland; 38,149

14-16 Sedgwick Street ● ● A
14-16 Sedgwick Street E9 6AA
→ Sat 10am-5pm. Regular architect-led half-hourly tours, first
come basis. Max 25 per tour. D G A
A 100% affordable housing development which has
established a sense of identity and quality of space in an area
of urban renewal. Eco Homes accredited, with solar panels
and virtually car-free. Stephen Davy Peter Smith Architects
2008. Entry: communal areas, 9th floor roof terrace, possible
access to flat(s).
Rail: Homerton; 308,394,292,38, W15

187 Brooke Road
187 Brooke Road E5 8AB
→ Sun 10am-5pm. First come basis. Max 10 at one time. G A
Timber-framed, hemp insulated extension to Victorian
end-of-terrace incorporating shuttered 'musical box' and
connecting other areas of the house with lightwell. Moving
Architecture 2008 (refurb). Entry: kitchen, extension, box
accessible via trapdoor and steep stairs, garden.
*Tube/Rail: Finsbury Park; Tube: Manor House; Rail: Clapton,
Rectory Road; 253,254,106,38,243,76*

89 Culford Road ● A
89 Culford Road N1 4HL
→ Sat/Sun 1pm-5pm. First some basis, queuing outside if
necessary. Last entry 4.40pm. Max 20 at one time. Q G A
Extreme low carbon refurbishment of 1840s terraced house
in conservation area. Insulation, airtightness, MVI IR, solar
thermal, triple glazing reduce emissions by 80%. Redesigned
contemporary interior. Prewett Bizley 2009.
*Tube: Angel; Tube/Rail: Highbury & Islington; Rail: Dalston
Kingsland; 76,73,141,149,243*

Adelaide Wharf ●
118/120 Queensbridge Road (main entrance) E2 8PD
→ Sat 1pm-5pm. Architect-led tours every 45 mins, pre-book
ONLY through Open House, see p15 for details. Max 25 per
tour. D T G A
Multiple award-winning Adelaide Wharf is a pioneering
mixed tenure residential scheme of 147 homes. U-shaped
court fronts onto a canal, an axial route and a park. Each
apartment has an outdoor room part hung, part cantilevered
out over the streets, courtyard or canal. Façade of layers of
roughly sawn larch making reference to the warehouses of
crates that once occupied this site. Allford Hall Monaghan
Morris 2008. Entry: courtyard, show flat, possibly roof.
Tube/Rail: Liverpool Street; 48,242,243,55,254,106

Eds Shed/Sunken House ●
75A De Beauvoir Road N1 4EL
→ Sat/Sun 10am-1pm. Tours every 20 mins, pre-book ONLY
through Open House, see p15 for details. Max 20 per tour. G
A cube clad in a cedar rainscreen, stained dark brown – a single
slot window at the front is all that indicates this is a house. The
entire site was excavated to basement level in order to create
the sunken foundation on which the house now sits. Hemp
insulation improves the thermal performance of the structure
while the solid timber frame provides a significantly reduced
carbon footprint. Adjaye Associates 2007.
*Tube: Old Street, Highbury & Islington; Rail: Dalston
Kingsland; 67,149,242,243,394*

Fairmule House ● ●
23-35 Waterson Street E2 8HE
→ Sat 12noon-5pm. First come basis. Last entry 4.30pm. Max
20-30 at one time. Architect and timber contractor on site.
Room Gallery (31 Waterson Street) hosts an exhibition by
Jane Prophet and in the park behind is Tom Wolseley's
'CABIN/ET' exhibition using shipping containers. d T G A
The largest solid-timber constructed mixed-use building in
the UK of 11 flats and 7 work units. Many green features and
bespoke public artworks throughout. Quay 2C 2006. Entry:
Room Gallery, common parts and 1st floor work unit.
*Tube: Old Street, Shoreditch; Tube/Rail: Liverpool Street;
26,55,67,149,48*

Hackney Empire Theatre
291 Mare Street E8 1EJ
→ Sat/Sun 10am-1pm. Tours at 10am, 12noon. D R T
Exuberant Grade II* listed auditorium and the most perfect
example of Edwardian variety theatre remaining in London.
Restored interiors added to the fly-tower and new back-stage
areas provided, topping it off with the sign 'Hackney Empire'
in massive terracotta capital letters that are 6.4 metres tall.
Frank Matcham 1901/Tim Ronalds (refurb) 2004. Entry: foyer,
auditorium, stage door, annex.
Tube: Bethnal Green; Rail: Hackney Central; 254,394,253,106,30

Hackney Town Hall
Mare Street E8 1EA
→ Sat 11am-4pm. Regular guided tours, first come basis. Last
entry 3.30pm. Max 25 at one time. D T
Exceptionally unaltered interiors in Art Deco style. Much
original work remains intact including fine light fittings,
panelling, floor surfaces and doors. Natural light pours in
from recently cleaned and restored glass ceiling. Lanchester &
Lodge 1934-1937. Entry: main reception areas, ground & first
floor, council chamber, main committee room.
*Tube: Bethnal Green; Rail: Hackney Central, London Fields; 48,55,
106,38,277,22,67,253,D6,30,236,276,W15*

Hothouse ▲
274 Richmond Road, London Fields E8 3QW
→ Sat/Sun 2pm-7pm. Regular tours, first come basis. D Q R T A
Hothouse, developed by Free Form Arts Trust, re-opened 2007
with expanded studios, workspaces and training facilities,
gallery and a roof top events terrace. Photo-voltaic roof on
studios and passive ventilation. Winner First London Planning
Awards 2008, Hackney Design Awards 2008 and RIBA Awards
2009. Ash Sakula Architects 2002.
*Tube: Bethnal Green; Rail: Hackney Downs, Hackney Central,
London Fields; 38,48,55,254*

Hoxton Hall
130 Hoxton Street N1 6SH
→ Sat/Sun 10am-5pm. D T
A unique survival, Grade II* listed saloon-style music hall.
Other rooms and halls added by Quakers 1910. Hoxton Street
frontage added 1980. Lovegrove & Papworth 1863. Entry: all
areas excluding offices.
Tube/Rail: Liverpool Street, Old Street; 67,149,243,242

Newington Green Unitarian Church
39 Newington Green N16 9PR
→ Sat 10am-5pm/Sun 1.30pm-5pm. Tours 2pm, 3pm, 4pm. d
Earliest active Nonconformist chapel in London (1708).
Includes 18C box pews and early monuments. Associated with
Mary Wollstonecraft, Joseph Priestley, Benjamin Franklin and
other prominent Unitarians. Entry: church.
Rail: Canonbury; 21,73,141,341,476

Redevelopment & Renovation of St Mary of Eton, Hackney Wick
Eastway E9 5JA
→ Sat/Sun 12noon-5pm. Regular tours, first come basis. D R A
Matthew Lloyd Architects LLP explain their proposed
redevelopment of this Grade II* listed church, tower and
mission hall and Eton House with models and drawings. The
existing church has battlemented parapet with traceried
panels, large bell-openings with flamboyant tracery and
several gargoyles. The proposed mix of landscaping,
residential units and modern community resources will act as
a catalyst for the area's regeneration.
Rail: Hackney Wick; 26,30,388,236,276

Restored Historic Almshouse at the Geffrye Museum
Kingsland Road E2 8EA
→ Sat 10am-5pm. Tours at 10.30am, 11.15am, 12.15pm, 2pm,
3.45pm, 4.30pm, first come basis. Last entry 4.30pm. Max
16 at one time. B C d R T
Grade I listed 18C almshouse restored to original condition.
Richard Halsaul and Robert Burford 1714/Branson Coates
Architecture 1998. Entry: almshouse, museum, gardens.
NB. Disabled access to museum & gardens only.
*Tube/Rail: Liverpool Street (Bishopsgate exit), Old Street (exit 2),
or; Rail: Dalston Kingsland, and then 67,149,242,243,394*

Rivington Place
Rivington Place EC2A 3BA
→ Sat/Sun 11am-6pm. Hourly tours. Max 15 per tour. C D R T G
An innovative new landmark building which won a 2008
RIBA award. The first permanent space dedicated to the
presentation of culturally diverse visual arts in the UK.
Sustainable architecture is achieved together with materials
and colours which mark it out as a beacon amongst the
surrounding older buildings. Adjaye Associates 2007. Entry:
ground, 1st, 2nd floors.
Tube/Rail: Old Street, Liverpool Street; 43,48,55,149,205,242,243

Eds Shed/Sunken House

Hackney Empire Theatre

Self-built Straw Bale Building, Hackney City Farm ●
Hackney City Farm, 1a Goldsmith's Row E2 8QA
→ Sun 11am-4pm. First come basis, queuing outside if necessary. Last entry 3.45pm. d T G
Built in 2007 with a 'no-compromise' policy, all materials used are environmentally sound. The classroom has straw bale walls, lime and clay render; other components are reclaimed/recycled materials. Entry: Straw Bale Building, farm site.
Tube/Rail: Bethnal Green, Liverpool Street; Rail: Cambridge Heath; 26,55,48

Shoreditch Prototype House ● A
4 Crooked Billet Yard (off Kingsland Road, opp Cottons Gardens) E2 8AF
→ Sun 10am-5pm. First come basis, queuing outside if necessary. Last entry 4.30pm. Max 20 at one time. d Q G A
Unique, award-winning, contemporary low energy house on brownfield site with striking glazed and planted façade hidden in the heart of Shoreditch, developed as a prototype for green urban terraced housing. Sustainable features include solar control façade with evergreen shading, lightweight steel, timber frame and solar thermal hot water system. Cox Bulleid Architects 2008. Entry: studio and house.
Tube/Rail: Old Street, Liverpool Street; 55,67,149,242,243

Shoreditch Town Hall
380 Old Street EC1V 9LT
→ Sat/Sun 10am-1pm. Regular tours, first come basis. Last entry 12.30pm. d T
Built as Shoreditch Vestry Hall in 1866 and one of the grandest of its type in London. Extended by William Hunt in 1902 incorporating an enlarged assembly hall and tower featuring statue of 'Progress'. Caesar Augustus Long 1866. Entry: assembly hall, council chamber, mayor's parlour, committee rooms, basement (some access may be restricted).
Tube/Rail: Liverpool Street, Old Street; 26,55,78,135,149,48,47,24

St Augustine's Tower ●
The Narroway, off Mare Street E8 1HR
→ Sat/Sun 11am-5pm. Max 30 at one time. New architectural exhibition.
Grade I listed, remaining tower of 13C parish church, with working late 16C/early 17C clock. Extensive views from roof. (Organised by Hackney Historic Buildings Trust). Entry: all areas including clock chamber and roof. NB. Very narrow winding stairs.
Tube: Bethnal Green; Rail: Hackney Central; 30,38,48,55,106,242 253,277,D6,W15,276

Sutton House, The National Trust
2 & 4 Homerton High Street E9 6JQ
→ Sat/Sun 12noon-4.30pm. Tours 1pm, 2pm, 3pm. Last entry 4pm. Max 25 per tour. B d R T
Rare example of Tudor red-brick house in East End. 18C alterations and later additions. Many early features including original linenfold panelling. Sir Ralph Sadleir 1535. NB. gallery, shop & café open from 12noon.
Tube/Rail: Bethnal Green, Highbury & Islington; Rail: Hackney Central; 30,38,48,55,253

The Bridge Academy, Hackney ●
Laburnum Street E2 8BA
→ Sat 10am-3pm. Architect-led tours at 11am, 1pm. D R T A
Bridge Academy rethinks the idea of the school as a piece of urban design integrated into the city fabric. Situated on the Regents Canal on an inner-city brownfield site the innovative vertical Academy creates a compact school shaped around a multi-level 'heartspace'. Conceived as a piece of architectural origami, the design displaces ground upwards taking advantage of magnificent roof-spaces for performance, learning and play. BDP 2008.
Tube/Rail: Old Street; Rail: Dalston Kingsland; 243,249,149,67

The Building Exploratory
8 Orsman Road N1 5QJ
→ Sat 10am-5pm. Hourly tours, first come basis. Max 25 at one time. D N T G A
Overlooking the Regent's Canal, office and exhibition space with bespoke furniture and exposed construction. Voluntary Design and Build.
Tube/Rail: Liverpool Street, Old Street; 242,149,243,67

The City Academy, Hackney ● ●
Homerton Row E8 6EA
→ Sat 10am-1pm. First come basis. Max 50 at one time. D R T G
A colourful glassy school ribbon, woven through clusters of mature existing trees, facing a Conservation Area and Grade II Sutton House. A strong sustainable approach has driven a concept that has reconciled aspirations, site and environmental performance, which includes passive environmental measures that rely on high standards of daylight and natural ventilation. BREEAM rating very good. Studio E 2009.
Tube: Bethnal Green; Rail: Hackney Central; 30,38,48,55,253

The Prince's Foundation
19-22 Charlotte Road EC2A 3SG
→ Sat 9.30am-1.30pm. Tours at 10am, 11am, 12noon. Guided tours visit areas usually closed to public. D T G
Former Victorian warehouse refurbished from old to functional modern with interiors by Robert Kime and furniture by Leon Krier. The Prince's Foundation for the Built Environment also provides accommodation for The Prince's Schools of the Traditional Arts, INTBAU and The Prince's Drawing School. Matthew Lloyd Architects (refurb) 2000. Entry: ground floor gallery, library, drawing studios.
Tube/Rail: Old Street, Liverpool Street 55,78,149,47,48

Village Underground ● ●
54 Holywell Lane EC2A 3PQ
→ Sat 10am-5pm. First come basis, queuing if necessary. G A
Recycled tube train carriages make affordable artists' studios on reclaimed land on top of an abandoned railway viaduct. Sustainable features include solar power. Auro Foxcroft & Nicholas Laurent 2007.
Tube/Rail: Liverpool Street, Old Street; 149,243,67,55,8

TALKS

Talk: 20 Dalston Lane ● ●
20 Dalston Lane E8 3AZ
→ Sun 3pm. Pre-book ONLY through Open House, see p15 for details. D T
20 Dalston Lane is an empty shop, being used as a temporary arts space. It is part of the on-going changes in the Dalston area, hosting events, talks and exhibitions. Join a conversation with architects, artists and arts organisations involved, with more about these developments and forthcoming changes.
Rail: Dalston Kingsland; 30,38,56,76,149,236,242,243,277

Supported by

⊕ Hackney

Hackney Design Awards
The Hackney Design Awards are held every two years and reflect the increasing awareness of high quality contemporary design in the borough. The 2008 Awards attracted 36 entries of which 20 were shortlisted, resulting in 4 winners (including the Hothouse building, Adelaide Wharf housing and the Shoreditch Prototype house), 2 commendations and 4 mentions. Nominations came from architects and building owners but also from individual residents and school pupils. This diversity of interest is at the heart of what the Awards are about – recognising and celebrating the inspiration that good design can bring to the lives of people in our community

Hammersmith & Fulham

Latymer Upper School: Performing Arts Centre

16 Ellingham Road
16 Ellingham Road W12 9PR
→ Sat 10am-5pm. Regular architect-led tours, pre-book ONLY through Open House, see p15 for details. Last tour 4.30pm. G A

The central theme of this architect's own house is 'Connections & Illusions'. A transformation of a standard London terraced house into a contemporary home, expanding, 'tardis-like', in every direction, juxtaposing new with old, cleverly designed literally down to the door knobs using handles Matt Keeler designed in collaboration with Nick Grimshaw. KSK Associates 2008.
Tube: Ravenscourt Park, Shepherd's Bush, Hammersmith; 94,237,207,266

26 Rylett Crescent
26 Rylett Crescent W12 9RL
→ Sun 10am-5pm. Regular architect-led tours, pre-book ONLY through Open House, see p15 for details. Last entry 4.30pm. Max 20 at one time. G A

A contemporary phoenix-like rebirth of a pretty but 'broken' Victorian semi, located in the heart of a Conservation area. A north facing modern wrap around garden extension sensitively but resolutely settles between two neighbouring extensions, and exploits every ray of available sunlight. Wide range of interesting contemporary finishes including polished concrete and recycled glass. KSK Associates 2008.
Tube: Stamford Brook, Ravenscourt Park, Hammersmith; 94,237,266

7 Hammersmith Terrace
7 Hammersmith Terrace W6 9TS
→ Sat/Sun tours at 11am, 12.30pm & 2.30pm. Pre-book ONLY in writing from 1 Sept, to: Manager, Emery Walker Trust, 7 Hammersmith Terrace, London W6 9TS, stating tour preference, if any, and giving full postal address and tel number. Max 2 tickets per applicant. Successful applicants will be advised by 8 Sept. Max 8 per tour.

The home (c1903) of Emery Walker, printer, antiquary and mentor to William Morris. A unique Arts and Crafts domestic interior. Entry: main rooms, garden.
Tube: Stamford Brook; 27,190,267,391,H91 to King's Street/ Goldhawk Road

All Saints Church
Church Gate (by Putney Bridge) SW6 3LA
→ Sat 11am-4pm/Sun 1pm-5pm. D N P R T

15C tower, 19C nave (designed by Sir Arthur Blomfield 1880-81) and many fine monuments. Good stained glass. Churchyard contains newly restored tomb of Granville Sharp, father of Abolitionist movement and tombs of Bishops of London.
Tube: Putney Bridge; Rail: Putney; 22,39,74,85,220,265,270,430

Charing Cross Hospital
Fulham Palace Road W6 8RF
→ Sun tours at 10.30am and 12.30pm. Pre-book ONLY on 020 8383 5226 or email Emelie.Salford@imperial.nhs.uk. Max 15 per tour. D R T

View the Riverside Wing (Ansell and Bailey 2006) with sculpture by David Mach, the hospital chapel (Ralph Rubbs) with stained glass by John Piper and West London Mental Health Centre (Frederick Gibberd Partnership) with sculpture and prints by Bill Woodrow. Other works by Peter Blake and Bridget Riley. NB. Visitors to be aware that they are visiting a working hospital.
Tube: Hammersmith; 190,211,220,295

Fulham Palace
Bishop's Avenue SW6 6EA
→ Sat 11am-2pm/Sun 11.30am-3.30pm. Sat tours of offices not normally open to the public on the half-hour, pre-book ONLY on 020 7610 7164. Sun tours of major ground floor public rooms on the hour (no pre-booking required). Exhibition in museum 'Edwardian Extravaganza: The Fulham Palace Pageant of 1909'. B D R T

Former residence of the Bishop of London. Tudor courtyard with Georgian additions and Butterfield chapel (1866). Reopened after Lottery funded restoration in 2006 with rooms around east courtyard restored and returned to late Georgian colour scheme. Stiff Leadbetter 1766.
Tube: Putney Bridge; 14,74,220,414,430

GlaxoSmithKline Clinical Imaging Centre
Burlington Danes, Du Cane Road W12 0HS
→ Sat tour 10.30am, pre-book ONLY on 020 8383 5226 or email Emelie.Salford@imperial.nhs.uk. Max 15 per tour. D R T

New clinical imaging centre – the result of a unique research collaboration between GlaxoSmithKline, Imperial College London and the Medical Research Centre. Artwork inside includes a series of photographs by Turner Prize nominated artists Zarina Bhimji and Catherine Yass. Sheppard Robson 2007.
Tube: East Acton, White City; Rail: Acton, Acton Central; 72,272,70,7

Godolphin and Latymer School: Rudland Music School
● A
Iffley Road (entrance in Cambridge Grove) W6 0PG
→ Sat/Sun 10am-3pm. Regular architect-led tours, first come basis, queuing outside if necessary. Last tour 2pm. Max 100 at one time. D T G A

A new music school for 11-18 year-olds constructed alongside a Grade II* listed church and linked via a glazed atrium. Acoustically designed with passive ventilation throughout. Shortlisted for a RIBA Award 2009. The Manser Practice 2008. Entry: Rudland Music School and The Bishop Centre (formerly St John the Evangelist Church).
Tube: Hammersmith; 220,283,295,266,267

Hammersmith and Queen Charlotte's Hospitals
Du Cane Road W12 0HS
→ Sat tour at 12.30pm, pre-book ONLY on 020 8383 5226 or email Emelie.Salford@imperial.nhs.uk. Max 15 per tour. D R T

Tour includes West London Renal Building (Ansell & Bailey 2005) with stained glass by Martin Donlin, radiotherapy department with prints by Julian Opie and Annie Albers and other works by Allan Ramsay, John Hoyland and Kate Whiteford.
Tube: East Acton, White City; Rail: Acton, Acton Central; 72,272,70,7

Hurlingham Club
Ranelagh Gardens SW6 3PR
→ Sat tours at 11am and 3pm.

Last of the grand 18C mansions which once fronted this part of the river, with magnificent interiors and extensive grounds. Dr William Cadogan/George Byfield 1760/1797-8.
Tube: Putney Bridge; 22,39,74,85,220,265,270,424

Latymer Upper School: Performing Arts Centre ●
237 King Street W6 9LR
→ Sat 1pm-5pm. Last entry 4.15pm. D T

Although freestanding, the building is linked to the original Arts Centre across two glazed bridges. The main recital space seats 100 while separate studios provide areas for dance, drama and music rehearsal. A fully glazed foyer opens to the newly landscaped heart of the school. Winner of the National Brick Award 2008. Arup were the acousticians. van Heyningen & Haward Architects 1999/2009. Entry: recital hall, dance/drama studio, music rooms, some classrooms.
Tube: Ravenscourt Park; Rail: Gunnersbury; 27,190,H91,391,267

Linden House ●
60 Upper Mall W6 9TA
→ Sun 1pm-5pm. Talks 1pm, 2pm, 3pm, 4pm about building's adaptation over the centuries and boating/rowing demonstrations. Max 60 at one time. R T

Grade II listed, elegant double-fronted Georgian riverside residence (1733) owned by The London Corinthian Trust. Original 18C frontage with 19C and 20C interior. Race starting box on river bank is Civic Trust Award winner. Entry: all principal rooms on ground and 1st floors, boatyard, race box.
Tube: Ravenscourt Park

Lyric Theatre Hammersmith
King Street W6 0QL
→ Sat 9.30am-1pm. Tours at 10.30am and 12noon. Pre-book ONLY on 0871 2211722. Max 25 per tour. d R T

Beautiful gilt and velvet auditorium rebuilt inside concrete exterior of 1970s development. New striking glass and steel entrance extension illuminated at night to create glowing box. Frank Matcham 1895/Rick Mather Architects 2003. Entry: backstage, auditoria.
Tube: Hammersmith; 9,10,27,33,72,190,209,211,220,266,267,28

Maggie's Centre
Charing Cross Hospital, Fulham Palace Road W6 8RF
→ Sun 11am-4pm. Regular tours, first come basis. Last entry 3.30pm. Max 100 at one time. D R T

A non-institutional 'open house', Maggie's is a flexible space designed to be welcoming, uplifting and thought-provoking. The raised roof allows natural light to enter the whole of the building. Partitions divide up the open structure, placing the kitchen at the heart of the building. RIBA Award Winner 2009. Rogers Stirk Harbour + Partners 2008.
Tube: Hammersmith, Baron's Court; Rail: Putney; 190,211,220,295

Palace Wharf
56 Rainville Road W6 9HS
→ Sat/Sun 1pm-6pm. d T

Built in 1907 as a wharf for marble importing, later a decorative plaster works, now artists' studios with river frontage. Entry: 36 artists' studios & riverside terrace.
Tube: Hammersmith, Fulham Broadway

The London Academy of Music & Dramatic Art (LAMDA)
155 Talgarth Road W14 9DA
→ Sat 10am-4.30pm. Regular tours of behind the scenes including classes in stage combat and director workshops. Last entry 4.15pm. Max 10 per tour. d T

Completed in 1894 and LAMDA's home since 2003. Black box studio theatre, rehearsal rooms, stage armoury and student common room. Redevelopment plans underway to create a world class drama campus, including a new state-of-the-art theatre. Niall McLaughlin Architects 2003.
Tube: Baron's Court, Hammersmith; 9,10,295,391

Voysey Studio, now Hungarian Reformed Church in UK
17 St Dunstans Road W6 8RD
→ Sat 10am-5pm. Tours every half hour, first come basis. Last entry 4.45pm. D R T A

One of Voysey's first and best buildings, designed for the artist WEF Britten and described by Pevsner in 'Pioneers of the Modern Movement' as being "remarkably novel". Currently being restored by TBD Architects. CFA Voysey 1892. Entry: hall, garden.
Tube: Barons Court

William Morris Society – Kelmscott House
26 Upper Mall W6 9TA
→ Sat/Sun 1pm-5pm. Max 40 at one time. Demonstration of printing on William Morris's Albion press. B d

Residence of Sir Francis Ronalds, George MacDonald and (from 1878-96) William Morris (organised by William Morris Society). Entry: basement and coach house only.
Tube: Ravenscourt Park; 27,190,267,391,H91

Supported by

h&f
hammersmith & fulham

Maggie's Centre

Hurlingham Club

Haringey

30 Cholmeley Crescent
30 Cholmeley Crescent N6 5HA
→ Sat 11am-5.30pm. First come basis. Max 20 at one time. d P Q A
A new take on the suburban semi. Lowering the garden to allow full width, double-height glass to flood the basement with light. Archplan Architects (refurb) 2006. Entry: ground, basement, garden.
Tube: Highgate, Archway; 263,210,143, W5

34 Barrington Road
34 Barrington Road N8 8QS
→ Sat 1pm-5pm. First come basis. d A
The house has been transformed, opened up to the garden, and the sky. Curved shapes and pods lead one easily through family spaces. Knott Architects 2009. Entry: ground floor.
Tube: Highgate; Rail: Hornsey; W7, W5,144

Bruce Castle Museum
Lordship Lane N17 8NU
→ Sat/Sun 1pm-5pm. Tours Sat and talks about Tudor falconry 1.30pm-4pm. Tours Sun half-hourly 1.30pm-4pm. Last entry 4pm. Max 20 per tour. B C D N P R T
Tudor Manor House built for Sir William Compton in 1514, substantially altered in 17C and 18C. A museum since 1906 housing local history and exhibitions of Bruce Castle. Entry: ground floor; other areas visited on tours. NB. All Hallows Church also open Sat/Sun 2-5pm.
Tube/Rail: Seven Sisters, Wood Green; Rail: Bruce Grove; 123,243

Coleridge Primary School ●
77 Crouch End Hill N8 8DG
→ Sat 10am-1pm. Last entry 12.30pm. Max 10 at one time. d P T
Conversion of the old Hornsey Art School (1880), retaining the central hall with the addition of new classroom wings. Balanced daylight is achieved through the use of clerestorey windows. Nicholas Hare Architects (conversion) 2008.
Tube/Rail: Finsbury Park; Tube: Archway; Rail: Crouch Hill; 41,91, W7

Highgate School Chapel & Big School
North Road N6 4AY
→ Sat 10am-1pm. Regular tours. Max 50 at one time. R T
The School Chapel and 'Big School' are of great architectural and historical significance to the centre of Highgate Village. F P Cockerell 1865/7. Entry: school chapel, 'Big School'.
Tube: Highgate, Archway; 143,210,271

Highpoint
Highpoint, North Hill N6 4BA
→ Sat 10am-5pm. Tours every 25 mins except between 12.30pm and 2.30pm. Pre-book ONLY through Open House, see p15 for details. Last tour 5pm. Max 12 at one time.
Grade I listed Modernist apartment blocks retaining many original features such as cork floors, concertina windows and metal doors. Tecton & Lubetkin 1935/1938. Entry: (by accompanied tour only) common parts, including recently restored foyers and interiors of a flat. NB. No photographs within the buildings or gardens, please.
Tube: Highgate; 143,271,210,134,43

Hornsey Library
Haringey Park N8 9JA
→ Sat 9am-5pm/Sun 12noon-4pm. Tour Sat 2pm, first come basis, approx 1 hour. Max 30 on tour. D N P R T
Open galleried Grade II listed library with internal courtyard. Engraved window by F Mitchell showing Hornsey architecture. Bronze sculpture by Huxley-Jones set in fountain outside. Ley and Jarvis 1965.
Tube: Finsbury Park; Rail: Crouch Hill; 41,91, W3, W7

Hornsey Town Hall
The Broadway N8 9JJ
→ Sat 10am-4pm. Regular tours. Last entry 3.30pm. Max 15 at one time. d T
Grade II* listed, about to undergo a renovation, the quintessence of municipal modernity of the period. Notable Ashburton marble staircases, fine wood panelled rooms and cork flooring. Marble & bronze foyers. Reginald H Uren 1934-5. Entry: most areas apart from council chamber and public halls.
Rail: Crouch Hill; 41,91, W5, W7

Linear House
70 Southwood Lane, Highgate N6 5DY
→ Sat/Sun 10am-5pm. Last entry 4pm. Max 8 at a time. D Q G
A modern insertion into the old fabric of Highgate Village, this single storey house is cut into and integrated with its steeply sloping site. Sleek in design and material with classical references. RIBA Downland Sustainability Award Winner 2008. Clague 2006.
Tube: Highgate; 43,134,271,210,143

Markfield Beam Engine and House
Markfield Road N15 4RB
→ Sat/Sun 11.30am-4pm. Tours of the engine house with engine steaming 12noon, 1pm, 2pm, 3pm. Last entry 3.30pm. Max 20 per tour of house. C D P R T
Grade II listed Victorian industrial building (1886) set within a park and next to the River Lee, with the original Wood Bros beam pumping engine. Newly restored Engine and House.
Tube/Rail: Tottenham Hale, Seven Sisters; Rail: South Tottenham; 41,123,230,279,341 to stations & High Road

Muswell Hill Odeon
Fortis Green Road N10 3HP
→ Sat/Sun 10am-1pm. Last entry 12.45pm. Max 20 at one time. R T
Grade II* listed Art Deco cinema, converted to three screens in 1974 but retaining its fine original decor. George Coles 1936. Entry: foyer and large main auditorium.
Tube: Highgate, East Finchley; 43,102,134,144,234, W7

Priory Yurt
82 Priory Gardens (access via side drive to garden) N6 5QS
→ Sat 2pm-6pm/Sun 11am-5pm. First come basis, queuing outside if necessary. d R G
Yurts are among the oldest nomadic structures. Their dome shape embodies an architectural archetype; their zero-footprint sustainably offers a creative solution to the contemporary housing crisis.
Tube: Highgate; 43,134,263

St Augustine of Canterbury
Corner Archway Road & Langdon Park Road N6 5BH
→ Sat/Sun 11am-5pm. B D P R T
High Victorian church with early 20C additions, restored after fire in 1924. Fine Hunter organ plus case. Imposing, sculptured west front. J D Sedding, Henry Wilson, J Harold Gibbons, Adrian Gilbert Scott 1888.
Tube: Archway, Highgate; 43,134,263

The Old Schoolhouse
Hornsey Historical Society, 136 Tottenham Lane N8 7EL
→ Sun 11am-4pm. Regular tours. Max 20 at one time. B d N P T
Early Victorian infant school, closed in 1930, and after conversion reopened in 1981 as HQ of Society. John Henry Taylor 1848. Entry: main school room.
Tube/Rail: Finsbury Park; Rail: Hornsey; 41,91, W3, W5

Theatre & Television Studios at Alexandra Palace
Alexandra Palace Way N22 7AY
→ Sat 10am-5pm. Regular tours. Max 35 at one time. R T
One of the few grand 19C leisure buildings to survive to the present day, this Grade II listed building houses a theatre (1875) and BBC studios where television was first broadcast. John Johnson 1875. Entry: theatre, television studios, via Ice Rink entrance. NB. children under 12 not admitted.
Tube: Wood Green; Rail: Alexandra Palace; W3

Tower and Churchyard of St Mary's Hornsey
Hornsey High Street N8 7PW
→ Sun 2pm-5pm. Regular tours. Max 15 at one time. B R A
Grade II* listed tower with restored chapel remaining from medieval parish church. Excellent views from top of tower. Organised by Friends of Hornsey Church Tower.
Tube: Turnpike Lane; Rail: Hornsey; 41,144, W3

Triangle Centre ● ●
91-93 St Ann's Road N15 6NU
→ Sat 1pm-5pm. Regular tours. Last tour 4pm. D P T G A
Purpose-designed children's, young people and community centre, notable for striking external cladding and wood-lined hall. Sustainable features include louvres, green roof, roof garden. Lasting benefit for the whole community. 2009 Civic Trust Special Award for Inclusive Design. Greenhill Jenner 2007.
Tube: Seven Sisters; Rail: Stamford Hill, Sth Tottenham; 67,73,259

WALKS/TOURS

Muswell Hill Walk
→ Meet: Sat 2pm at Muswell Hill Library, Queen's Avenue N10 3PE. Duration approx 2 hours. Max 35 on tour.
Tour takes in early and late Victorian, Edwardian and 1930s buildings, and gives an historical interpretation of how a rural enclave changed into a unique Edwardian suburb. (Organised by Hornsey Historical Society.)
Tube: East Finchley, Highgate; 43,102,134,144,234, W7

Tottenham High Road Historic Corridor Walk
→ Meet: Sun 11am outside Old Tottenham Town Hall, Town Hall Approach Road N15 4RY. Duration approx 2 hours.
Tour exploring the area's history including 19C Jewish Hospital, Georgian town houses, Town Hall complex including 21C Bernie Grants Arts Centre, High Cross monument, Palace Theatre.
Tube: Seven Sisters; 41,123,149,230,243

Tower Gardens Garden Suburb
→ Information pick up point: 5 Tower Gardens Road N17 7PX (open Sun 9am-5pm). Self-guided exterior tour.
One of the first garden suburbs in the world, with 2-storey terraced cottages retaining many architectural features. The LCC created a 'housing of the working classes' role for the architects' department. W E Riley 1910-24.
Tube: Turnpike Lane; Wood Green; Rail: Bruce Grove; 123,231,243,217

Supported by

Haringey Council

Harrow

All Saints' Church
90 Uxbridge Road, Harrow Weald HA3 6DQ
→ Sat 10am-4pm/Sun 12noon-5pm. Regular guided tours. Contemporary art exhibition. B D P R T
Excellent early example of the work of one of the best Victorian church builders. Good stained glass by William Morris (3), Charles Kempe (2) and Whitefriars. Monument to WS Gilbert and sculpture by Josephine de Vasconcellos. Grade II* listed. William Butterfield 1845 and 1889.
Tube: Harrow on the Hill, Stanmore; Tube/Rail: Harrow & Wealdstone; 340, H12, H19, H18

Church of St Lawrence, Little Stanmore
1 St Lawrence Close, Whitchurch Lane, Edgware HA8 6RB
→ Sat 10am-4.30pm/Sun 11am-5pm. Regular tours. d C P T
Unique Continental Baroque church almost entirely rebuilt in 1715 by James Brydges, first Duke of Chandos. Walls and ceiling covered with paintings of biblical scenes with trompe-l'oeil effect. Fine wood carvings (much of it attributed to Grinling Gibbons) and the organ on which Handel played. John James 1715-1721. NB. Children's worksheets and guides available.
Tube: Canons Park, Edgware; 186, 340, 79

East End Farm Cottage
Moss Lane, Pinner HA5 3AN
→ Sat/Sun 10am-5pm. Regular tours, first come basis, queuing if necessary. Last entry 4.30pm. Max 6 at one time.
Three-bay timber-framed yeoman house built c1420 with list of previous owners dating back to 1429. Part wall painting of hunting scene on dining room wall (16C). Tudor upstairs window and a smoke room still intact. Entrance porch dates from 16C. Entry: front room, hall, garden only.
Tube: Pinner

Former Grosvenor Cinema, now Zoroastrian Centre For Europe
440-442 Alexandra Avenue, Harrow HA2 9TL
→ Sat 10am-1pm. Regular tours, first come basis. D T
Grade II* listed Art Deco building with well-preserved interior. Auditorium with deep coved ribs; proscenium arch flanked by fluted columns. F E Bromige 1936. Entry: auditorium, foyer.
Tube: Rayners Lane; 398

Fourth Form Room, Harrow School: Old Schools
Old Schools Church Hill, Harrow-on-the-Hill HA1 3HP
→ Sun 1pm-5pm. Regular tours, first come basis. Max 20 at one time. T
Best preserved 17C schoolroom in the country. Wainscot panelling, benches, tables and chairs for Masters and Monitors. Original fireplace replaced in 1730, oriel window inserted in 1820. Walls carved with names of every Harrow pupil attending school until 1847 when name-boards were installed above the panelling. Sly 1615. Entry: 4th form room.
Tube/Rail: Harrow-on-the-Hill, Harrow & Wealdstone; 258, 114, 140

Grim's Dyke
Old Redding, Harrow Weald, Middlesex HA3 6SH
→ Sun tours at 12noon, 1pm, 2pm, pre-book ONLY on 020 8385 3100. Max 30 per tour. P T
One of Shaw's best known 'Olde English' style country residences and once the home of WS Gilbert. Listed gardens. Richard Norman Shaw 1872.
Tube: Harrow-on-the-Hill, Stanmore; Rail: Watford Junction; 258

Headstone Manor House
Pinner View, Harrow (in grounds of Headstone Manor recreation ground) HA2 6PX
→ Sat/Sun 10am-4pm. Tours bookable only in person at Harrow Museum reception on 19 & 20 Sept from 10am for tours starting 10.30am, duration 45 mins. Last tour 4pm. Max 20 per tour. B d P R T
Opportunity to see much of the interior of this 14C Grade I listed moated Manor House, following major restoration work. Built early 13C and former residence of the Archbishops of Canterbury, it is the oldest surviving timber-framed building in Middlesex. Entry: Manor House (on guided tour only), tithe barn, small barn, granary, museum grounds. Visitors must be able to walk unaided.
Tube/Rail: North Harrow, Harrow-on-the-Hill, Rayners Lane, Harrow & Wealdstone; H10, H9, H14

Museum of Harrow School Life
Football Lane, Harrow-on-the-Hill HA1 3EA
→ Sun 2.30pm-5pm. Max 25 at one time. D P
Museum building dating from 1873 showing historical and modern life at Harrow School.
Tube/Rail: Harrow-on-the-Hill; Rail: South Harrow then 258 bus; 258, H17

Old Speech Room Gallery, Harrow School
Old Schools Church Hill, Harrow-on-the-Hill HA1 3HP
→ Sun 1pm-5pm. First come basis. Max 35 at one time. P
Purpose built room intended for the teaching of public speaking which figured prominently in the classical curriculum. Converted 1976 by Alan Irvine into modern gallery with mezzanine floor. C R Cockerell 1819-1821. Entry: gallery displaying selections from school's distinguished collection of antiquities and fine art.
Tube/Rail: Harrow-on-the-Hill, Harrow & Wealdstone; 258, 114, 140

Pinner House
Church Lane, Pinner HA5 3AA
→ Sat 10am-4pm. Regular tours, first come basis. D R T
Grade II listed early Georgian house (1721) with pilastered front and magnificent oak-panelled dining room. Former rectory of the vicar of Harrow. Entry: ground and 1st floors.
Tube: Pinner; 183, H11, H12, H13

Pinner Parish Church Hall
Church Lane, Pinner HA5 3AA
→ Sat 10am-4pm/Sun 1pm-5pm. Last entry Sat 3.45pm, Sun 4.45pm. D T
RIBA Award-winning glass and steel extension to existing church hall. Adjacent 14C Grade II* listed church also open. Weston Williamson (extension) 1994. Entry: main hall, side rooms, kitchen. NB. Activities taking place in hall.
Tube: Pinner; 183, H11, H12, H13

Former Grosvenor Cinema

St Mary's, Harrow-on-the-Hill
Church Hill, Harrow HA1 3HL
→ Sun 12noon-5pm. Regular tours, first come basis. D N P R T
Grade I listed dating to 12C, and in Medieval times the most important church in Middlesex, with notable views over London. Excellent monuments by Flaxman and Westmacott and a burial tablet of Byron's daughter Allegra. George Gilbert Scott (restored) 1846-9.
Tube/Rail: Harrow-on-the-Hill, Harrow & Wealdstone; 258, H17

Sweetmans Hall
90 West End Lane, Pinner HA5 3NT
→ Sun 10am-1pm. Half-hourly tours, pre-book ONLY through Open House, see p15 for details. Max 8 per tour. P G
16C timber-framed house with a smoke bay. Georgian and Victorian additions including interesting features. The timber frame is intact on upper storey and roof. Winner of Harrow Architectural Trust Award 2008 for restoration works undertaken by the owners. Sustainable features include use of lime mortars and other eco-friendly products in renovation programme. Entry: house, garden.
Tube: Pinner; Rail: Harrow; 183, H11, H12, H13

WALKS/TOURS

Pinner Walk
→ Meet: Sun 2pm corner of Chapel and Bridge Street, Pinner HA5 3HR. Duration 1 1/2 hrs. Max 50 on tour.
Guided walk including Pinner's historic High Street with its 15C and 16C buildings and Pinner parish church.
Tube: Pinner; 183, H11, H12, H13

Supported by

Havering

Bower House
Orange Tree Hill, Havering-atte-Bower, Romford RM4 1PB
→ Sat 10am-5pm. P R T
Grade I listed Mansion House commanding the most extensive southerly views over Essex towards Kent. Leading landscape designer Charles Bridgman and Sir James Thornhill (best known for his wall paintings at Blenheim Palace) were involved with the design. Henry Flitcroft 1729. Entry: mansion house, grounds.
Rail: Romford; then bus 375

Bretons Manor House
411 Rainham Road, Hornchurch RM13 7LP
→ Sat 10am-1pm. First come basis, queuing outside if necessary. Max 6 at one time. D P Q R T
Grade II listed Manor House built 1740 by gentleman farmer on ruins of Tudor house. Restored 1975. Entry: main house, brick barn, part of walled garden.
Tube: Elm Park; Rail: Rainham; 103,165,365

CEME (Centre for Engineering and Manufacturing Excellence)
Marsh Way, Rainham RM13 8EU
→ Sat/Sun 10am-5pm. Regular tours, first come basis. Max 20 per tour. D P R T G
CEME is a dynamic hub of education, enterprise and manufacture for east London; a flagship project for the Thames Gateway regeneration. Its futuristic design alludes clearly to its role as a vehicle for innovation and growth in the new millennium. Sheppard Robson 2003. Entry: all areas, grounds.
Tube: Dagenham Heathway; Rail: Rainham, Dagenham Dock; 174

Fairkytes
51 Billet Lane, Hornchurch RM11 1AX
→ Sun 10am-3pm. Regular tours, first come basis. Last entry 3pm. Max 20 at one time. d N P T
Grade II listed Georgian house, interesting chimneys, and probably the only listed mound in the world. Links with Quaker prison reformer Elizabeth Fry. Now an arts centre.
Tube: Hornchurch; Rail: Upminster, Romford; 248,252,256,324,370,373

Havering Town Hall
Main Road, Romford RM1 3BD
→ Sat 10am-4pm. Regular tours, first come basis. Photographic exhibition. D T
Grade II listed, the design was the result of an architectural competition won by Collins & Geens. Unique fittings using Bath stone, red cedar wood and Tasmanian oak, with full-height entrance hall and tall central staircase window and flagpoles. HR Collins & AEO Geens 1935. Entry: ground and 1st floor.
Tube: Hornchurch; Rail: Romford; 252,248,175,128,66

Langtons House
Billet Lane, Hornchurch RM11 1XJ
→ Sun 10am-5pm. Regular tours, first come basis. Last entry 4.45pm. Max 30 at one time. Exhibition of historic photographs. D P T
Grade II listed neo-Georgian house from c1760 with later additions. Landscaped garden with lake, orangery and gazebo. Entry: marriage rooms, orangery. Gardens only on Sat.
Tube: Hornchurch; Rail: Emerson Park; 248,252,256,324,370

Rainham Hall
The Broadway, Rainham RM13 9YN
→ Sat 11am-5pm. Regular tours, first come basis. Last entry 4.15pm. Max 20 at one time.
Built in 1729 for merchant and ship owner John Harle, it is a fine example of 18C domestic architecture, with wrought-iron gates, carved porch, interior panelling, splendid staircase and plasterwork. Entry: ground floor of house, garden.
Rail: Rainham; 103,165,287,372

Royal Liberty School (formerly Hare Hall)
Upper Brentwood Road, Gidea Park, Romford RM2 6HJ
→ Sun 10am-5pm. First come basis. Tours by historian. Last entry 4.15pm. P T
Grade II listed Palladian villa with a west facing five-bay front of Portland stone with two wings. Interior contains fine original staircase. James Paine 1768. Entry: ground, 1st, 2nd floors.
Tube: Hornchurch; Rail: Gidea Park; 496,674

St Andrew's Parish Church
222 High Street, Hornchurch RM12 6QP
→ Sat 2pm-5pm/Sun 1pm-5pm. Regular tours, first come basis. D N P R T
Grade I listed church partly built in 14C. Noted for its bull's head and horns on the east end of the church which gives Hornchurch its name. Entry: church, churchyard.
Tube: Hornchurch, Upminster Bridge; Rail: Upminster; 248,370

St Helen and St Giles
The Broadway, Rainham RM13 9YW
→ Sat 10am-12.30pm. B D T
Grade I listed Norman church with notable chancel arch with chevron and nailhead ornament, built by Richard De Lucy. Entry: vestry, chancel.
Tube: Elm Park, Dagenham East; Rail: Rainham; 103,165,287,324

The Queen's Theatre
Billet Lane, Hornchurch RM11 1QT
→ Sat 10am-1pm. Backstage tours on the hour, every hour (may not be suitable for wheelchair users). Bookable in advance from Box Office on 01708 443333. Max 30 per tour. Children's activities running till 1pm. C d P R T
Opened by Sir Peter Hall, a robust example of 1970s civic architecture and a vibrant and successful producing theatre. Norman Brooks 1975. Entry: all front of house areas, and backstage with tour.
Tube: Hornchurch; 193,248,252,256,324

The Round House
Broxhill Road, Havering-atte-Bower, Romford RM4 1QH
→ Sun tours at 10.30am, 12noon, 2pm, 3.30pm, pre-book ONLY through Open House, see p15 for details. Max 15 per tour. P T
Grade II* listed late Georgian elliptical 3-storeyed stuccoed villa. Attributed John Plaw 1792-4.
Rail: Romford

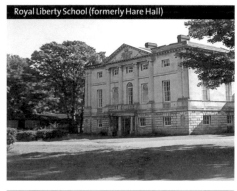
Royal Liberty School (formerly Hare Hall)

Upminster Old Chapel
70 St Mary's Lane, Upminster RM14 2QR
→ Sat 12noon-4pm/Sun 2pm-4pm. Max 15 at one time. B D R T
Grade II timber-framed former Dissenters' Meeting House with pedimented façade. Two blank windows flank the Doric entrance porch. Due for major restoration. Entry: front lobby to view interior.
Tube: Upminster Bridge; Tube/Rail: Upminster; 248,348,370,373

Upminster Tithe Barn Museum
Hall Lane, Upminster RM14 1AU
→ Sat/Sun 10am-5.30pm. Regular external/internal tours including exhibits. Last entry 5.15pm. Demonstrations of historical exhibits & outdoor event on Sunday. B C D N P R T
15C box-framed, 9-bay, aisled barn, weatherboarded with crown-post, collar-tie reed-thatched roof. Ancient monument, now Museum of Nostalgia.
Tube/Rail: Upminster; 248

Upminster Windmill
St Mary's Lane, Upminster RM14 2QH
→ Sat/Sun 2pm-5pm. Regular tours. Last tour 5pm. Max 10 per tour. B P Q
Fine Grade II* listed wooden smock windmill in use until 1934 and containing much original wooden machinery. (Organised by Friends of Upminster Windmill.) James Nokes 1803. Entry: mill interior.
Tube/Rail: Upminster; 248,370

WALKS/TOURS

Gidea Park Garden Suburb Walk
→ Meet: Sat 10.15am at entrance to Balgores Square car park, (immediately north of Gidea Park Station) RM2 6AU. 2hr duration. For information call 01277 219 892. Max 40 per tour. B D
The first Gidea Park Garden Suburb houses were built as a result of an open competition in 1910 for architects. Many of the houses were in Tudor styles, roughcast, colour-washed, or sometimes half-timbered. Further developments took place up until the mid-1930s. Tour takes in Gidea Park exhibition houses and Hare Street buildings.
Rail: Gidea Park

Supported by

Hillingdon

Swakeleys House

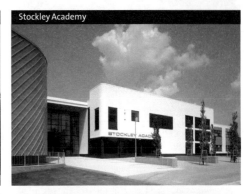
Stockley Academy

Cranford Stable Block & St Dunstan's Church
Cranford Park, The Parkway, Cranford TW5 9RZ
→ Sat/Sun 9am-5pm. Max 20 at one time. Tours of church at 1pm & 4pm. Special children's activities at 11am, 2pm, history quiz throughout the day. C D P R T
Restored 18C stable block of now demolished Cranford House, former seat of the Earl of Berkeley. The front has arches with stone keystones facing a cobbled yard. Entry to ground floor area (west stable). Also open 18C St Dunstan's Church with Saxon and Norman remnants including 1380 bell – the oldest in diocese of London. Berkeley family tombs in cemetery.
Tube: Hatton Cross, Hounslow West; Rail: Hayes & Harlington; 105,111,81,222,498,E6,195

Drayton Hall
Church Road, West Drayton UB7 7PS
→ Sat/Sun 10am-4pm. Regular tours, first come basis. Past and Present local photographic exhibition and GWR exhibition. D P
18C manor house where Napoleon III lived in 1872. Inside a hallscreen of 2 fluted Doric columns, some early 19C enriched door cases, and cornices with acanthus scroll or anthemion pattern. Entry: house, grounds.
Tube: Uxbridge, Hounslow West; Rail: West Drayton; 222,U5,350

Harefield Academy ●
Northwood Way UB9 6ET
→ Sat/Sun 10am-1pm. First come basis, queuing outside if necessary. Last entry 12.30pm. D P T
A rectangular horizontal strip timber-clad building with volume over three stories houses a synthetic pitch protected from the elements under a large span structure which lets in extensive natural light. Two central atriums are separated by a drum containing a theatre. AEDAS Architects 2008. Entry: house, grounds.
Tube: Northwood, Rickmansworth; Rail: Denham; 331,R21

Ickenham Manor
Address upon booking, Ickenham, Uxbridge UB10 8QT
→ Sat tours at 10am, 11am, 12noon. Pre-book ONLY through Open House, see p15 for details. Max 6 per tour.
Four-bay timber-framed Tudor Manor House, connected to a Medieval hall. Later additions include 16C stair tower and two 18C brick wings. Entry: ground floor, gardens.
Tube: Ickenham, Hillingdon

Indoor Athletics Centre, Brunel University
Kingston Lane, Uxbridge UB8 3PH
→ Sat/Sun 10am-5pm. First come basis. Last entry 4pm. Max 20 at one time. d N T
Indoor athletics and netball facilities in a building shape defined by the volumetric requirements of the sports within. The curved roof is a catenary arch supported on wishbone steels, halving the foundations required. David Morley Architects 2006. Entry: all areas except offices.
Tube: Uxbridge; Rail: West Drayton; U1,U3,U4,U7,222,A10

Old Coach House and Dovecot
Eastcote House, High Road, Eastcote HA5 3AL
→ Sun 10am-4pm. d P T
Timber-framed, 17C coach house, dovecot and walled garden are remnants from Eastcote House. Home of Eastcote Billiards Club since 1929, the interiors are largely as originally constructed.
Tube: Eastcote (10-15 min walk), Ruislip; bus from station

St Mary the Virgin Church
High Street, Harmondsworth UB7 0AQ
→ Sat 10am-5pm/Sun 12noon-5pm. Arts and Crafts exhibition. D N R T
St Mary's Church has parts dating back to 11C, a fine Norman doorway and a Saxon sundial outside on the south wall.
Tube: Heathrow Central; Rail: West Drayton; U3

St Mary's Church, Harefield
Off Church Hill, Harefield UB9 6DU
→ Sat 10am-4pm/Sun 11.30am-12.30pm. Regular tours, first come basis. Max 100 at one time. D P R T
Exceptionally fine 12C medieval church, surrounded by large country churchyard, including Anzac Cemetery from WWI. Many notable monuments including Lady Spencer, Countess of Derby. Fine 18C 3-decker pulpit. Grade I listed. Entry: all areas except upper levels of the tower.
Tube: Uxbridge, Northwood then 331 or U9 bus; Rail: Denham (then 331)

St Peter & St Paul Harlington
St Peter's Way, High Street, Harlington UB3 5AB
→ Sat 10am-4pm/Sun 1pm-5pm. Regular tours. D N P T
Grade I listed church (16C) with Norman font and Norman stone arch carved with cats' heads. Interesting monuments including Easter sepulchre. Ancient yew tree in churchyard. Good restoration between 1830 and 1860.
Tube: Hatton Cross; Rail: Hayes & Harlington; 140,U4

Stockley Academy ●
Park View Road, Yiewsley UB8 3GA
→ Sat 10am-2pm. Max 12 per tour. D T G
A newly-built aspirational school building designed around a central atrium linking a 2-storey E-shaped teaching wing and a 3-storey performance arts block. Central atrium space that can be used for exhibitions, dining and assembly. Other spaces include a four court sports hall, gymnasium, drama space, learning resource centre, general and specialist teaching spaces. AEDAS Architects 2007.
Tube: Uxbridge; Rail: West Drayton; U3,U5

Indoor Athletics Centre, Brunel University

Swakeleys House
Swakeleys Road, Ickenham (from Milton Road) UB10 8NS
→ Sat 10am-1pm. First come basis. d P T
By far the most important house in Ickenham and an outstanding example of a Jacobean country house built in the 1630s. The house is constructed of red brick, laid in English bond on an H plan. The Great Hall includes the 1655 Harrington Screen, 18C marble fireplace and original panelling. Entry: Great Hall, gardens.
Tube: Ickenham, Uxbridge; Rail: West Ruislip; U1,U2,U10

The Great Barn, Harmondsworth
Manor Court, High Street, Harmondsworth UB7 0AQ
→ Sat/Sun 10.30am-5pm. d P
This great Medieval barn (1426), over 190 feet long and nearly 40 feet high, is the last of a series of enormous, cathedral-like barns built on this site in Harmondsworth. Peter McCurdy (restored) 1986. Entry: barn, grounds adjacent to barn.
Tube/Rail: Heathrow T1,2,3 or West Drayton, then U3,350

Uxbridge Quaker Meeting House
York Road, Uxbridge UB8 1QW
→ Sat 11am-4pm. Last entry 3.30pm. Max 20 at one time. Exhibition on 'Quakers and Uxbridge from 1658'. R T
Grade II listed typical Georgian Quaker meeting house (1818), retaining its original features with an elders' gallery and full size opening screens. Entry: large meeting house.
Tube: Uxbridge; 222,331,427,607,U4

Supported by

HILLINGDON
LONDON

Hounslow

Walking Through Shared Heritage

Boston Manor House
Boston Manor Road, Brentford TW8 9JX
→ Sat/Sun 2pm-5.30pm. Half-hourly tours, first come basis. Last tour 5pm. Max 30 per tour. B T
Jacobean Manor House (1623) set in parkland with lake and ancient trees. Richly decorated 17C plaster ceilings in State Rooms. Donald Insall carried out the restoration in 1963. Entry: state room, dining room.
Tube: Boston Manor; Rail: Brentford; E8

Cavalry Barracks
Beavers Lane, Hounslow TW4 6HD
→ Sat 1pm/Sun 11am tours, pre-book ONLY on 020 8818 6757 (vehicle registration, type and colour needed along with full names). Tours by local historians. Max 20 per tour. P T
Historic London barracks with notable mid 19C additions under L B Ewart. James Johnson 1793. Entry: selected buildings.
Tube: West Hounslow

Chiswick House ●
Burlington Lane W4 2RP
→ Sun 10am-5pm. Tours at 11am, 12noon, 2pm on the house's art and architecture. 3pm talk on the symbolism of the house, hidden in the art and architecture. Last entry 4.30pm. Max 40 per tour and talk, first come basis. B d T
Glorious example of 18C English architecture, designed to emulate the style and elegance of the houses and gardens in the suburbs of ancient Rome. Lord Burlington/William Kent 1727. NB. Disabled access only booked in advance on 020 8995 0508.
Tube: Turnham Green; Rail: Chiswick

Chiswick Parish Church
Church Street W4 2PJ
→ Sun 1pm-6pm. Tours at 2pm, 4pm. Last entry 5.30pm. Archive display. B D P R T
Grade II* listed church on site for 1,000 years (tower 1435), rebuilt by J L Pearson 1883. Many notable monuments including Hogarth, Whistler, de Loutherbourg tomb by Soane, Chaloner and tomb of Sir Charles Tilston Bright.
Tube: Turnham Green; Rail: Chiswick

Chiswick Town Hall
Heathfield Terrace W4 4JN
→ Sun 1pm-5pm. First come basis. P T
Built initially as a vestry, later extended. Victorian and Edwardian interiors with rich tiles and stunning stained glass, one of the most beautiful Victorian interiors in London. W J Trehearne 1876/Arthur Ramsden 1901. Entry: main hall, Hogarth hall, vestibule, old council chamber, committee room.
Tube: Chiswick Park; Rail: Gunnersbury; 27,237,267,391,E3,H91

Gunnersbury Park Museum & Park
Gunnersbury Park W3 8LQ
→ Sun 11.30am-4pm. Ground floor tours 1pm-4.30pm. B D P R T
Former home to the Rothschild family, now a lively museum set in beautiful 19C mansion on an elevated terrace overlooking lawns and parkland. Alexander Copland 1802/ Sydney Smirke (extended) 1835. Entry: Georgian bathhouse and temple in park, usually closed to public.
Tube: Acton Town; E3

Osterley Park House
Jersey Road, Isleworth TW7 4RB
→ Sun 1pm-4.30pm. Timed tickets may apply. Last entry 4pm. Max 200 in house at one time. d R T
One of Britain's most complete examples of the architect's work. Set in over 350 acres of park, garden and farmland. Robert Adam 1761. Entry: house, park, garden.
Tube: Osterley; Rail: Isleworth; H28,H37,H91

St Mary's Convent
10 The Butts, Brentford TW8 8BQ
→ Sat tours at 10am, 12noon, 2.30pm. Pre-book ONLY on 020 8568 7305. Duration approx 1 hour. Max 8 per tour. d P T
Convent in 18C Grade II listed house with original features. Various additions including west wing (1913-15) and harmonious care home facilities and chapel by PRP Architects (1998-2001). Entry: lobby, community room, chapel, Heritage room and Foundress' room (no wheelchair access to Heritage & Foundress' rooms). NB. Archival exhibition and historical talk.
Tube: Boston Manor; Rail: Brentford; 235,237,267,E2,E8

Voysey House/Acanthus L W Architects
Barley Mow Passage W4 4PN
→ Sat 10am-5pm. Max 20 at one time. D T A
The former Sanderson factory, now an architects' office. Voysey's only industrial building, in white glazed brick with horizontal black banding and distinctive scalloped parapet. CFA Voysey 1902. Entry: entrance lobby, 2nd floor.
Tube: Chiswick Park, Turnham Green; Rail: Gunnersbury; 27,190,237,267,391,E3,H91

West Thames College (former Spring Grove House)
London Road, Isleworth TW7 4HS
→ Sat 10am-4pm. Regular tours, first come basis. Last tour 3.30pm. Max 15 per tour. d P T
Remarkably intact prime example of late Victorian architecture and interior design, including stained glass windows and mosaics. Grade II listed with one remaining fine Georgian room. Previous owners include Pears 'Soap' family and Sir Joseph Banks, founder of Kew Gardens. Sir John Offley/ various 1645 onwards. Entry: house and key rooms.
Tube: Osterley, Hounslow East; Rail: Isleworth; 117,H37,235,237 stop outside

Chiswick House

WALKS/TOURS

Bedford Park Tour
→ Meet: Sun 2pm at Victorian Society, 1 Priory Gardens W4 1TT. Tour lasts approx 2hrs. T
Bedford Park was the first garden suburb. Some 400 homes, mostly in red brick with red tiled roofs, Dutch-style gables, balconies and artists' studios. Norman Shaw, E W Godwin, E J May and Maurice B Adam 1875-1886.
Tube: Turnham Green; 94

Old Chiswick Walk
→ Meet: Sat 3.30pm at the George and Devonshire Public House, Hogarth Roundabout W4 2QE
Discover an Elizabethan house and other houses, ranging from the 17C-20C that have been home to the aristocracy as well as celebrities.
Rail: Chiswick; 190,E3

The Royal Manor of Hanworth walk
→ Meet: Sun 3.30pm at Hanworth Library (Junction of Hounslow Road & Hampton Road West) TW13 6AW. Duration approx 1 hour.
Walk includes Hanworth Palace, used by Henry VIII as a hunting lodge, and Hanworth Park House which replaced the Manor House destroyed by fire in 1797.
Rail: Feltham; 111,285,490,H25

Walking Through Shared Heritage
→ Meet: Sun 2.30pm at Chiswick Business Park, Building 3, 566 Chiswick High Road W4 5YA. Duration 1 1/2 hours. T
The starting point of the walk is the RIBA award winning business centre (Richard Rogers Partnership 2000) and at the other end is the house of William Willett (1856-1915), builder and originator of Daylight Time, located in Mill Hill Park Estate, an English Heritage conservation area.
Tube: Chiswick Park, Acton Town; Tube/Rail: Gunnersbury; Rail: South Acton; 27,237,267,391,440

Supported by

London Borough of Hounslow

Islington

30 Thornhill Road
30 Thornhill Road N1 1HW
→ Sat 10am-1pm. Architect-led tours every half hour, pre-book ONLY through Open House, see p15 for details. Last tour 12.30pm. Max 20 per tour. A G
Remodelling and extension of Georgian terraced house into contemporary light-filled flat and retail unit with double-height living space and three levels of planted timber clad terraces/courtyard. Sustainable features include passive solar gain from large windows and rooflights, stack effect ventilation, and high levels of insulation and double-glazing. Jake Ireland Architects (refurb) 2007. Entry: flat.
Tube: Angel; Rail: Caledonian Road & Barnsbury; 671,271,205,153,38

56 Whistler Street
56 Whistler Street N5 1NJ
→ Sat 10am-1pm/Sun 10am-5pm. First come basis, queuing outside if necessary. A G
A terrace transformed in a conservation area – the existing structure of a typical 2-up 2-down has been renovated to link with its past whilst incorporating modern amenities. Exposed brickwork, in-site concrete and glass stairs. A house full of light and space. Sustainable features include passive ventilation and grey water collection. Phil Coffey Architects 2008.
Tube/Rail: Highbury and Islington; Rail: Drayton Park; 4,19,43,271,393

83 Calabria Road
83 Calabria Road N5 1HX
→ Sat 10am-5pm. Tours every 45 mins. Pre-book ONLY through Open House, see p15 for details. Max 6 at a time. A
A vertical garden grows around a double height library space to the rear of a remodelled Victorian house. Designed to fill the house with light and maximise views to the garden through a fluid sequence of spaces. Waghorn Gwynne Architects (extension) 2006.
Tube/Rail: Highbury & Islington; 4,19,30,43,271,277

85 Mildmay Park A
85 Mildmay Park N1 4NB
→ Sat 10am-5pm. First come basis, queuing outside if necessary. Max 20 at one time. G A
New house making optimum use of tiny derelict site. Intricate series of interior spaces with purpose-made joinery and 3-storey timber staircase. Prewett Bizley Architects 2005.
Tube/Rail: Highbury & Islington; Rail: Dalston Kingsland, Canonbury; 21,73,141,341,476

Almeida Theatre
Almeida Street N1 1TA
→ Sat 10am-12.30pm. Tours every half hour, first come basis. Max 12 per tour. d R T A
Built as reading rooms and a lecture hall in 1830s, it was renovated and opened as the Almeida Theatre in 1980. Recent major refurbishment. Burrell Foley Fischer (refurb) 2003. Entry: front of house, stage area, dressing rooms, green room, wardrobe department, sub stage, auditorium, box office, bar, workshop.
Tube: Angel; Tube/Rail: Highbury & Islington; 4,19,30,38,43

Bennetts Associates Architects

BDP Studios
16 Brewhouse Yard EC1V 4LJ
→ Sat 11am-4pm. Last tour 3.30pm. D R T A E
Late 19C brewery building housing BDP's studios. Original features remain including glazed brick walls, steel columns and vaulted ceilings. Bradford & Sons 1889/BDP 2003. Entry: studios (via tours), gallery, reception, café.
Tube/Rail: Farringdon, Barbican; 243,55,153,4,56

Bennetts Associates Architects ●
1 Rawstorne Place EC1V 7NL
→ Sat 10am-5pm. Regular tours. Last entry 4.30pm. Max 20 at one time. Displays of current projects including the Royal Shakespeare Theatre, Stratford-upon-Avon. d T G A
RIBA Award-winning architects' office combining a revitalised group of redundant industrial buildings and an 18C barn with new contemporary elements. Sustainable features include re-use of existing buildings and green roofs. Bennetts Associates with Baynes & Mitchell 2002.
Tube: Angel, Farringdon; 4,19,38

Charterhouse Chapel
Charterhouse Square EC1M 6AN
→ Sun 2pm-5pm. Last entry 4.45pm. Max 30 at one time. Founded as a Carthusian Monastery in 1371, later sold as a Tudor mansion. Elizabeth I and James I both spent time here. In 1611 endowed as a school (now in Godalming) and almshouse, which it remains to this day. Entry: Chapel Court, Chapel Cloister, Chapel.
Tube: Barbican; 4,56,153

Conisbee
1-5 Offord Street N1 1DH
→ Sun 10.30am-4.30pm. Half hourly tours. Last tour 3.30pm. Max 15 per tour. T G E
Innovative mixed use redevelopment with sustainable features around a courtyard 'oasis' with water, vegetated wall, towering ferns, outdoor terraces, living 'rubble' roof and natural ventilation/light shafts. Pyle Boyd (architects' office), The McFarlane Partnership (residential) 2004. Entry: ground and 1st floors, courtyard, terrace.
Tube: Caledonian Road; Tube/Rail: King's Cross St Pancras; 17,91,259

Cypher House
2A Dalmeny Road N7 0HH
→ Sat/Sun 1pm-5pm. First come basis, queuing if necessary. One of the architects will be on site. Last entry 4.45pm. Max 15 at one time. Q A
Carved out of a small restrictive site, the house maximises light and space by using three half-levels which extend on three sides to the boundary walls. Top lighting, internal courtyards and a double height ceiling add to the sense of space. The 'architectural promenade' includes three staircases. David Wild and Sacks & Maguire 2008. Entry: all areas.
Tube: Tufnell Park; 29,253,4,134,390

Finsbury Town Hall
Rosebery Avenue EC1R 4RP
→ Sun 10am-5pm. Regular tours. Last entry 4.45pm. Max 10 at one time. D T
Opened by Lord Rosebery, an ornate building with elegant decor influenced by the Art Nouveau movement. Several notable rooms including the Great Hall with unique stained glass, antique mirrors and Clerkenwell Angel statuettes. E Vaughan 1895. Entry: great hall, council chamber, marriage room, staircase.
Tube: Angel; Tube/Rail: Farringdon; 19,38,341

Golden Lane Campus ●
101 Whitecross Street EC1Y 8JA
→ Sat 10am-1pm. Regular tours, first come basis. D T
Sitting next to the Barbican with a robust outside presence, the campus is home to a children's centre, primary school and special school and is also a community resource. The design, on a tight urban site, allows for maximum interaction between the different components while maintaining the sense of identity of each. Nicholas Hare 2008. Entry: whole campus.
Tube: Barbican; Tube/Rail: Old Street; 153,4,43

John Thompson & Partners ●
23-25 Great Sutton Street EC1V 0DN
→ Sat 10am-5pm. Regular architect-led tours, first come basis. Max 20 at one time. Architectural exhibition about the building and other JTP projects. d T G A
Refurbishment of a former 1920s warehouse into an architects' studio, fitted out with the latest green technology such as photovoltaics and solar hot water microgeneration, water conservation and eco materials as a demonstration of sustainable office design. John Thompson & Partners (refurb) 2008. Entry: reception, studios, courtyard, annexe.
Tube: Barbican; Tube/Rail: Farringdon, Old Street; 4,55,153,243

Kings Place
90 York Way N1 9AG
→ Sat/Sun 9.30am-11pm. Tours 10am, 11am, 12noon of public areas, concert venues. Max 20 per tour. D N R T G A
An iconic mixed-use building comprised of three basic components: a smaller scale block on Battlebridge Basin; The Rotunda, a long rectangular block facing York Way and running west to east a street-like atrium. RIBA Award Winner 2009. Dixon Jones 2008. Entry: galleries, ground floor, concert level, terrace.
Tube/Rail: King's Cross St Pancras; 10,17,91,214,390,259

Laycock Street Housing and Doctors Surgery ●
28 Laycock Street N1 1SW
→ Sat 10am-5pm. Architect-led tours on the hour apart from 1pm, first come basis. Max 15 per tour. Q G A
Contemporary design of 70 new homes, private and affordable. The social housing has been designed as blind tenure and has the same quality materials of copper and timber cladding throughout the project. The different materials are overlaid in varying depths across the façades giving depth and modelling with further movement provided by recessed and projecting balconies. Project includes new doctors' surgery. Brady Mallalieu 2009.
Tube/Rail: Highbury & Islington; 4,19,30,43,271,393

London Canal Museum
12-13 New Wharf Road N1 9RT
→ Sat 10am-4.30pm. Regular tours. Exhibitions on 'London's waterways and the ice trade' and 'Wartime waterways'. B C D R T G
Canalside building built 1862 as an ice warehouse for Carlo Gatti. The unique ice wells may still be seen.
Tube/Rail: King's Cross St Pancras; 10,17,91,259,390,476

London Metropolitan Archives
40 Northampton Road EC1R 0HB
→ Sat 10am-5pm. Building tours of LMA at 10.30am, 12noon, 2pm, 3.30pm (max 20 per tour). Pre-book ONLY for tours on 020 7332 3857 Mon-Fri. Family event 1pm-5pm – Creative Art Workshop: 'My Place, Your Place, Our Place!' exploring designs of Golden Lane Estate and Barbican. Pre-book ONLY for workshop on 020 7332 3857 Mon-Fri. Self-guided family walk exploring shapes, colours and textures in different buildings. Last entry 3.30pm. C D N T
Current LMA building was purpose built in the late 1930s for the Temple Press. Many original features with public rooms recently remodelled by Bissett Adams. F W Troup 1939. Entry: research and reading areas and areas not normally open.
Tube: Angel, Chancery Lane; Tube/Rail: Farringdon, King's Cross St Pancras; 19,38,341,63,55,243

Marx Memorial Library
37a Clerkenwell Green EC1R 0DU
→ Sat/Sun 11am-4pm. Regular tours and talks. Last entry 3.30pm. Max 50 at one time. B d T
Grade II listed, built as a Welsh Charity School, a library since 1933. Lenin worked here 1902-03 and his office is preserved. Fresco on 1st floor. Late 15C tunnels. Sir James Steere 1737. Entry: Lenin Room, lecture hall, reading room, basement tunnels.
Tube/Rail: Farringdon, King's Cross St Pancras; 55,63,243

no-House ●
43A Mercers Road N19 4PP
→ Sat/Sun 1pm-5pm. Tours every 10mins, queuing outside if necessary, first come basis. Max 10 per tour. D G A
Contemporary family home set in a conservation area – a striking glass and timber box over three floors. A timber screen in front of the glass curtain façade captures the Victorian features of the neighbouring houses, but expresses them in a modern vocabulary. Sustainable materials are used throughout. no-Architects 2009.
Tube: Tufnell Park, Holloway Road; Rail: Upper Holloway; 134,390,17,43,263,271

Kings Place

Pollard Thomas Edwards architects offices
Diespeker Wharf, 38 Graham Street N1 8JX
→ Sat 10am-5pm. Regular architect-led tours. Last entry 4.30pm. Max 25 at one time. A
Conversion of a canalside Victorian warehouse, formerly a timberyard, into spacious offices, garden and glazed extension with one of the best waterside views in London. Pollard Thomas Edwards 1990s/2003. Entry: upper & lower ground floors, courtyard.
Tube: Angel; Rail: Essex Road; 43,214

Sadler's Wells Theatre
Rosebery Avenue EC1R 4TN
→ Sat 10am-5pm. Regular tours. Pre-book ONLY through Open House, see p15 for details. Max 15 per tour. D N R T A
There has been a theatre on this site for over 300 years. The 20C design features a full height glazed screen façade that allows passers-by to view the public spaces within. The auditorium is lined with metal gauze panels that take dramatically transforming light and image projection, uniting audience and performers. There are three foyer galleries with bars, plus rehearsal and teaching spaces. FGM Chancellor 1931/RHWL and Nicholas Hare Architects 1998. Entry: all areas including stage and back of house.
Tube: Angel; Tube/Rail: Farringdon, King's Cross St Pancras; 19,38,341

St Joseph's Church
Highgate Hill N19 5NE
→ Sat 11.30am-6pm (closed between 1pm & 3pm)/Sun 4pm-6.30pm. Historical exhibition. B C D N P R T
Romanesque and Byzantine styles, 2000-ton copper dome, baldachino, 228 ceiling tiles by Nathaniel Westlake. Grade I listed 1898 organ by William Hill & Son. Arts and Crafts Stations of the Cross. Albert Vicars 1889. Entry: church and organ gallery.
Tube: Archway; Rail: Upper Holloway; 143,210,271,W5

Stanton Williams Architects' Offices
36 Graham Street N1 8GJ
→ Sat 12noon-5pm. Architect-led tours half-hourly. Last tour 4.30pm. Max 25 per tour. Model making for children. C D T A
Architects' studio with panoramic views over the Regent's Canal. Opportunity to learn more about major projects including sites in King's Cross, with models on display. Pollard Thomas Edwards (Stanton Williams fit-out) 2003.
Tube: Angel; 30,38,73,214,205

Sadler's Wells Theatre

The Look Out, Vittoria Primary School Community Building ● ●
Half Moon Crescent N1 0TJ
→ Sat 10am-5pm. Max 25 at one time. D G
School/community hall sited at school entrance addressing the surrounding neighbourhood. Cross-laminate timber construction, zinc and timber clad with glazed cantilever roof connection to main school. Sustainable features include rain water harvesting and heating recovery units. Entry: all areas. Charles Barclay Architects 2009.
Rail/Tube: King's Cross St Pancras; Tube: Angel; 17,91,153,259

Union Chapel
Compton Terrace N1 2XD
→ Sat 10am-6pm/Sun 12.30pm-6pm. Tours on the hour. Sat 12noon-4pm performances. B d T
Octagonal Grade II* listed Congregational chapel, containing vast and theatrically balconied interior. Now a concert space, as well as church and day centre. James Cubitt 1877. Entry: main auditorium, chapel, ancillary rooms.
Tube/Rail: Highbury & Islington; 4,19,30,43,271

W. Plumb Family Butchers
493 Hornsey Road N19 3QL
→ Sat/Sun 10am-5pm. First come basis. Max 25 at one time. D
Grade II listed, ornate former butcher's shop c1900 with art nouveau wall tiling, scrolled meat rails, geometric tiled floor and mahogany cashier's booth. Very well preserved. Entry: butcher's shop.
Tube: Archway; Rail: Upper Holloway; 41,91,210

Wesley's Chapel and House
49 City Road EC1Y 1AU
→ Sat 10am-4pm/Sun 12.30pm-2pm. Regular tours. NB. Groups over 10 persons should book in advance on 020 7253 2262. Last entry Sat 3.30pm/Sun 1.30pm. Max 50 at one time (15 in Wesley's house). B d N T
Fine Georgian complex built by John Wesley as his London base. George Dance the Younger 1778. Entry: chapel, museum, John Wesley's house, gardens.
Tube: Old Street (Exit 4); Tube/Rail: Moorgate, Liverpool Street; 21,43,76,141,205,214,271

Supported by

🏛 ISLINGTON

Kensington & Chelsea

18 Stafford Terrace
18 Stafford Terrace W8 7BH
→ Sat 10am-1pm. Tours every half hour. Timed tickets for all tours allocated on first come basis at 9.45am. Last tour 1pm. Max 12 per tour. B Q T
Uniquely well-preserved Victorian house with original interior decoration and contents. Unrivalled example of late 19C 'artistic' interior, with Morris wallpaper, light fittings by Benson and eclectic furniture. Joseph Gordon Davis 1868-74. Entry: ground and 1st floors only.
Tube: High Street Kensington; 9,9A,10,27,33,49

188 Portland Road ● ●
188 Portland Road W11 4LU
→ Sat 10am-1pm. First come basis, queuing outside if necessary. Last entry 12.30pm. Max 20 at one time. d Q G
New build eco-development of 3 houses built within a constrained land locked site. Outwardly refined, the modernist white rendered buildings have large open plan living spaces, shared courtyard and private decked roof terraces. Sustainable features include super insulated walls filled with shredded newspaper, heating and hot water is provided by 12 geothermal bore holes 65m deep, photovoltaic cells, grey water recycling. Michaelis Boyd Associates 2009.
Tube: Ladbroke Grove, Latimer Road; Tube/Rail: Kensal Green; 52,302,18,295

26 Victoria Road
26 Victoria Road W8 5RG
→ Sat 1pm-4pm. Tours on the hour. Last tour 4pm. Pre-book ONLY through Open House, see p15 for details. Max 10 per tour. A
Refurbishment of a 1950s modern terrace house with a spectacular garden, dramatic staircase and intriguing volumes. Gumuchdjian architects 2008.
Tube: Gloucester Road; Rail: West Brompton; 9,10,49,52,70

61 Courtfield Gardens
61 Courtfield Gardens SW5 0NQ
→ Sun 10am-5pm. First come basis. Max 20 at one time. Q A
Radical transformation of large dark basement into modern family home, including innovative products such as computer controls, rubber floors and colour change lights. Winner of Best Apartment on C4's 'Britain's Best Homes' and featured on 'Other People's Homes' programme. Hogarth Architects 2001.
Tube: Gloucester Road, Earl's Court; Rail: West Brompton; 49,74,328

Brompton Cemetery Chapel, Colonnades and Memorials
Old Brompton Road SW5 or Fulham Road SW10 9UG
→ Sat/Sun 1pm-5pm. Tour at 2pm starting at the cemetery chapel, no booking needed. For information on tours ring 020 7351 1689. Max 35 at one time. B d T
London's finest Victorian cemetery of 40 acres with many memorials, designed by architect who had previously worked on rebuilding of Windsor Castle. Original records dating back to 1840. Benjamin Baud 1840. Entry: chapel, cemetery grounds.
Tube/Rail: West Brompton; 14,74,190,211,328,C3,414

Cadogan Hall
5 Sloane Terrace SW1X 9DQ
→ Sat 10am-12noon. Tours at 10am & 11am, first come basis. Max 15 per tour. D T
Completed in 1907 as a Christian Science Church, the Hall is a dramatic mixture of Byzantine, Romanesque and Indo-Saracenic elements. Later additions include stained glass on a Celtic knot theme by Tiffany designer Rosenkrantz. R F Chisholm 1908/Paul Davis & Partners 2003. Entry: front of house, backstage.
Tube: Sloane Square; 11,19,22,211,319,C1,137

Cremorne Riverside
Cremorne Gardens, Lots Road SW10 0QH
→ Sat 10am-5pm. First come basis, queuing outside if necessary. Last entry 4.45pm. D R T G
This RBKC boating centre takes the form of two lozenge-shaped structures nudging up to the river defence wall. The buildings are clad in Cor-Ten steel and are designed to resemble rusty upturned boats moored on the riverbank. Although the two buildings are identical in plan, the roofs are complementary shapes: one gently pitched, the other a valley gutter – one to house offices and meals, the other changing rooms. Entry: both buildings. Sarah Wigglesworth Architects 2008.
Tube: Fulham Broadway, Sloane Square; 11,22,328,345

Institut français du Royaume-Uni
17 Queensberry Place SW7 2DT
→ Sat/Sun 12.30pm-5.30pm. Tours every half hour. Max 15 at one time. Documentaries showing. N R T
1930s building by French architect, refurbished in 1950, then later restructured and modernised. Contains a newly refurbished cinema by architect Stefanie Fisher, conference room, multimedia library and bistro. Patrice Bonnet 1939/Jean-Francois Darin 1996. Entry: library, hall.
Tube: South Kensington; 14,49,70,74,345,C1

Kensal Green Cemetery, Dissenters' Chapel
Kensal Green Cemetery, Ladbroke Grove W10 4RA
→ Sun 10am-5pm. Max 20 at one time. B d P R T
Grade II* listed Dissenters' Chapel built by General Cemetery Company as an Ionic Temple and restored 1997. John Griffith of Finsbury 1837.
Tube: Ladbroke Grove; Tube/Rail: Kensal Green; 52,302,18,295

Kensington Palace
Kensington Gardens (meet at William III statue, close to Golden Gates) W8 4PX
→ Sat/Sun tours at 11am, 12noon, 2pm, 3pm, led by Historic Royal Palaces' historians and building surveyors. Pre-book ONLY through Open House, see p15 for details. NB. 3pm Sat tour only BSL interpreted. Max 20 per tour. B R T
Originally a Jacobean house, Kensington was adapted for Stuart and Georgian monarchs between 1689-1715 by the likes of Wren and Hawksmoor. Other alterations were made for future princesses residing at the palace. It is currently about to embark on a new capital build project to transform the visitor experience for a grand re-opening in 2012.
Tube: High Street Kensington; Notting Hill Gate; 9,10,14,52,70

Lindsey House
100 Cheyne Walk SW10 0DQ
→ Sat 2pm-4pm. First come basis, queuing outside if necessary. Last entry 4pm. Max 20 at one time. Q
Built on the former site of Sir Thomas More's garden, the house has a fine 17C exterior and many notable past residents including Whistler and I K Brunel. Entry: entrance hall, garden.
Tube: Sloane Square, South Kensington; 239,19,49,345

The Octagon

Michaelis House ●
95a Oxford Gardens W10 6NF
→ Sun 1pm-5pm. Tours every 15 mins. Pre-book ONLY through Open House, see p15 for details. Max 20 per tour. d G A
Low-build 5-bedroom house with swimming pool, grass/sedum roof, borehole/heat pump hot water/heating system with solar panels (thermal and PV) and electric car. Michaelis Boyd Associates 2006. Entry: house, garden.
Tube: Ladbroke Grove; Tube/Rail: Paddington; 7,23,52,295

Peter Jones
Sloane Square SW1W 8EL
→ Sat/Sun 12noon-5pm. Tours on the hour. Meet in customer services, 6th floor. Last tour 4pm. Max 20 per tour. D N Q R T
Grade II* listed building, with 5-year renovation programme. Britain's first ever curtain walling and various features listed between 1969-71 such as spiral staircase. Sloane Room has one of best views over Chelsea. RIBA Award Winner 2005. Crabtree, Slater & Moberley 1936-8/John McAslan + Partners 2004. Entry: main building, Sloane Room, behind the scenes areas.
Tube: Sloane Square; 11,19,22,211,319,C1,137

Portobello Dock ●
343 Ladbroke Grove W10 5BU
→ Sat 10am-1pm. Last entry 12.30pm. Max 40 at one time. D T G
Elegant new landmark office building, with sustainable features including displacement ventilation and solar hot water panels of 2,250sqm. A major commercial and residential urban regeneration by Derwent London. Stiff & Trevillion Architects 2008. Entry: lobby, ground floor, 5th floor.
Tube: Ladbroke Grove; Tube/Rail: Kensal Green; 7,23,295,52,452,18

Royal Court Theatre
Sloane Square SW1W 8AS
→ Tours Sat 11am & 1pm, pre-book ONLY on 020 7565 5000. Max 15 on tour. B D R T
Interior refurbishment with vermilion-painted wall by artist Antoni Malinowski. Old panelling removed to expose Victorian ironwork and brickwork in a mix of old and new. RIBA Award Winner. Emden and Crewe 1887-8/Haworth Tompkins 2000. Entry: front of house, auditoriums and backstage.
Tube: Sloane Square; Tube/Rail: Victoria; 11,19,22,137,211,319,C1

St Columba's Church of Scotland
Pont Street SW1X 0BD
→ Sat 10am-5pm/Sun 1pm-5pm. Regular tours. B d P R T
Distinctive listed white building in 'Swiss' style replacing earlier Victorian building destroyed in WWII. Sanctuary retains sense of modernity. Sir Edward Maufe 1955. Entry: sanctuary, chapel, library, Kirk Session room, lower hall, Columbarium, tower.
Tube: Knightsbridge, South Kensington, Sloane Square; 137,19,22,452,C1

The Yellow Building – Monsoon Accessorize HQ

St Thomas' C of E Primary School

St Thomas' C of E Primary School ●
Appleford Road W10 5EF
→ Sat 1pm-5pm. Regular tours. Max 20 per tour. D T A
Innovative new school in landscaped playspace and gardens. Predominantly funded by creating 69 flats, with separate entrances, above school. The school is approached through central, curved, zinc-clad entrance. Pollard Thomas Edwards Architects 2009.
Tube: Westbourne Park, Paddington; 23,18,28

Stack Houses A
264 Westbourne Park Road/1 Basing Street W11 1EJ
→ Sat/Sun 10am-5pm apart from between 12noon-3pm when they will be closed. First come basis, queuing outside each property if necessary. Last entry 15 mins before closing times. G A
The design emphasises the fact that this new building consists of two independent houses placed on top of each other. While contemporary in design the building draws from the tectonic composition of the adjacent Victorian houses with their clearly expressed bases. Sustainable features include rain water harvesting, extensive roof garden, air to water heat pump, solar water heating and heat recovery. Studio Bednarski 2008.
Tube: Ladbroke Grove, Westbourne Park; Rail/Tube: Paddington; 7,70,452,52,123

The Ismaili Centre
1-7 Cromwell Gardens SW7 2SL
→ Sat 10am-4.30pm. Regular tours. Last tour 4pm. Max 100 at one time. D T
Part of an international family of Ismaili Centres, the London centre is the first religious, cultural and social space for the Shia Imami Ismaili Muslim community in the West. From the serenity of the entrance fountain to the remarkable roof garden, it draws upon Islamic traditions in architecture and design while remaining conscious of its context. Casson Conder Partnership 1983. Entry: first, second and third floors.
Tube: South Kensington; 14,70,74,345,414,C1

The LuxPod
Mezzanine, 38 Gloucester Road SW7 4QT
→ Sat/Sun 10am-5pm. Regular tours every 15mins, pre-book ONLY through Open House, see p15 for details. Last tour 5pm. Max 3 per tour. G A
Described as a luxury room on the rocket hotel to Mars, The LuxPod is an ingenious, fully functional, new build studio flat of 9 square metres. It is urban living of the future perched atop a 19C building. Studio Bednarski 2008. Entry: studio flat only.
Tube: Gloucester Road; 49,74

The Octagon
36c The Limes, Linden Gardens W2 4ET
→ Sat 10am-5pm. First come basis, queuing outside if necessary. Last entry 4.30pm. d Q
The existing building was an unusual octagonally shaped 2-storey house which was retained in the redesign to create a central kitchen/dining area with the rectangular annex of the house extended to form a master bedroom, dressing room and bathroom. Internally the feel is rustic with polished concrete screed throughout the ground floor, and the octagonal first floor living room having an antique oak floor and a wood burning stove. Michaelis Boyd Associates 2008.
Tube: Notting Hill Gate, Holland Park; 52,452

The Roof Gardens & Babylon Restaurant (formerly Derry & Toms)
6th & 7th Floor, 99 Kensington High Street (entrance on Derry Street) W8 5SA
→ Sun 8am-11am. First come basis, queuing outside if necessary. Last entry 10.45am. Max 500 at one time. d Q
A fine example of 30s architecture, the former Derry & Toms building is home to The Roof Gardens – one and a half acres of beautifully themed gardens, comprised of a Spanish Garden, Tudor Courtyard and English Woodland Garden. Recently undergone a year's extensive refurbishment. Bernard George 1938. Entry: 6th and 7th floors.
Tube: High Street Kensington; Tube/Rail: Victoria, Paddington; 9,10,27,28,49,52,328

The Tabernacle
Powis Square W11 2AY
→ Sat/Sun 10am-1pm. Last entry 12.30pm. D N T
Grade II listed former chapel in Romanesque style built in bright orange terracotta. Recent sympathetic interior refurbishment retains the stunning cast iron ornate beamed roof. Now a music/dance/community venue in the heart of Notting Hill. Habershon & Fawckner 1887.
Tube: Notting Hill, Ladbroke Grove, Westbourne Park; 7,70,52,452,23

The Yellow Building – Monsoon Accessorize HQ ●
1 Nicholas Road W11 4AN
→ Sun 10am-1pm. First come basis, queuing outside if necessary. D Q T A
The Yellow Building is the 15,000m2 landmark headquarters for fashion company Monsoon Accessorize. Intended to read as a creative powerhouse, the building has a dramatic top-lit atrium with a stunning open staircase running from top to bottom. Allford Hall Monaghan Morris 2008. Entry: all external areas, ground floor atria, internal main staircase to 5th floor – no access onto floors.
Tube: Latimer Road; 316,295

Trellick Tower
5 Golborne Road W10 5UT
→ Sun 10.30am-4.30pm. Tours every half hour. Pre-book ONLY through Open House, see p15 for details. Last entry 4.30pm. Max 8 per tour. d R T
Goldfinger's 31-storey "Unité d'Habitation" built as social housing and now one of London's most desirable addresses. Monumental in style, with its free-standing service tower and surreal boiler house, it retains beautiful detailing and a rich use of materials. Ernö Goldfinger 1972. Entry: lobby, 2 or 3 flats.
Tube: Westbourne Park; 18,23,28,31,52,70,328

Upside Down House
20 Portobello Road W11 3DH
→ Sat 10am-1pm half-hourly architect-led tours, pre-book ONLY through Open House, see p15 for details. Max 8 per tour. A
A contemporary reinterpretation of a traditional 2-storey terrace house retaining the original façade. Bedrooms at ground floor enable three interconnecting living spaces above to enjoy space and light. Pitman Tozer Architects 2008. Entry: whole house.
Tube: Notting Hill; 52,28,328,27,148

Wilmotte UK Architects Offices
133 Oxford Gardens W10 6NE
→ Sat/Sun 10am-5pm. Max 30 at one time. d T A
Refurbishment of old Litchfield studios into an art gallery and architectural practice. Current and past work on display.
Tube: Latimer Road, Ladbroke Grove; 228,295,316

Supported by

THE ROYAL BOROUGH OF
KENSINGTON
AND CHELSEA

Lambeth

The Michael Tippett School

1901 Arts Club
7 Exton Street SE1 8UE
→ Sat 10am-5pm. Regular hourly architect-led tours, first come basis. Tours include musical performance. Last tour 4pm. Max 30 at one time. A R T
Late Victorian schoolmaster's house elegantly converted into a European salon-inspired arts club providing performance, rehearsal, meeting space and bar. Waugh Thistleton (refurb) 2005. Entry: salon, bar/lounge, meeting room, deck/terrace.
Tube/Rail: Waterloo; Rail: Waterloo East; 1,59,139,176,211

5 Chestnut Road – The Clock House
5 Chestnut Road SE27 9EZ
→ Sat 10am-2pm. Tours on the hour, first come basis. Last tour 2pm. Max 40 at one time. d P T A
Victorian house extended with large contemporary, highly colourful living space. Pre-patinated copper roof, large areas of glass, douglas fir detail, housing art collection and clock museum visible through glass floor. Michael Crowley Architect 2001. Entry: lower 2 floors.
Tube/Rail: Brixton; Rail: West Norwood, Tulse Hill, West Dulwich; 2,432,196,68,468

All Saints Church
Lovelace Road, West Dulwich SE21 8JY
→ Sat 10am-4pm. D P R T
Recently completed contemporary remodelling including provision of enhanced facilities and repair of fire-gutted Grade I listed Gothic revival church. George Fellowes-Prynne 1891/ Thomas Ford & Partners (refurb) 2006. Entry: nave, part crypt, choir gallery (max 15 at one time).
Tube/Rail: Brixton then 3,201,P13; Rail: West Dulwich, Tulse Hill

Angell Town ●
Angell Town Estate Housing Office, Langport House, Overton Road SW9 7HN
→ Sat 11am-4pm. Regular tours of estate. Max 20 per tour. d T G A
Housing estate, formerly unsafe and unpopular, now regenerated to create a traditional street pattern with new and refurbished homes. Includes RIBA award winning homes at Marcella Road and sustainable development at Boatemah Walk with solar roof, rainwater harvesting, natural paints. Anne Thorne Arc/Mode One/Burrell Foley Fischer/Levitt Bernstein/Greenhill Jenner 1991-2005. Entry: tours include exterior views of work by all 5 architectural practices.
Tube: Brixton; 3,159,133,333

Beaconsfield
Lambeth Ragged School, 22 Newport Street, Vauxhall SE11 6AY
→ Sat/Sun 11am-5pm. Max 200 at one time. Sat 2pm-3pm a collective performance with various artists; Sun 2pm Bob & Roberta Smith's Apathetic Afternoon; Sat/Sun Soundtrap IV: John Wynne; Sat/Sun Ragged Canteen. d N R T
The remaining girls' wing of the former Lambeth Ragged School built 1851 by local philanthropist Lord Beaufoy – now a unique space for contemporary art. Entry: all areas
Tube: Lambeth North; Tube/Rail: Vauxhall, Waterloo; 77,344,360

Beefeater Distillery
20 Montford Place, Kennington Lane SE11 5DE
→ Sat/Sun 12.30pm-5pm. Tours every half hour. Pre-book ONLY through Open House, see p15 for details. Max 15 per tour. Last tour 4.30pm. NB. Regret no disabled access.
The distillery is home to the only globally recognised gin still made in the capital. Merging the old with the new, its architecture combines Victorian style with the work of Douglas and J D Wood who extended the building in the 1960s. NB. 1 G+T (1 unit) or soft drink available for visitors.
Tube: Kennington; Tube/Rail: Waterloo, Victoria; 36,436,185,2,148

BFI IMAX
Waterloo Roundabout SE1 8XR
→ Sat/Sun tours of projection booth at approx 11.15am, 12.45pm, 2.15pm, 3.45pm. Pre-book tours ONLY by email: lucy.jennings@bfi.org.uk. R T
Multi-storey, glass-enclosed cylinder, illuminated by coloured lighting at night, with most sophisticated motion-picture projection system in the world. Avery Associates Architects 1999. Entry: ground and 1st floor foyers.
Tube/Rail: Waterloo; 1,4,26,59,68,76,77,168

Brixton Windmill
Blenheim Gardens SW2 5ET
→ Sat 10am-3pm. Regular tours. Max 10 per tour. d
One of a very few windmills in existence in London, built 1816 when Brixton Hill was open fields. Was a working mill until the early 20C but fell into disuse. Entry: windmill.
Tube/Rail: Brixton; 45,59,109,118,133,159,250,333

Brockwell Lido, Brockwell Park
Dulwich Road SE24 0PA
→ Sat 10am-5pm. Regular tours, first come basis. (Pool open at normal charge). Last tour 4pm. Max 8 per tour. D P R T
Classic 1930s open air swimming-pool restored to former glory with addition of a single story extension replicating the original design. H A Rowbotham & T L Smithson 1937/Pollard Thomas Edwards (refurb) 2007. Entry: lido pool side, reception.
Tube/Rail: Brixton; Rail: Herne Hill; 3,37,68,196,201,322,468

Carnegie Library
188 Herne Hill Road SE24 0AG
→ Sat/Sun 10am-5pm. Tours on the hour. Last tour 4pm. D R T
Grade II listed building combining classical framework with Tudor-style mullioned and transomed windows. Red brick with terracotta. Bell cupolas and lakeland slate roof. Wakeford & Son 1905. Entry: public areas, despatch room, garden.
Rail: Denmark Hill, Herne Hill, North Dulwich; 3,42,68,468,P4

Christ Church, Streatham
Christ Church Road SW2 3ET
→ Sat 10am-4pm/Sun 12.30pm-4pm. Self-guided tours. d P T
Grade I listed pioneering brick polychromy, "Byzantium on the South Circular". Display on recent restoration of Owen Jones' paint scheme and mosaics. James W Wild 1840-1.
Tube/Rail: Brixton; Rail: Streatham Hill; 109,133,159,201,59,137,5

Clapham Manor Primary School ●
Belmont Road SW4 0BZ
→ Sat/Sun 10am-1pm. First come basis, queuing outside if necessary. Last entry 12.30pm. Max 20 at one time. D T A
A polychromatic extension inserted into a tight urban context offering this DCSF outstanding school a new identity with much-needed new learning spaces and an organisational hub, whilst maintaining external play space. de Rijke Marsh Morgan (dRMM) 2008.
Tube: Clapham Common; Rail: Clapham High Street; 35,37,417,137,345

Coin Street neighbourhood centre
108 Stamford Street SE1 9NH
→ Sun 1pm-5pm. Tours on the hour, first come basis. Under 16 years to be accompanied by adult. Max 20 per tour. D P T G
Forming the fourth side of Iroko Housing Co-operative, the 3500sqm centre includes a day-nursery, programmes for adults, older people, parents, young people and children as well as conference and meeting spaces. Using the same combination of untreated timber and painted steel on the residential side but with the southern side incorporating solar 'chimneys' within a multi-coloured façade. Haworth Tompkins 2007.
Tube: Southwark; Tube/Rail: Waterloo; Rail: Waterloo East; RV1,381

Conservation Extension
21 Lambourn Road SW4 0LS
→ Sat 1pm-5pm. Architect-led tours every 15 minutes, pre-book ONLY through Open House, see p15 for details. Last tour 4.45pm. Max 4 per tour. P T G A
Existing building in a Conservation Area opened up to create a kitchen/dining/living area in an extension with two roof lights, a glazed roof and rear elevation incorporating sliding folding doors leading to a new terrace and garden, all executed in a eco-friendly design. Anthony Thomas Architects Ltd 2009. Entry: ground floor and lower ground floor.
Tube: Clapham Common; Rail: Wandsworth Road; 35,77,87,137

Effra Surestart Early Years Centre ●
Effra Parade SW2 1PL
→ Sat 10am-1pm. Last entry 12.30pm. Max 20 at one time. D T G A
With its visually striking entrance, this Early Years Centre of Excellence combines a nursery and community centre within a tight urban site. Great example of stimulating spaces for children, with bespoke lighting and environmentally friendly agenda. Sustainable features include good natural daylight and ventilation, low energy lighting throughout, non-toxic finishing materials. Architype 2005.
Tube/Rail: Brixton

National Theatre

Garden Museum (former Museum of Garden History)
Lambeth Palace Road SE1 7LB
→ Sat/Sun hourly tours 11.30am-4.30pm, max 25 per tour, first come basis. Max 150 in museum at one time. B d R T

A contemporary gallery space, made entirely from prefabricated timber, inserted into the historic fabric of the building. Described by Building Design as a 'triumph of the architectural imagination'. Shortlisted for a RIBA Award 2009. Dow Jones Architects (refurb) 2008.
Tube: Lambeth North, Westminster; Rail/Tube: Waterloo; 3,77,344,C10,507

Garden Pavilion ●
44 The Chase (tour access through side gate) SW4 0NH
→ Sun 11am-5pm. Half-hourly tours led by architect, joiner (Lignum Joinery) or engineer (Elliott Wood), pre-book ONLY through Open House, see p15 for details. Last tour 4.30pm. Max 30 at one time. D G A

Like a gazebo this garden pavilion detaches from parent house and sets its design within the main corner diagonal which faces near due south across the garden. Six windows fully roll back and away from the cantilever entrance corner. The floor is set level with garden. Materials are Douglas fir structural roof and frames, rattrap brick walls, concrete floor. Roof is sedum vegetation. RIBA Award Winner 2009. Andrew Pilkington Architects 2008.
Tube: Clapham Common; Rail: Queenstown Road; 37,88,137,155,345

Lambeth Palace
Lambeth Palace Road SE1 7JU
→ Sat 10am-3pm. Regular tours. Last tour 3pm. Max 25 at one time. Queue closes 12noon. d Q

Archbishop of Canterbury's London home, dating from 13C; 19C work by Blore, and crypt vestibule opened 2000. Entry: chapel and crypt courtyard, Great Hall (17C), guardroom, picture gallery. NB. No toilets available.
Tube: Lambeth North; Tube/Rail: Waterloo; Rail: Vauxhall; 3,77,344,C10

Lambeth Town Hall
Brixton Hill SW2 1RW
→ Sat/Sun 12noon-2pm. Regular tours. D N T

Edwardian civic pride in brick and Portland stone with restored interiors. Chunky Baroque façades with corner entrance tower and elegant council chamber. Grade II listed. Septimus Warwick & H Austin Hall 1906. Entry: ante chamber, council chamber, reception areas.
Tube/Rail: Brixton; 59,159,109,118,250,P4,35,37,P5,2,3,45,133,333

National Theatre
South Bank SE1 9PX
→ Sat 10am-1pm/Sun 12noon-2pm. Short 'Secret Tours', first come basis, meet ground floor cloakroom. Last tour Sat 12.45pm & Sun 1.45pm. Max 10 per tour. B d N R T

A key work in British Modernism (Grade II* listed), Lasdun's NT incorporates 3 theatres, workshops, rehearsal and admin rooms with public areas of interlocking spaces, inside and out. RIBA Award Winner. Denys Lasdun and Partners 1967-76/ Stanton Williams (refurb) 1997.
Tube/Rail: Waterloo: Rail: Waterloo East; 1,4,26,59,68,171,176,18

National Theatre Studio
83-101 The Cut SE1 8LL
→ Sat 11am-4pm. First come basis. Last entry 3.30pm. Max 100 at one time. d T G

New Brutalist style building which opened as workshop annexe to Old Vic Theatre. Since 1984 it has been the developmental arm of the National Theatre. Sustainable features include natural ventilation, sedum roof, energy efficient lighting and use of reclaimed features from original building. Lyons Israel Ellis Partnership 1958/Haworth Tompkins (refurb) 2007. Entry: rehearsal spaces, studio, writers' rooms, education space, roof.
Tube: Southwark, Lambeth North; Tube/Rail: Waterloo; Rail: Waterloo East; 68,168,171,176

Pullman Court
Streatham Hill SW2 4SZ
→ Sun 12noon-5pm. Max 10 at one time in flats.

Grade II* listed Modern Movement building, with balcony walkways and period internal features. Frederick Gibberd 1936. Entry: flats (differing types), communal parts, gardens.
Tube/Rail: Brixton (then bus); Rail: Streatham Hill; 159,137,133,109,250

Roots & Shoots ●
Walnut Tree Walk SE11 6DN
→ Sat/Sun 1pm-5pm. Tours at 1.30pm, 2.30pm, 3.30pm. Max 50 per tour. Exhibition and displays. D N R T G A

Training centre providing environmental education for all, built on an inner city site. The building has a large photovoltaic roof, solar water heating, three planted roofs and a rubble roof. Paul Notley/CPP Architects 2008. Entry: plant nursery, wild garden.
Tube: Lambeth North; Rail: Waterloo; 159,59,3,360

Royal Festival Hall
Festival Square, Belvedere Road SE1 8XX
→ Sat/Sun behind the scenes tours at 10am, 11am, 12noon, first come basis, duration 45 mins. B N P R T

The major refurbishment of Royal Festival Hall has enhanced the acoustics and comfort to world class standards, increased audience facilities and accessibility, and created an entirely new education and learning centre. LCC Architects Department 1951/Allies and Morrison (refurbishment) 2007.
Tube: Embankment; Tube/Rail: Charing Cross, Waterloo; 172,181,1

South London Theatre
2A Norwood High Street SE27 9NS
→ Sat/Sun 1pm-5pm. Regular guided tours with opportunities to view improvisation and rehearsals. R T

Grade II listed former fire station (1881) with prominent watch tower. Owen Luder (conversion) 1967. Entry: all areas except watch tower roof.
Rail: West Norwood, Tulse Hill; 2,68,196,315,322,432,468

The London Eye ●
County Hall, Belvedere Road SE1 7PB
→ Sun 9am-9.45am: Lecture with David Marks including a 15 minute Q&A. 10am-10.30am: Guests to board the first flight of the day for a standard flight on the London Eye. Pre-book ONLY through Open House, see p15 for details. 150 tickets maximum allocation. D T A

The London Eye is the world's tallest cantilevered observation wheel and has rapidly become a much loved symbol of modern Britain. RIBA Award Winner. Marks Barfield Architects 1999.
Tube: Westminster; Tube/Rail: Waterloo; RV1,211,24,11

The Michael Tippett School ● ●
Heron Road SE24 0HZ
→ Sat 10am-1pm. Tours at 10am, 11am, 12noon, first come basis. D T G

Multiple award-winning design for the first BSF school to open in London accommodating up to 80 secondary school students with profound and multiple learning problems. The form of the building is determined by the section through classrooms which maximises natural light and ventilation with concrete soffits to maximise thermal mass. Colourful external louvres provide solar protection and the school also has a sedum roof. Marks Barfield Architects 2008.
Rail: Loughborough Junction; P5,345

Tree House ●
1a Bedford Terrace, Lyham Road SW2 5DJ
→ Sat/Sun 9.30am-4.30pm. First come basis, queuing outside if necessary. Max 20 at one time. d G

A net zero energy house which makes the most of a small plot, integrating inside and outside spaces. The top room opens into the canopy of the tree that inspired the form, details and performance of the house. Constructive Individuals 2006.
Tube: Clapham North; 35,37,137,417,88

West Norwood Cemetery & Greek Chapel
→ Meet: Sun at 2pm, 2.30pm, 3pm inside main cemetery gate, Norwood Road SE27 9JU. Duration 1 1/2 hours. Max 35 per tour. B P

Opened 1837, with monuments to famous Victorians. 65 Grade II/II* listed monuments, including Greek Chapel attributed to John Oldrid Scott, c1872.
Tube/Rail: Brixton; Rail: West Norwood, Tulse Hill; 2,68,196,322,432,468

Young Vic
66 The Cut, Waterloo SE1 8LZ
→ Sun 11am-4pm. Regular tours, first come basis. Max 12 per tour. D R T A

Major £12.5 million rebuilding project completed October 2006. Main auditorium retained with extra height and with 2 newly built smaller, naturally-lit studios. Foyer has double-height mezzanine. Exterior includes mesh façade and painted screen by artist Clem Crosby. RIBA Award Winner 2007 and shortlisted for the RIBA Stirling Prize 2007. Haworth Tompkins 2007.
Tube/Rail: Waterloo; Tube: Southwark; Rail: Waterloo East

Supported by

Lambeth

Lewisham

APT – The Art in Perpetuity Trust
Harold Wharf, 6 Creekside SE8 4SA
→ Sat/Sun 1pm-5pm. First come basis. d N P R T
Originally a rag sorting warehouse, now converted to new use as art studios and gallery. Steel frontage and atrium form recent additions. Alfred Roberts 1911/Campbell Jackson Architects (refurb) 2000. Entry: gallery, 37 studios, yard.
DLR: Deptford Bridge; Rail: Deptford, Greenwich; 47,53,177,453

Boone's Chapel
Lee High Road SE13 5PH
→ Sat 10.30am-5pm/Sun 12noon-5pm. First come basis. Max 20 at one time. Exhibition to celebrate the first 40 years of the Churches Conservation Trust. d G A
Grade I listed former almshouse chapel restored in 2008 using salvaged materials with organic insulation. Brick and Portland stone chapel (1682) in grounds of former almshouse gardens with recreated physic garden. Entry: chapel.
Rail: Blackheath, Lewisham, Lee; 321,178,261,122 (Brandram Road)

Crossways Sixth Form ●
Sprules Road, Brockley SE4 2NL
→ Sat 11am-2pm. Regular tours, first come basis. Last entry 1.45pm. Max 20 at one time. D T G
As a new type of school building, this Academy offers its students 21C learning facilities in a striking and contemporary working environment. Sustainable features include recycled rainwater, sunlight travel pipes reducing use of artificial lighting and 'smart' building materials. IID Architects 2004.
Tube/Rail: New Cross, New Cross Gate; Rail: Brockley; 484,172,122

Horniman Museum – Behind the Scenes of Natural History
100 London Road SE23 3PQ
→ Sun tours at 2pm & 3pm, duration 1 hour, pre-book ONLY by email to marketing@horniman.ac.uk, or ring 020 8699 1872 ext 196. D N R T
See some rarely seen natural history specimens and learn about the architecture of the North Hall Gallery, with Jo Hatton the Natural History Curator. C H Townsend 1901.
Tube/Rail: New Cross Gate; Rail: Forest Hill; 176,185,197,356,P4,122

Lewisham Arthouse/Deptford Library
140 Lewisham Way SE14 6PD
→ Sun 1pm-5pm. Tours every 15-20 mins. Last tour 4.45pm. Max 10 per tour. Small historical display. d P T
Former library, converted to studios. Grade II listed building in classical Renaissance style with curved glass vaulted roof. A Brumwell Thomas 1914. Entry: all except restricted access to studios.
Tube/Rail: New Cross, New Cross Gate; DLR: Lewisham, Deptford Broadway; 21,136,321,436,171,172,53,453

Manor House Gardens Ice House
Manor House Gardens (Old Road) SE13 5SY
→ Sat/Sun 2pm-5pm. Last entry 4.50pm. Max 10 at a time. P R T
Grade II listed ice well (1773) and underground chambers in park, which provided ice for nearby Manor House, former home of Sir Francis Baring. Cited in 2002 Civic Trust Awards.
DLR/Rail: Lewisham; Rail: Lee, Hither Green; 122,261,278,321

Crossways Sixth Form

Manor House Library
Old Road SE13 5SY
→ Sat 10am-5pm/Sun 10am-4pm. General access during opening hours. For architectural tours, pre-book ONLY on 020 8852 0357 or email manorhouselibrary@lewisham.gov.uk. Max 10 on tours. Exhibition of history of Manor House. D N P T
Grade II listed classical design (attributed to Richard Jupp 1771-2) with 5 bay façade, 4 column portico and two Adam-style plasterwork ceilings on the ground floor, recently reopened after extensive renovation. Now state-of-the-art library and children's centre with the restored fixtures and fittings illustrating the elegance of the original design. Entry: library, basement area, main lobby, 1st and 2nd floors.
Rail: Hither Green, Blackheath; 122,178,261,321

St Margaret's Church & Churchyard
Lee Terrace (corner of Brandram Road) SE13 5DL
→ Sat 10.30am-5pm/Sun 12noon-5pm. Regular tours. B D P T
A Grade II* listed early Victorian Gothic church recently restored. Graveyard contains 23 listed monuments. John Brown 1839/James Brooks 1875. Entry: Main nave, chancel and Lady chapel.
DLR/Rail: Lewisham; Rail: Blackheath; 54,89,108

St Paul's Church, Deptford
164-166 Deptford High Street SE8 3DS
→ Sat 11am-5pm/Sun 1pm-4.30pm. Last entry Sat 4.45pm/Sun 4.15pm. d N P R T
England's finest baroque church, superbly restored (2004). Grade II listed. Circular steeple with semi-circular portico. Splendid apse murals, William Drake organ in 1748 case and vaulted crypt. Thomas Archer 1712-23. Entry: church and crypt.
Rail: New Cross; DLR: Deptford Bridge; 47,199

Stone House
281 Lewisham Way SE4 1XF
→ Sat/Sun tours at 12noon, 1.15pm, 2.30pm, 3.45pm, 5pm, pre-book ONLY through Open House, see p15 for details. Max 20 per tour. d T
One of London's best Palladian Villas with fine portico, saloon with painted ceiling c1830 and dining room with murals by Peter Kent (1995). Grade II* listed. Recently restored. George Gibson the Younger 1771-3. Entry: dining room, staircase, saloon, 2 other rooms, lantern and garden with water feature remodelled by Todd Longstaffe-Gowan.
DLR: Elverson Road; Rail/DLR: Lewisham; Rail: New Cross; 21,136,321,436

Walter Segal Self-Build House with Eco-refurbishment

The Capitol (formerly Forest Hill Cinema)
11-21 London Road SE23 3TW
→ Sat/Sun 10am-5pm. Regular architectural tours including behind-the-scenes to largely untouched first floor area. Pre-book ONLY on 020 8291 8920. Last tour 4pm. Max 8 per tour. d R T
Formerly Capitol Cinema, Grade II listed rare survival of a complete 1920's cinema in Art Deco Egyptian style, later a bingo hall and now a pub. Stanley Beard 1929.
Rail: Forest Hill; 185,176,122

Walter Segal Self-Build House with Eco-refurb ●
8 Walters Way, Honor Oak Park SE23 3LH
→ Sat 12noon-5pm. Regular tours, first come basis. Last entry 4.45pm. Max 20 at one time. R T G
A close of 13 self-built houses. Each house is unique and built using a method developed by Walter Segal, who led the project in the 1980s. The open house has benefitted from extensive eco-refurbishment including super-insulation, triple glazing and solar hot water and heating. Walter Segal 1987. Entry: house.
Rail: Honor Oak Park; P4,P12,185

Supported by

Lewisham

Merton

31b St Mary's Road
31b St Mary's Road SW19 7BP
→ Sun 10am-5pm, half-hourly tours except for 1pm-2pm. Pre-book ONLY through Open House, see p15 for details. Max 12 per tour. d T
One of a small number of Peter Foggo houses, single storey, flat roofed house inspired by Mies van der Rohe's Farnsworth House, with skylights, two wings, mahogany panelling and floor-to-ceiling windows. A large open-plan living room looks out onto landscaped gardens. Peter Foggo 1965. Entry: all except 1 bedroom, utility room.
Tube: Wimbledon Park, Southfields; Rail: Wimbledon; 493,93,200

9 Parkside Avenue
9 Parkside Avenue SW19 5ES
→ Sun 12noon-4pm. Architect-led regular tours, first come basis, queuing if necessary. A
Complex series of interlocking spaces within a simple overall volume, the house has references to the dramatic and hidden sources for lighting spaces seen in Baroque churches and the work of Soane. Holden + Partners 1999. Entry: house, garden.
Tube/Rail: Wimbledon

Baitul Futuh Mosque
181 London Road, Morden SM4 5PT
→ Sat 10am-5pm. Regular talks and tours, pre-book ONLY on 020 8648 5255. B D N R T
Purpose-built mosque (2003) and the largest in Europe, with 15m diameter dome and minarets 36m and 23m high, and accommodating 13,000 worshippers. The building is a blend of Islamic and modern British architecture and incorporates much of the structure of an old dairy site. Facilities include halls, library, crèche, studios. Voted one of top 50 buildings in the world by Independent magazine. Entry: all areas.
Tube: Morden; Rail: Morden South; 93,154,213,80

Buddhapadipa Temple
14 Calonne Road SW19 5HJ
→ Sat 9am-5pm/Sun 9am-4pm. Regular 10-minute tours. Last entry 3pm. Max 30 per tour. B P T A
Complex of buildings on 4 acres of land with Buddhist Theravada Temple in Thai style – one of only two outside Asia. Interior walls with excellent mural paintings by Thai artists, depicting aspects of Buddha's life. Praves Limparangsri Architect w/Sidney Kaye Firmin Partnership 1980. Entry: temple, gardens.
Tube/Rail: Wimbledon; 93

Merton Civic Centre
London Road, Morden SM4 5DX
→ Sat/Sun 10am-4pm. Regular tours, first come basis. G
Council offices with tower and modern council chamber. The roof has dramatic views over London's skyline together with wind turbines. Monitors in lobby display the amount of electricity being generated. A Green 1960-2/Organised Office Developments 1985. Entry: roof viewing platform, office areas, council chamber.
Tube: Morden; Rail: Morden South; 93,154,80,293,118

Morden Hall Park
→ Meet Sat 2pm outside Riverside Café, Morden Hall Park SM6 8LD. First come basis. Max 25 per tour. B D P R T
A tour around buildings in Morden Park including the Stables, a quadrangle built c1886 around a cobbled courtyard including clocktower, where up to 12 horses were stabled and the Snuff Mill c1750 which ceased operating as a mill in 1922. NB. Proposals for Green Living Centre in stable block.
Tube: Morden; Tram: Phipps Bridge; 93,157,154,118,164,80,163,421,420,293,493,413

Morden Park House
London Road (behind Merton College), Morden SM4 5QU
→ Sun 10am-1pm. Interactive/multimedia tours available. Last entry 12.30pm. Max 50 at one time. D P T
Grade II listed fine 1770 house in extensive grounds built for John Ewart on part of the Morden Hall Estate, now the Borough Register Office.
Tube: Morden; Rail: Morden South; 93,80

New Wimbledon Theatre
The Broadway SW19 1QG
→ Sat 10am-1pm. Pre-book ONLY on 020 8545 7901 or email sambain@theambassadors.com. Last entry 1pm. Max 20 per tour. NB. Tours include many steps. T
Striking Edwardian theatre with beautiful main auditorium in classic three-tier design, seating 1,652. Recent major refurbishment. Cecil Masey & Roy Young 1910. Entry: main auditorium, stage.
Tube/Rail: Wimbledon; 57,93,219,493

St Lawrence Church
London Road, Morden SM4 5QT
→ Sat 9am-6pm. First come basis. Max 15 at one time. D T
Grade I Norman, possibly Saxon, brick-built church consisting of a nave and chancel. Tower at the west end. Gothic-style stone windows from the old church inserted into the present 1636 structure. East window stone likely to be from Merton Priory.
Tube: Morden; Rail: Morden South; 93,80

St Mary's Church, Merton Park
Church Path, Merton Park SW19 3HJ
→ Sat 10am-5pm/Sun 12noon-5pm. Tours Sat 11am, 3pm/Sun 3pm. d P T
Grade II listed gem of a country church built in 1115, now in the heart of a suburban conservation area. Norman features, William Morris glass and associations with famous people including Nelson.
Tramlink: Merton Park; Tube: South Wimbledon; Tube/Rail: Wimbledon; 163,164,152

The Chapter House, Merton Priory
Merton Abbey Mills, Merantun Way SW19 2RD
→ Sat/Sun 10am-5pm. First come basis. Max 50 at one time. NB. The remains lie under the A24 Merantun Way, between Merton Abbey Mills and Sainsbury's. Adjacent Merton Abbey Mills market will be open. C D P
Fascinating excavated remains of the Chapter House of Merton Priory c1100-1200, one of the most important of all Augustinian foundations prior to its destruction in 1538 by Henry VIII. Entry: Chapter House archaeological relic.
Tube: Colliers Wood; Rail: Wimbledon; 57,131,152,200,219,470

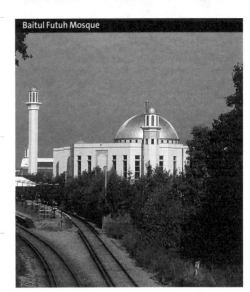
Baitul Futuh Mosque

New Wimbledon Theatre

Wimbledon Windmill
Windmill Road SW19 5NR
→ Sat 10am-5pm. Regular tours, first come basis. Max 50 at one time. Architect for restoration and curator on site. B C d P R T A
Rare example of a hollow post mill (1817). Grade II* listed, it now contains a museum depicting the history and development of windmills in Britain. Many working models, windmill machinery, equipment and tools.
Tube/Rail: Wimbledon; 93

Supported by

merton

Newham

East Thames Group Headquarters ◐ ●
29-35 West Ham Lane E15 4PH
→ Sat 9am-2pm. Tours on the hour 10am to 1pm. Max 10 per tour. Multimedia exhibition on history of design in social housing, including a section on the Open House My City Too! (see p11 for more details). D R T G A
A newly-built landmark building providing the headquarters of one of the largest housing associations in London and a welcoming community space. Includes a one-stop-shop, café, exhibition, roof terrace and meeting and event facilities. Sustainable features include brown roof. Fletcher Priest Architects 2008. Entry: reception, foyer. Other floors on tour only.
Tube/Rail: Stratford; 86,104,108,158,238,241,257,262,425,473,D8

Grassroots ◐
Memorial Park, Memorial Avenue (building just inside park entrance) E15 3DB
→ Sat 10am-2pm. Last entry 1.30pm. Max 50 at a time. C D P R T G A
Partially subterranean, energy-efficient building of cutting-edge design with grass roof and internal courtyard, set in a park. Community and nursery use. Eger Architects 2005. Entry: all main areas, Early Start area and inner courtyard.
Tube: West Ham

House Mill
Three Mill Lane E3 3DU
→ Sat/Sun 11am-4pm. Regular tours. Last tour 3.30pm. Max 18 per tour. B D P R T
The UK's oldest and largest tidal mill. 5-storey, timber-framed, brick-clad watermill with four waterwheels, originally built 1776 to mill grain for distillery trade. Operational until 1940. (Organised by River Lea Tidal Mill Trust). Entry: ground, 1st, 2nd and 3rd floors of mill and rebuilt house.
Tube: Bromley by Bow; DLR: Devons Road; 25,108,D8,S2

London 2012 Olympic Park
Meet: The Score Complex, Oliver Road, Leyton E10 5JY
→ Sat/Sun 8.30am to 6pm. Regular tours departing from Score. Max 45 per tour. Minimum age of 8 years will apply. Pre-book ONLY on 0300 2012 550. Flat soled shoes must be worn.
The Olympic Park which is being created on a 2.5sqkm site in the Lower Lee Valley will be at the heart of the London 2012 Games. It is one of the largest construction and engineering projects in Europe. The site will transform during legacy into one of the largest new urban parks in Europe for 150 years. Construction work is well underway on the 'big five' venues – Olympic Stadium, Velodrome, Olympic Village and International Broadcast Centre/Main Press Centre. Entry: limited to bus tours.
DLR/Tube/Rail: Leyton

London Regatta Centre
Dockside Road E16 2QD
→ Sat/Sun 10am-5pm. First come basis. d P R T
Robust and sharply angular boathouse. A 2-storey building with glass façade overlooking the Royal Dock, containing a gym, indoor rowing tank, restaurant and accommodation. Ian Ritchie Architects 1999.
DLR: Royal Albert

Olympic Park Viewing Gallery at Holden Point
Holden Point, Waddington Road, Stratford E15 1QN
→ Sat/Sun 10am-12noon. 1 hour slots, pre-book ONLY on 020 8430 5992. Max 15 at one time. No wheelchair access.
See spectacular birdseye views of the Olympic Park from the viewing gallery, constructed for the International Olympic Committee's visit during London's bid to host the London 2012 Olympic Games and Paralympic Games. Newham Council officer on site to answer questions. NB. Viewing gallery sits on 21st floor of housing block, please respect residents.
Tube/Rail: Stratford; 25,69,86,104,108

St Mary Magdalene Church & Nature Reserve
High Street South/Norman Road E6 6HN
→ Sat 10am-4pm. Regular tours, first come basis. D P R T
Grade I listed 12C church, with London's largest churchyard and one of the best-preserved Norman archways in the country, as well as other interesting features, including 750-year-old wall paintings. Entry: church, churchyard, parish hall, nature reserve.
Tube: East Ham; DLR: Beckton; 101,104,474

St Mary the Virgin
Church Road, Manor Park, Little Ilford E12 6HA
→ Sat 10am-5pm/Sun 12noon-5pm. D P T
Small Grade I listed 12C chapel in lovely churchyard setting, it retains original architectural features and has interesting brasses, monuments and stained glass windows.
Tube: East Ham; Tube/Rail: Manor Park; 25,86,101,104,147

Stratford Circus
Theatre Square E15 1BX
→ Sat/Sun 10am-1pm. Tours at 10am, 12noon, 1pm of theatre spaces, technical booths. Max 10 per tour. D R T
Space, light, inspiration – a contemporary building achieves the original vision to create a modern user-friendly facility with multi-functional spaces. Levitt Bernstein 2001. Entry: foyer, café, theatres.
Tube/DLR/Rail: Stratford; 25,69,27b,108,473

Stratford Picture House
Gerry Raffles Square, Salway Road E15 1BN
→ Sat/Sun 2pm-4pm. Tours on the hour. Last tour 4pm. Max 10 per tour. D R T
Contemporary cinema in the heart of Stratford, a linear east-west glass and steel building, dramatically revealing its structure and functions to the passer by. Four screens with state-of-the-art sound. Burrell Foley Fischer Architects 1997.
DLR/Tube/Rail: Stratford; 25,69,86,104,108,158,238,241,257,262

The Children's Garden Early Years Centre ◐ ●
University of East London Docklands Campus, University Way E16 2RD
→ Sat 10am-5pm. First come basis, queuing outside if necessary. Regular tours, first come basis. Max 10 at one time. D T G
Constructed from recycled and refurbished building modules, the nursery is a calm and welcoming environment for children in a landscaped garden clad in untreated Scottish larch. Windows overlooking the garden provide a natural light and the interior is free from reception desks, corridors and signage to simplify the children's experience with angled walls for the playrooms, bespoke geometric furniture and colour-washed surfaces for the different areas of activity. Arts Lettres Techniques 2007.
DLR: Cyprus Docklands; Rail/DLR: Stratford; 366

London 2012 Olympic Park

The Hub
123 Star Lane, Canning Town E16 4PZ
→ Sat 10am-4.30pm. Last entry 4pm. Max 50 at one time. Community events taking place. D P R T G
Community resource centre with glazed façade and a Crawford door that creates open aspect for café/lounge/reception areas. Winner 2005 Regeneration Award and Runner-up 2005 Prime Minister's Building of the Year Award. Eger Architects 2005. Entry: all main areas.
DLR/Tube: Canning Town; 69

Theatre Royal Stratford East ●
Gerry Raffles Square E15 1BN
→ Sat tours at 10am, 11am, 12noon/Sun 10am and 11am, first come basis. Max 15 per tour. Talk Sun 12noon in auditorium by Murray Melvin, theatre archivist and Dawn Reid, associate director. D R T
Built as a playhouse and entertaining audiences for over 100 years. Having undergone a £7.5million refurbishment it now has the best of both worlds: an original Victorian auditorium with beautiful Frank Matcham interior; and state-of-the-art backstage and front of house facilities. Grade II* listed. JG Buckle, Frank Matcham 1884. Entry: theatre, backstage areas.
DLR/Tube/Rail: Stratford; 25,108,69

University of East London Docklands Campus
University Way E16 2RD
→ Sat/Sun 10am-4pm. Tours on the hour. D R T G A
An imaginative composition of brightly coloured residential towers and faculty buildings designed by award-winning architects. A flagship of sustainable design in the heart of the London Docklands. Planned sustainable features include solar panels, wind turbine, solar-thermal panels. Edward Cullinan Architects 1999/Building Design Partnership (Phase 2) 2006. Entry: all common areas except offices and some laboratories.
DLR: Cyprus

West Ham Parish Church of All Saints
Church Street, Stratford E15 3HU
→ Sat 10am-6pm. D R T
Grade I listed Norman church (1138) much enlarged reveals the building styles of many periods. Many notable monuments with sanctuary by Sir George Gilbert Scott. Entry: nave, chancel, north & south aisles, tower with guide.
Tube: Plaistow, West Ham; DLR/Tube/Rail: Stratford; 69,241,262,276

Supported by

Redbridge

Bancroft's School
611 High Road, Woodford Green IG8 0RF
→ Sat 10am-2.30pm. Last entry 2pm. d P T
A dignified and impressive design with later additions. Spiral staircase leads to the top of the tower, giving excellent views of East London. Formerly a Drapers' Company charitable school in Mile End Road, Bancroft's moved to its present site in 1889. Sir Arthur Blomfield 1889. Entry: chapel, great hall, library, dining hall, tower, grounds.
Tube: Woodford; Rail: Chingford; 20,179, W13

Barnardo's Village
Tanners Lane, Barkingside, Ilford IG6 1QG
→ Sat/Sun 10am-5pm. Regular hourly tours, first come basis. Max 40 in cottage, 200 in church. Exhibition and archived film relating to the Village in the past and Barnardo's work today in church and cottage. D P T
The Victorian 'village' was started in the 1870s and had expanded to over 70 'cottages' on 60 acres by Barnardo's death in 1905. The Church is the only remaining children's church in the country with lower pews and child-themed stained glass windows. Monument to Barnardo with bronzes by Sir George Frampton and iconic spired clock contained in village. Ebenezer Gregg 1876-1895. Entry: partial entry to one of the original cottages and Children's Church.
Tube: Barkingside; Rail: Ilford; 150,169,128,167,462

Christ Church
Wanstead Place E11 2SW
→ Sat 10am-5pm/Sun 11am-5pm. D P T
Grade II* listed church with ragstone tower, spire, good stained glass by Kempe and newly restored William Hill organ. A characteristic work of Scott. Diocesan Architectural Committee Award Winner 2009 for the reordering of the navel and chancel. Sir George Gilbert Scott 1861.
Tube: Wanstead, Snaresbrook; 66,101,145,308, W13, W14

Ilford War Memorial
Ilford War Memorial Gardens, Eastern Avenue, Newbury Park IG2 7RJ
→ Sat/Sun 11am-4.30pm.
Grade II listed memorial hall incorporating an entrance to the now demolished children's ward of the Ilford Emergency Hospital, recording names of those killed during WWII. C J Dawson & Allardyce 1927.
Tube: Newbury Park; 66,169

Quaker Meeting House, Wanstead
Bush Road E11 3AU
→ Sat 10am-5.30pm. Last entry 5.15pm. Display celebrating local Quaker history. C D P R T
Modernist building based on four hexagons within an Epping Forest setting. Contains a sunny meeting room for Quaker worship facing onto a wooded burial ground of simple headstones, including that of Elizabeth Fry. Norman Frith 1968. Entry: foyer, meeting room, social room, kitchen, grounds, wildflower meadow.
Tube: Leytonstone; 101,308

Valentines Mansion

Redbridge Town Hall, Council Chamber
128-142 High Road, Ilford (Oakfield Road entrance) IG1 1DD
→ Sat 10am-5pm. Tours on the hour 11am to 2pm, first come basis. Max 15 per tour. D T
Built in 3 stages consisting of the Old Town Hall (1901) with façade in free classic style and some original decorations, library (1927) and additional buildings (1933). B Woolard 1901. Entry: ground and 1st floors.
Tube: Gants Hill; Rail: Ilford; 25,86,123,128,129,145,147,150,167,169,179,296,364

St Mary's, Wanstead
Overton Drive E11 2LW
→ Sat 10am-5pm/Sun 1pm-5pm. D P T
Grade I listed, fine example of a small Georgian church with original box pews, next door to the now vanished Wanstead House. One of London's best Baroque monuments (to Sir Josiah Child of the East India Company) in chancel. Thomas Hardwick 1790.
Tube: Wanstead; 66,101,145,308, W13, W14, W12

Temple House
14 The Avenue, Wanstead E11 2EF
→ Sat 10am-1pm. Tours every 40 minutes. Pre-book ONLY through Open House, see p15 for details. Max 10 per tour.
One of the few pieces of Wanstead Park to survive, this Grade II* listed Ionic temple c1730-40 now sits in a residential garden.
Tube: Wanstead, Snaresbrook: Rail: Ilford

The Gazebo
20 The Avenue E11 2EF
→ Sat/Sun 10am-1pm. Pre-book ONLY on 020 8989 3639. Last entry 12.30pm. Max 8 per tour. P
Brick-built gazebo standing upon small cruciform grotto, all that remains of Wanstead Grove. Early 18C. Entry: gazebo, grotto.
Tube: Wanstead; 66,101,145,308, W13, W14

The Hospital Chapel of St Mary & St Thomas
48 Ilford Hill, Ilford IG1 2AT
→ Sat 10am-4pm/Sun 1pm-5pm. Regular tours. B D R T
Founded c1145 by the Abbess of Barking as a hospice for 13 old and infirm men, the present building is 12C and 19C. Grade II* listed with many interesting monuments, including Burne-Jones windows. (Organised by Friends of the Hospital Chapel.)
Tube: Gants Hill; Rail: Ilford; 25,86,123,150,179

The Temple
Wanstead Park E11 2LT
→ Sat/Sun 12noon-5pm. Tour of grounds 1pm and 3pm. Last entry 4.45pm. C d T
18C garden building in style of a Doric temple, one of the last remaining structures surviving from Wanstead Park's days of grandeur. Discover the history of the Park from its earliest years to the last 125 years under the City of London management. Entry: ground and first floor.
Tube: Wanstead; 66,101,145,308, W13, W14

Uphall Primary School Nursery
Uphall Road, Ilford IG1 2JD
→ Sat/Sun 10am-1pm. Max 10 at one time. D P T
Unusual 1930s ship-shaped school building, converted to nursery. Dropped ceilings and child-height porthole windows give suitable scale of space whilst complementing external elevations. Grade II listed. Civic Trust commendation 2000. Tooley and Foster c1927. Entry: nursery, playground.
Tube: Barking; Rail: Ilford

Valentines Mansion
Emerson Road, Ilford IG1 4XA
→ Sun 11am-4pm. Tours 11.30am, 2pm. C D P R T
Large, late 17C Grade II* listed house with fine staircase and Venetian window and with Georgian additions, used as a family dwelling until the early 1900s. Recently restored with period furnished rooms, Victorian kitchen and pantry, temporary exhibition gallery and interactive family room. Entry: ground & 1st floors.
Tube: Gants Hill; Rail: Ilford; 123,129,150,167,179,296

Supported by

London Borough of
Redbridge

Richmond

7 The Green
7 The Green, Twickenham TW2 5TU
→ Sat/Sun 10am-5pm. First come basis, queuing outside if
  necessary. d P A
Conversion of a Georgian-style house in Twickenham
conservation area with extensive contemporary single-storey
extension with kitchen, dining and lounge embracing a zen-
style courtyard. 3s architects & designers (refurb) 2009.
Tube/Rail: Richmond; Rail: Twickenham; R68,490,33,H22,110

All Hallows Parish Church
Chertsey Road (close to RFU stadium), Twickenham TW1 1EW
→ Sat 10am-5pm/Sun 12noon-5pm. B C D P R T
A City of London church, previously in Lombard Street. Moved
to present site in 1940 with original tower and richly carved
interior furnishings. Christopher Wren 1694/Robert Atkinson
(rebuilt) 1939-40. NB. Sun services at 10am, 6.30pm.
Tube/Rail: Richmond; Rail: Twickenham; 281,H37

Classroom of the Future – Ingenium, Meadlands Primary School ●
Broughton Avenue TW10 7TS
→ Sat 10am-1pm. First come basis. Children's activity 'Arts
  Challenge' taking place. C D P R T G
A flexible, organic, light, colourful learning space. Made of
prefabricated moulded GRP, the building is high-tech and
energy efficient and features a large curved teaching space lit
by openable roof windows and a wall of glass opening onto a
terrace. Future Systems 2005. Entry: classroom.
Tube/Rail: Richmond; 371 from Richmond, 65 to Ham Common

Eco House Sherland Road ▲
65 Sherland Road, Twickenham TW1 4HB
→ Sun 10am-5pm. First come basis, queuing outside if
  necessary. Architect will be on site. Max 6 at one time. G A
Part of the 'Old Home Superhome Network', the property
demonstrates how eco-friendly extensions can help reduce
carbon emissions from existing Victorian housing stock.
Green specification used throughout including sheep's wool
insulation, thermowood cladding and sedum roofs. CO_2
emissions have been reduced by 50%. ECDA 2006. Entry: all
areas except bedrooms.
Rail/Tube: Richmond; Rail: Twickenham; 281,33,H22,R70,R68

Garrick's Temple to Shakespeare
Temple Lawn, Hampton Court Road, Hampton TW12 2EN
→ Sat/Sun 10am-5pm. Last entry 4.45pm. Max 30 at one
  time. Garrick/Shakespeare exhibition includes replica of
  Roubiliac statue. B C D R T
Octagonal Temple in the Ionic manner, built 1756 for David
Garrick in honour of his idol William Shakespeare. Capability
Brown landscape restored to 18C appearance. Civic Trust
Award commendation. Entry: temple, lawn by riverside.
*Ferry: Hampton pedestrian ferry from Molesey; Rail: Hampton,
Hampton Court; 111,216,R68,267*

The Glasshouse

Marble Hill House

Grove Gardens Chapel
**Richmond Cemetery, Grove Gardens, off Lower Grove Road
(entrance opposite Greville Road) TW10 6HP**
→ Sun 1pm-5pm. Max 30 at one time. D P T
Small, charming Gothic chapel of imaginative design with
plate tracery and mosaic triptych. Former cemetery chapel,
now restored for mixed community use. Thomas Hardy
was apprenticed to architect of chapel Blomfield. Sir Arthur
Blomfield c1873.
Tube/Rail: Richmond; 371

Ham Children's Centre ●
**St Richard's with St Andrew's CE Primary School,
Ashburnham Road, Ham TW10 7NL**
→ Sun 10am-5pm. Architect-led regular tours, first come
  basis. D T G A
The Children's Centre provides support services for young
parents in a calm, welcoming and sustainable building
adjacent to a new nursery and garden. Sustainable features
include timber frame, prefabricated timber cladding panels,
ground source heat pump, green roof, external blinds.
IID Architects 2008.
Tube/Rail: Richmond; 371

Ham House
Ham Street, Ham TW10 7RS
→ Sat 12noon-4pm. Gardens also open 11am-5pm. Last entry
  to house 3.30pm. Max 300 in house at one time. B C D P R T
Built in 1610 for a Knight Marshall of James I, Ham House was
greatly extended in the 1670s. At the forefront of fashion,
its interior decoration rivalled a small palace. Entry: areas of
house, garden, outbuildings.
Tube/Rail: Richmond; Rail: Kingston; 371,65,K5

Hampton Court Palace: Tennis Court Lane
Hampton Court Palace, East Molesey KT8 9AU
→ Sat/Sun 10.30am-4pm. Entry by guided tours every 20 mins
  only, first come basis. B D R T
A guided tour of Tennis Court Lane – the more functional
side of the palace. Visitors will see a variety of different
architectural styles from Tudor to Victorian.
Rail: Hampton Court; 111,216,411,R68

Heathfield Children's Centre and Nursery ●
Powder Mill Lane TW2 6EX
→ Sat 10am-5pm. D G P T A
A new vibrant and accessible children's centre and nursery
with coloured timber cladding and gabion wall façades
using recycled aggregate with a brown roof deck. Sarah
Wigglesworth 2008.
Tube/Rail: Richmond then H22 bus; Rail: Whitton; H22,110

Jindals' Pavilion
95 Lonsdale Road SW13 9DA
→ Sat 1pm-5pm. First come basis, queuing outside if
  necessary. Last entry 4.30pm. R T
A space for meditation at the end of a large garden. The
pavilion is conceived as a set of four exterior walls that are not
joined, but which shield the glass within. This creates a private
but open space and a small walled courtyard. Paul Archer
Design 2007. Entry: pavilion in back garden only.
Tube: Hammersmith; Rail: Barnes Bridge; 419,72,33,209,283

Kilmorey Mausoleum
275 St Margaret's Road (opposite Ailsa Tavern) TW1 1NJ
→ Sat 1pm-5pm. Max 5 inside mausoleum. d
Egyptian-style, pink and grey mausoleum for the second Earl
of Kilmorey. The form relates to the shrines at the heart of
Egyptian Temples. HE Kendall 19C. Entry: mausoleum, main
grounds.
Tube: Hounslow East; Rail: Richmond, St Margaret's; H37

Langham House Close, Flats
Langham House Close, Ham Common TW10 7JE
→ Sat 10.30am-5pm. First come basis, queuing if necessary.
  Last entry 5pm. Max 20 inside flats at one time. P Q
A landmark in 'Brutalism'. Exposed shuttered concrete and
brick construction with iconic oversized concrete 'gargoyles'
and geometric fenestration. Interior features exposed brick
chimney/mantle/squint and architect-designed cupboards.
Stirling and Gowan 1958. Entry: entrance hall to flats 25-30,
and flat 7.
Rail: Richmond, Kingston; then 65 bus to Ham Common

Marble Hill House
Richmond Road, Twickenham TW1 2NL
→ Sun 10am-5pm. Last entry 4.30pm. Tours at 10.30am,
  12noon, 2pm, 3.15pm on Marble Hill House focusing on the
  life of Henrietta Howard. Max 15 per tour, first come basis.
  Jam and wine testing and the Marble Hill Society Book Sale
  throughout the day. B R T
Magnificent Thames-side Palladian villa, set in beautiful
parkland. Built for Henrietta Howard, Countess of Suffolk and
mistress of George II. Colen Campbell 1724-29.
*Tube: Richmond; Rail: St Margaret's, Twickenham;
33,490,H22,R68,R70*

Heathfield Children's Centre and Nursery

Normansfield Hospital Theatre
2A Langdon Park TW11 9PS
→ Sat/Sun 11am-4pm. Regular tours, first come basis. Last entry 3.45pm. B D P R T
Grade II* listed theatre which has recently been restored to its former glory and was a progressive concept for its time. Gothic proscenium arch and elaborate stage and scenery. Originally built as part of the Normansfield Hospital for patients/ students with learning disabilities. Rowland Plumbe 1877. Entry: theatre, basement.
Rail: Hampton Wick; 281,285 (from Kingston)

Orleans House Gallery, Octagon Room and New Arts Education Centre
Riverside TW1 3DJ
→ Sun 1pm-5pm. Max 60 at one time. Family activities 2-4pm. B C D N P R T
Louis Philippe, Duc d'Orleans, lived here between 1815-17. Gibbs' Octagon room and adjoining gallery/stable block are remaining parts of Orleans House. Coach house education centre opened 2006, using a design strategy of new pieces complementing the old. Further developments 2007-08 including café. John James 1710/James Gibbs 1720/Patel Taylor (new centre) 2008. Entry: Octagon Room, main gallery, stables gallery.
Tube/Rail: Richmond, Rail: St Margaret's, Twickenham; 33,490,H22,R68,R70

Richmond Lock Building (Surrey Side)
The Towpath, Richmond TW9 2QJ
→ Sun 10am-4pm. Regular talks by lock keeper. Last entry 3.30pm. Max 10 at one time.
Example of good-quality late-Victorian functional design (1894). Entry: lock cottage and lock side.
Tube/Rail: Richmond; Rail: St Margaret's; 33,65,490,H22,R68,R70

Richmond Theatre
The Green, Richmond TW9 1QJ
→ Sat tours at 10.15am and 12noon, pre-book ONLY on 08448 717 651, max 20 per tour. Family activities at 11am and 12noon, pre-book only on 08448 717 651, max 15 per session. d R T
A typical Matcham design, this beautiful 840 seat theatre was exhaustively researched and then restored in 1989 to a fabulous crimson, cream and gold. All original mouldings restored and renewed. Frank Matcham 1899. Entry: auditorium, backstage, foyers.
Tube/Rail: Richmond; 65,371,419,437,493

Royal Botanic Gardens, Kew: Architectural Tour
Meet at Main Gate, Kew Green, Royal Botanic Gardens, Kew TW9 3AB
→ Sat/Sun tours at 11am, 12noon, 1pm, 2pm, 3pm, pre-book ONLY on 020 8332 5604 or email tours@kew.org. Max 15 per tour. D T
Buildings highlighted are Nash Conservatory, Orangery, Kew Palace, Princess of Wales Conservatory, Davies Alpine House, Palm House, Waterlily House and Museum No 1.
Tube/Rail: Kew Gardens; Rail: Kew Bridge; 65,237,267,391

Royal Botanic Gardens, Kew: Herbarium, Library, Art and Archives
Royal Botanic Gardens, Kew TW9 3AE
→ Sat/Sun 10am-4pm. Last entry 3pm. Max 70 at one time. Staff available to talk about collections and purpose of building. D
Originally occupying a domestic house c1720 with purpose built wings naturally lit with atria added 1877-2000 to house library and 7,000,000 plant specimens. Victorian wings have elegant spiral staircases and ornamented metal pillars. View of new wing by Edward Cullinan Architects recently completed. Entry: Herbarium.
Tube/Rail: Kew Gardens; Rail: Kew Bridge; 65,237,267,391

Royal Botanic Gardens, Kew: Jodrell Laboratory
Meet at Main Gate, Kew Green, Royal Botanic Gardens, Kew TW9 3AB
→ Sat 10am, 12noon, 2pm, 4pm/Sun 1pm, 3pm, architect-led tours, pre-book ONLY through Open House, see p15 for details. Max 10 per tour. A D T G
Housing reference collections, offices and laboratories, the Laboratory fits in with the local environment – horizontal cedarboard cladding will mellow to similar colour of trunks of eucalyptus trees outside. Louvred exterior and computer-controlled windows to regulate heating/cooling. Wilkinson Eyre Architects 2006. Entry: all laboratories on ground floor, basement of Wolfson Wing.
Tube/Rail: Kew Gardens; Rail: Kew Bridge; 65,237,267,391

Sandycombe Lodge
40 Sandycoombe Road, St Margaret's, Twickenham TW1 2LR
→ Sun tours 10.30am, 11.15am, pre-book ONLY through Open House, see p15 for details. Max 12 per tour. B d T
Small rustic villa built to Turner's own designs, with inspiration from John Soane, for his own use as a rural retreat. JMW Turner 1812. Entry: ground floor, garden, basement.
Tube/Rail: Richmond; Rail: St Margaret's; H37,R70,R68,H22,33

Royal Botanic Gardens, Kew: Jodrell Laboratory

Shell Grotto
Hampton Court House, The Green, East Molesey (opposite Hampton Court Palace) KT8 9BS
→ Sun 12noon-4pm. Max 15 in grotto, more in gardens. D P
Designed as a Summerhouse for Hampton Court House, with fire places for moonlit parties, merging Roccoco garden design and shell collecting, Grade II listed. Thomas Wright 1757-67. Entry: Shell Grotto, gardens.
Rail: Hampton Court; 411,R68,R70

The Glasshouse
River Lane, Petersham TW10 7AG
→ Sat 10am-5pm. Half-hourly tours. Pre-book ONLY through Open House, see p15 for details. Max 10 per tour. Last tour 4.30pm. d P
Contemporary courtyard style house with a low profile of just 7m. The house is a linear arrangement of rooms accessed from the 40m long double-height gallery surrounded by established trees and shrubs which also creates a boundary wall enclosing the garden. Terry Farrell & Partners 2004. Entry: ground floor, part of 1st floor.
Tube/Rail: Richmond; 65

Twickenham Museum
25 The Embankment TW1 3DU
→ Sat/Sun 11am-5pm. Last entry 4.30pm. Max 25 at a time. B P T
Grade II listed former waterman's cottage c1720. Recently restored and converted by Anthony Beckles Willson into museum celebrating rich local history.
Tube/Rail: Richmond; Rail: Twickenham; H22,R68,R70,290,490

York House
Richmond Road TW1 3AA
→ Sun 12noon-4pm. D P T
Mid-17C house with fine staircase and 18C additions. Entry: ground floor: parlour, council chamber, other rooms.
Tube/Rail: Richmond; Rail: Twickenham; 490,33,H22,R68,R70

Supported by

LONDON BOROUGH OF RICHMOND UPON THAMES

Southwark

1 Morocco Street
1 Morocco Street SE1 3HB
→ Sat 10am-1pm. Regular tours. Max 15 per tour.
A working Victorian engraving studio on the ground floor of a four-storey former leather warehouse in the heart of the old leather district in Bermondsey. Houses a massive 1900s' copperplate printing press engineered in London's East End. Artist/engraver will be present.
Tube/Rail: London Bridge; 21,35,40,43,47,48,133,149,SL1,SL2

15 and a half Consort Road
15 and a half Consort Road SE15 2PH
→ Sat/Sun 10am-5pm. First come basis, queuing if necessary. Queue closes 3.30pm. Last entry 4.45pm. Max 20 at one time. Architects available for discussion. Q G A
As seen on Grand Designs, the opening roof and sliding bath typify this unique and extraordinary response to various constraints and opportunities of a tight budget on an 'unusable' brownfield site. Shortlisted RIBA Awards 2006. One of six voted as Nation's favourite Grand Designs' houses. DVD available showing how to take the dream from an idea to reality. Richard Paxton Architects/MOOARC/Flower Michelin 2005. Entry: whole house.
Rail: Peckham Rye, Queens Road

3 Acorns Retro Eco-house ●
2 Coleman Road, Camberwell SE5 7TG
→ Sat/Sun 10am-5pm. Last entry 4.30pm. Max 20 at one time. P Q G
Victorian terrace two-bedroomed house, converted into London's first retro carbon-negative home. It sells more green electricity to national grid than it imports fossil fuels. Sustainable features include solar electric and hot water panels, wind-turbine, wood-burner, rain-harvester, range LED bulbs. Display on green-lifestyle. Owner is leading eco-author and business eco-auditor. Entry: ground floor and garden.
Tube: Elephant & Castle; Tube/Rail: London Bridge then 343; Rail: Rye Lane; 36,12,171

4 Carmarthen Place ●
4 Carmarthen Place SE1 3TS
→ Sun 12noon-4pm. First come basis. Max 15 at one time. d G
One of two eco wooden houses with sedum roof. New to UK and prefabricated in Europe to exacting designs, the complete panels were craned into site. E Doherty & A Menage 2006.
Tube: Oval; Tube/Rail: Elephant & Castle; Rail: Denmark Hill; 12,25,36,40,45

49 Camberwell Grove ●
49 Camberwell Grove SE5 8JA
→ Sat 1pm-5pm/Sun 10am-5pm. First come basis, queuing outside if necessary. Max 20 at one time. D T G
This tiny terraced house has been remodelled to provide a light, flexible interior, full disabled access, with rainwater harvesting, air-source heat pump and PV panels. Eger Architects (refurb) 2009.
Tube: Oval; Tube/Rail: Elephant & Castle; Rail: Denmark Hill; 12,25,36,40,45

6 Pond Cottages
6 Pond Cottages, College Road SE21 7LE
→ Sat/Sun 1pm-5pm. First come basis. d A P
Grade II listed late 17C weather-boarded workers' cottage which has been restored in 2006 by the current owners, an interior stylist/designer and developer. Although the original part of the property retains its cottage charm, a new modern extension together with tropical planting in the garden gives it a modern twist.
Rail: West Dulwich, North Dulwich; 3

67 Grange Walk
67 Grange Walk (opposite no. 29 & 30) SE1 3DT
→ Sun 9am-1pm. First come basis. Max 20 at one time. Q
Grade II* listed double-fronted Queen Anne house c1700 largely restored and now used as a family home.
Tube/Rail: London Bridge; 1,188,78,42

Allies and Morrison Studio ●
85 Southwark Street SE1 0HX
→ Sat/Sun 10am-1.30pm. Regular tours, first come basis. Last entry 1.15pm. Max 8 at one time. D A
Purpose-designed studio with fully glazed front arranged on 5 floors linked by a stepped, externally-planted atrium. RIBA Award Winner 2004. Allies and Morrison 2003.
Tube/Rail: London Bridge, Blackfriars; Tube: Southwark; 381,RV1

Bermondsey Square ▲
Bermondsey Square SE1 3FD
→ Sat/Sun 11am-5pm. First come basis, queuing outside if necessary. East Architects will be present. D N R T G A
The new trio of buildings by Munkenbeck + Marshall create the central square designed by East in 2008. Residents have use of a bespoke-designed bikestore by Sarah Wigglesworth. Dive Architects have produced the desk and bench in the central reception. A renewed public space with programme of events for local community incorporating many green features. Entry: Bermondsey Square, Shortwave Cinema, Bermondsey Square Hotel.
Tube: Borough; Tube/Rail: London Bridge; C10,188,78,42,381

Blue Fin Building ● ●
110 Southwark Street SE1 0SU
→ Sat/Sun 10am-4pm. First come basis. Last entry 3.45pm. Architectives tour by Alex Wraight from Allies and Morrison Sat 2pm. Talk by Tim Makower Sat 3pm. B C D Q R G
The crystalline form of the building is generated from the overlaid geometries of the site and the historic grain of this part of Southwark. Its surface is intensely textured and enlivened with a vibrant, random pattern of angled shading fins whose appearance changes constantly through day and night. Winner BCO Best Corporate Workplace 2008. Allies and Morrison 2007. Entry: reception, atrium, bridges, office floor, meeting room suite, terrace, café.
Tube: Southwark; Tube/Rail: Blackfriars, London Bridge, Waterloo; RV1,381

Brunel Museum
Railway Avenue SE16 4LF
→ Sat/Sun 10am-5pm. Regular tours. Last entry 4.50pm. B d P R T
Views of the Grand Entrance Hall to the Thames Tunnel and roof gardens with panoramic views. The entrance hall is half the size of the dome of St Paul's but hidden underground. Crawl through a tunnel to view from a high platform. River gardens contain a Frankenstein tree and award-winning sculptures. Sir Marc Brunel 1842.
Tube: Canada Water; Tube/Rail: London Bridge; 47,188,381

Oxo Tower Wharf

Cathedral ●
St Thomas's Church, St Thomas Street SE1 9RY
→ Sat 10.30am-4.30pm. First come basis. d T A
The beautiful 300 year-old St Thomas's Church (Grade II* listed) has just been completely refurbished by Cathedral Group plc and is now the company's headquarters. Allford Hall Monaghan Morris 2008. Entry: main office.
Tube/Rail: London Bridge; 21,35,40,43,47

City Hall ●
The Queen's Walk, More London (from Tower Hill, walk across Tower Bridge) SE1 2AA
→ Sat/Sun 9am-6pm. Last entry 5.30pm. Sat/Sun 10am-1pm City of 1000 Architects activity for children, see p13 for full details. C D Q R T G A
Home of the Mayor of London and London Assembly, an environmentally-aware building with innovative spiral ramp and fine views across London. Foster and Partners 2002. Entry: London's Living Room, spiral ramp, chamber.
Tube: Tower Hill; Tube/Rail: London Bridge; 47,42,78,381,RV1

Dog Kennel Hill Apartments ●
8 Dog Kennel Hill SE22 8AA
→ Sat/Sun 10am-5pm. Regular tours, first come basis, queuing outside if necessary. Last entry 4.30pm. D P G
'DKH' is a new build, private housing development with 19 apartments creating a beacon housing scheme utilising timber louvres, mesh panelling and stone gabions. RIBA Award Winner 2008. John Smart Architects 2007. Entry: courtyard, duplex, penthouse.
Tube: Elephant & Castle; Rail: Denmark Hill, East Dulwich; 176,40,185,P13,484

Dulwich College
Dulwich Common SE21 7LD
→ Sun tours at 10am & 11.15am, pre-book ONLY on 020 8299 9284. Max 40 per tour. d P T
Founded in 1619 and rebuilt in the 1860s, the buildings are large, symmetrical and ornate, in the Italian Renaissance style. Charles Barry Junior 1866-70. Entry: Great Hall, Lower Hall, Boardroom, Masters' Library, North Cloister.
Tube: Brixton; Rail: West Dulwich; P4,P13,3

Dulwich Picture Gallery
Gallery Road SE21 7AD
→ Sun 11am-5pm. Tours of gallery 3pm. B C D P R T
Britain's oldest purpose-built public art gallery. At the centre of this seminal building Soane designed a mysterious mausoleum for the gallery's founders. Recent glass, bronze and brick extension. RIBA Award Winner. Sir John Soane 1811/ Rick Mather (extension) 2000. Entry: gallery, Christ's Chapel of God's Gift also open 12.30pm-4.30pm, dating to 17C with pictures after Raphael, fine stained glass and carvings.
Rail: West Dulwich (from Victoria), North Dulwich (from London Bridge); P4 (from Brixton)

Dulwich Wood Nursery School & Children's Centre ● ●
Lyall Avenue SE21 8QS
→ Sun 1pm-5pm. Regular tours, first come basis. Last tour 4.30pm. Max 10 per tour. D T G A
Childcare, education, family and health services are integrated in Southwark's new-build Children's Centre that features a glazed atrium around which children's rooms give onto woodland play areas. Eger Architects 2007.
Tube: Brixton; Rail: Sydenham Hill, Gipsy Hill

Friendship House (LHA)
Belvedere Place, off Borough Road SE1 0AD
→ Sat 9.30am-4.30pm. Tours every half hour. Max 10 per tour. D T
Angular walls of dramatic zinc tiles and bright render enclosing a quiet courtyard with reflective pool as modern self-catered accommodation for 179 residents. RIBA Award Winner 2005. MacCormac Jamieson Prichard 2003. Entry: common rooms, dining areas, bedsits, garden.
Tube: Borough, Elephant & Castle; Tube/Rail: Southwark, London Bridge; 344,35,40,133

Imperial War Museum (Dome Reading Room and Family Event)
Lambeth Road SE1 6HZ
→ Sat/Sun 1pm-5pm. Tours on the hour. Max 15 at one time. Family tours Sat/Sun 1pm and activities throughout. B C R T
Formerly the central portion of the Royal Bethlem Hospital or 'Bedlam'. Smirke's Dome containing the chapel now used by researchers consulting the Museum's book and archival collections. James Lewis 1815/Sidney Smirke 1846/Arup Associates 1989/2000. Entry: reading room, boardroom, museum.
Tube: Lambeth North; Tube/Rail: Waterloo; 1,3,12,45,59

Jerwood Space
171 Union Street SE1 0LN
→ Sat/Sun 10am-6pm. Tours 2pm, 3pm, 4pm, 5pm. Rehearsals and professional dance workshops taking place. D P R T
Former Victorian school converted in contemporary idiom (Paxton Locher Architects 1998) to provide theatre/dance rehearsal facilities, plus striking gallery (currently exhibiting the Jerwood Drawing Prize 2009), alongside a café and glazed courtyard (the Glasshouse – Satellite Architects 2003). New studios and meeting rooms (Munkenbeck & Partners 2007) on the restored top floor (lost to wartime bombing).
Tube: Southwark; Tube/Rail: London Bridge; 40,45,63,344,RV1

Kingswood House
Seeley Drive (by car approach only from Kingswood Drive), Kingswood Estate SE21 8QR
→ Sun 1pm-4.30pm. Talks at 2pm, 3.30pm followed by tours. Last entry 4.15pm. d P R T
Substantial villa built in form of stone-faced baronial castle for the founder of Bovril. Now library and community centre. HV Lanchester 1892. Entry: normally closed areas.
Rail: Sydenham Hill; 450,3,322

Kirkaldy Testing Works
99 Southwark Street SE1 0JF
→ Sat 10am-4.30pm. Regular tours, first come basis. Last entry 4pm. Max 20 at one time. T
Grade II listed industrial building, purpose-built to house D Kirkaldy's unique materials testing machine, now restored. T Roger Smith 1873. Entry: ground floor, basement.
Tube: Southwark; Tube/Rail: London Bridge; 45,63,100,381

Lavender Pond Pumphouse
The Pumphouse Educational Museum, Lavender Pond and Nature Park, Lavender Road SE16 5DZ
→ Sat/Sun 10am-5pm. Tours of designated nature reserve 11am, 1pm & 3pm. Last entry 4.30pm. Social history exhibitions and Peek Frean Collection talks. D N P R T G
Yellow stock brick pumphouse originally regulated water levels in Surrey Commercial Docks, now houses Rotherhithe Heritage Museum. Lavender Pond provides a unique oasis of tranquillity among urban sprawl.
Tube/Rail: London Bridge; DLR: Canada Water; 381,C10

Nunhead Cemetery
Linden Grove SE15 3LP
→ Sat/Sun 1pm-5pm. Tours at 2pm, 3pm. B D N P T G
Magnificent Victorian cemetery with Gothic chapel and ruined lodges. One of London's wildest and most overgrown cemeteries, a square mile of inner city forest. Recently restored with the help of a lottery grant. Unique in London – 50 acres of wilderness, complete with bats, owls, foxes, squirrels. Thomas Little & JJ Bunning 1840. Entry: cemetery, chapel, east lodge.
Rail: Nunhead; 484,P3,P12

Old Operating Theatre Museum & Herb Garret
9a St Thomas Street SE1 9RY
→ Sat/Sun 10.30am-5pm. Max 60 at one time. B
St Thomas' Church (1703) once part of old St Thomas' Hospital, houses the herb garret and Britain's only surviving 19C operating theatre. Thomas Cartwright 1703. NB. Access via 32 step spiral staircase.
Tube/Rail: London Bridge; 21,35,40,43,47,48,133,149,SL1,SL2

Oxo Tower Wharf
Bargehouse Street, Southbank SE1 9PH
→ Sat 11am-5pm. Tours on the hour including into the tower and outside access at top. Last tour 4pm. Max 16 per tour. Q T
Built for the Oxo company in 1928, it became a familiar feature on the London skyline thanks to its tower, which broke draconian advertising laws by spelling out the company logo as an architectural feature. In the 90s Coin Street Community Builders began a major refurbishment project transforming the building into an award-winning mixed use development. Albert W Moore 1929/Lifschutz Davidson Sandilands (refurb) 1995. Entry: tower by tour only, design shops, restaurants, cafés, bars, Gallery@oxo exhibition.
Tube: Southwark; Tube/Rail: Waterloo; RV1,45,63,100,381

Quay House

City Hall

Peckham Library
122 Peckham Hill Street SE15 5JR
→ Sat 11am & 2pm & Sun 2pm tours to non-public areas. Max 25 per tour. D N G
A dramatic design resembling an upside-down 'L' of coloured glass and green copper. A pure 21C building. RIBA Award Winner. Alsop and Stormer 2000.
Tube: Elephant and Castle (then bus 12,63,171,343); Rail: Peckham Rye; all buses via Peckham Square

Quay House
2C Kings Grove (Queens Road end) SE15 2NB
→ Sun 12noon-5pm. First come basis. Last entry 4.30pm. d P R T G A
As seen on Channel 5's 'I Own Britain's Best Home', conversion of 1930s milk depot into architect's office, sculpture studio and home with new-build development of three flats above. Exhibition in m2 gallery and throughout building by Stuart Mayes. Sustainable features include re-use of existing derelict building with recycling of materials. Quay 2C 2001. Entry: ground floor house/office/studio.
Tube: New Cross; Rail: Queens Road, Peckham; 436,171,12,63

Retro-eco House ●
36 Wansey Street SE17 1JP
→ Sat/Sun 10am-5pm. Regular tours on the hour, first come basis. Last entry 4.30pm. Max 30 per tour. P G
Extensive residential eco-retrofit of early Victorian townhouse with air source heat pump, solar thermal panels, underground rainwater harvesting system and insulation techniques including sheep's wool and internal wall cladding. Garden includes hens and examples of permaculture design. Featured in BBC2's 2009 series 'It's Not Easy Being Green.' Entry: house and garden.
Tube/Rail: Elephant and Castle; 12,35,68,171,176

Rooftop Retreat ● A
Flat 1, 2 D'Eynsford Road SE5 7EB
→ Sat 10am-5pm. First come basis, queuing outside if necessary. D P G A
Built on a flat roof, changing light and shade, natural materials and tree top views are the keynote elements of this super-insulated, timber frame rooftop home and its strikingly planted terrace garden. Eger Architects 2009.
Rail: Denmark Hill; 36,12,45,68,176

Rye Oak Children's Centre ● ● ●
Whorlton Road, SE15 3PD
→ Sat 1pm-5pm. Regular tours, first come basis. D T G
This fully sustainable children's centre provides an elegant counterfoil to the Victorian primary school with which it shares an entrance and community facilities. Zero carbon rated construction, natural ventilation, brown roof, water recycling, energy saving lighting, non-toxic finishes and green playground with trees for solar shading. Eger Architects 2009.
Rail: Peckham Rye; 343,12,37,78,63

Sands Films Studios & Rotherhithe Picture Research Library
82 St Marychurch Street SE16 4HZ
→ Sat/Sun 10am-5pm. Tours on the hour. Last entry 5pm. Max 25 per tour. B d P R T
Grade II listed riparian granary converted in 1970s to a picture research library, film studios, prop and costume workshops. 2008 Southwark blue plaque winner. Entry: picture research library, film studio, cinema, costume and prop workshops.
Tube: Bermondsey, Canada Water; Tube/Rail: London Bridge; 47,188,381,C10

Siobhan Davies Studios
85 St Georges Road SE1 6ER
→ Sat 1pm-6pm. First come basis, queuing if necessary. Last entry 5.30pm. Max 150 at one time. D T G
A landmark home for dance, the daring design with 2-storey atrium and undulating ribbon roof breathes life into an old school building. RIBA Award Winner 2006. Sustainable features include re-use of existing building, materials from sustainable sources, earth tubes cooling air, natural ventilation, high-tech double-glazing and high levels of thermal insulation. Sarah Wigglesworth Architects 2006.
Tube: Elephant & Castle, Lambeth North; Tube/Rail: Waterloo; 12,53,148,344,360,453

St Giles Parish Church, Camberwell
Camberwell Church Street SE5 8RB
→ Sat/Sun 10am-6pm. Last entry 5.30pm. B d T
A large Grade II listed parish church – one of Scott's finest designs. Key features include the magnificent east window by Ruskin. Interior recently redecorated and restored together with recently restored spire. Sir George Gilbert Scott 1844. Entry: church, crypt.
Rail: Denmark Hill; 12,171,36,68,436

St Peter's, Walworth
Liverpool Grove SE17 2HH
→ Sat 10am-4pm. D N T
Best-preserved example of a church by Soane. Wedgwood blue interior restored after WWII damage. Sir John Soane 1825.
Tube/Rail: Elephant & Castle; 12,35,40,45,68,171,176,468,148

Sunshine House (Southwark Child Development Centre)
27 Peckham Road SE5 8UH
→ Sat/Sun 10am-5pm. Regular tours, first come basis. D T
The entrance foyer, reception and play and family resource facilities form the public heart at the centre. A garden provides a place for children and young people and their families to relax. The building maximises the use of the site while remaining sensitive to its location next to a listed building. A key element of the external design is the use of colour on all windows and metal work. Allford Hall Monaghan Morris 2007.
Rail: Peckham Rye; 12,171,36

The Glasshouse
Melior Place, Snowfields SE1 3SZ
→ Sat/Sun 1pm-5pm. Max 30 at one time. Architect on site Sun only. T A
Under the sun-trapping glass roof of a converted garage, architect Michael Davis has created a dazzling setting for Andrew Logan's sculptures. Michael Davis 1989.
Tube/Rail: London Bridge; RV1

The Old Mortuary
St Marychurch Street SE16 4JE
→ Sat/Sun 10am-5pm. Regular tours. Last entry 4pm. Max 10 per tour, max 25 at one time. B D P R T
Erected in 1895 and situated in Rotherhithe Conservation Area. Retains many original features including a vaulted ceiling in Russell Hall, original doors, lantern skylight, and iron girder in Varney Room (formerly post-mortem room), wooden panelling in chapel. Now community centre with local history group (Time and Talents Association). Entry: former mortuary, post mortem room, chapel.
Tube: Bermondsey, Canada Water; Tube/Rail: London Bridge; 1,47,188,225,381

The Pioneer Health Centre
St Mary's Road SE15 2EE
→ Sun 10am-2pm. Hourly tours, first come basis. Last tour 1pm. Max 50 at one time. D P R T
Grade II* listed Modernist building, famously described by Walter Gropius as "an oasis of glass in a desert of brick". Originally built to house 'The Peckham Experiment' an innovative health centre in the 30s. It was converted to private dwellings in 2000, retaining the original indoor pool. Sir E Owen Williams 1935.
Tube/Rail: New Cross Gate; Rail: Queens Road, Peckham; 36,136,436,171,177

The Rose
Park Street SE1 9AR
→ Sat/Sun 11am-6pm. Tours every hour with video screening. Last entry 5pm. D
Archaeological site of the first Elizabethan theatre on Bankside, where Shakespeare performed and learnt his craft. Philip Henslowe 1587. Entry: viewing platform via exhibition foyer.
Tube: Mansion House, Southwark; Tube/Rail: London Bridge; RV1,381

Weston Williamson Architects Offices
43 Tanner Street SE1 3PL
→ Sat 1pm-5pm. Max 30 at one time. T G A
Practice's own offices built on site of Sarson's Vinegar works as part of a mixed-use inner-city development scheme. Views of City from roof terrace. Sustainable features: low-energy building. Weston Williamson 2000. Entry: offices, roof terrace.
Tube/Rail: London Bridge; 47

WALKS/TOURS/TALKS

Behind the scenes tour and talk of the South London Gallery's extension – by 6a Architects ●
65 Peckham Road SE5 8UH
→ Sat/Sun 12noon-6pm. 'Hard hat' tours led by 6a Architects Sat/Sun 3pm. P A
Opportunity to find out more about the gallery's expansion project as well as its history. 6a will outline their plans to turn a domestic terraced property into a café, artist's flat and exhibition spaces, as well as a build a new extension at the rear of the SLG's original Grade II listed late Victorian Arts and Crafts building (Maurice Adams 1896). Also on view is 'Beyond These Walls', an international group exhibition prompting fresh perspectives on the SLG's building and environment.
Tube: Elephant & Castle then 171,12,P3; Rail: Peckham Rye; 12,36,345,436

Landscape Institute Walks
→ 'Pottery, Politics, Prison and Power': meet Sat 1pm at front Gate of Potters Fields Park, Tooley Street, SE1. 'Theatre, festivals, beef cubes and bridges': meet Sun 1pm next to Golden Jubilee Footbridge, Festival Terrace, RFH SE1. Pre-book ONLY through Open House, see p15 for details. Max 25 per tour.
Tours which show how landscape architecture is changing the public face of London: Saturday's tour includes the streets and places around City Hall, Clink Prison and Tate Modern; Sunday's tour takes in the streets and places around RFH, NT, OXO Tower and the Millennium Bridge.
Tube/Rail: London Bridge, Waterloo

Peckham Space – by Architects Penson Group ● ●
Peckham Library, 5th Floor, 122 Peckham Hill Street SE15 5JR
→ Sat 12.30pm-2pm. Pre-book ONLY on 020 7514 2299 or email info@peckhamspace.com. D R T
Peckham Space is an arts initiative developed by Camberwell College of Arts, University of the Arts London and Southwark Council. It commissions new multimedia, location-specific projects connecting art, people and place through creative experience. Join the architects Penson Group and launching artists in conversation with the Director about the forthcoming launch of Peckham Space.
Tube: Elephant and Castle (then bus 12,63,171,343); Rail: Peckham Rye; all buses via Peckham Square

The South Bank: Improving London's River Relations
→ Meet: Sat 11am at Scoop Amphitheatre adjacent to City Hall SE1 2AA. Pre-book ONLY on 020 7467 1470 or email marketing@lda-design.co.uk. Duration approx 1 hour. Max 30 per tour.
The Thames is forging a stronger relationship with London due to a renaissance in public space and life. Explore two vanguard spaces – Potter's Field and More London – and discover what makes this area one of London's superlative achievements in contemporary design.
Tube: Tower Hill; Tube/Rail London Bridge; 47,78,381,RV1

Supported by

Southwark.
Council

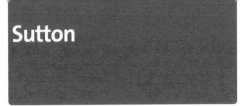

Sutton

All Saints Carshalton
High Street, Carshalton SM5 3AQ
→ Sat/Sun 9am-6pm. Regular tours. Max 50 at one time. Sat 1pm talk about monuments in church. History talks, bell ringing, music during afternoons, displays. B D N R T
12C south aisle and former chancel. Enlarged by Blomfield in 1894. Bodley woodwork, Kempe glass, astonishing Comper decorations, brasses and monuments of interest. Entry: all areas including bell tower at certain times, subject to services.
Rail: Carshalton

BedZED ● ●
24 Helios Road, Wallington SM6 7BZ
→ Sat/Sun 11am-3pm. Tours on the hour. Pre-book ONLY through Open House, see p15 for details. Max 15 per tour. N T G A
Peabody Trust's urban eco-village with 100 homes and 10 workspaces, designed to reduce residents' energy and water usage. Roofs with photovoltaic panels are topped with colourful distinctive cowls that circulate air. BedZED is the most comprehensive example of sustainable development in the UK. Bill Dunster Architects/Bioregional (environmental consultants) 2002. Entry: show-home, exhibition.
Rail: Hackbridge, Mitcham Junction; 127,151

Carshalton House
West Street SM5 3PS
→ Sun 3pm-5pm. d T
The principal rooms of the Mansion contain 18C decoration including a unique painted room. The early grounds were designed by Charles Bridgeman, and include a water tower by architect Henry Joynes. Entry: painted room, oak room, library.
Tube: Morden, then 157; Train: Carshalton; 127,157,407,X26,154

Carshalton Park Grotto
Carshalton Park, Ruskin Road SM5 3DE
→ Sat 2pm-4pm. First come basis. Last entry 3.45pm. d P
A surviving element from a major incomplete early 18C landscaping project, it stood at the end of a long canal, designed to be seen from mansion that was never finished. Built of brick, the interior decoration was removed in 1914.
Tube: Morden then 15; Rail: Carshalton; S3,407,X26,127,157

Carshalton Water Tower and Historic Gardens
West Street, Carshalton SM5 2NR
→ Sat/Sun 2pm-5pm. Last entry 4.30pm. B D R T
Early 18C Grade II listed building incorporating plunge bath with Delft tiles, Orangery, saloon and pump chamber with part-restored water wheel. Hermitage in grounds. Entry: Orangery, saloon, bathroom, pump chamber.
Tube: Morden; Rail: Carshalton; 157,127,407,X26,154

Honeywood
Honeywood Walk, Carshalton SM5 3NX
→ Sat/Sun 10am-5pm. Last entry 4.45pm. B C d T
Historical house dating to 17C with many later additions including major extensions of 1896 and 1903. Rich in period detail and much of the interior recently restored to the 1903 colour scheme, including a billiard room with original Edwardian table and fittings. Now a local museum.
Rail: Carshalton; 127,157,407,X26

Little Holland House
40 Beeches Avenue, Carshalton SM5 3LW
→ Sat 10am-1pm. First come basis, queuing outside if necessary. Max 25 at one time. B d N T
Grade II* listed building whose interior was created entirely by Dickinson, inspired by the ideals of John Ruskin and William Morris and contains Dickinson's paintings, hand-made furniture, furnishings, metalwork and friezes, in Arts and Crafts style. Frank Dickinson 1902-4. Entry: ground floor, master bedroom, back bedroom, bathroom, garden.
Tube: Morden, then 154 bus; Rail: Carshalton Beeches; 154

Lumley Chapel
St Dunstan's Churchyard, Church Road, Cheam SM1 1EA
→ Sat/Sun 11am-4pm. d N
Medieval former chancel of parish church, part 12C, with many important post-Reformation memorials.
Rail: Cheam

Nonsuch Mansion
Ewell Road, Cheam SM3 7DZ
→ Sat/Sun 2pm-5pm. First come basis. Last entry 4.45pm. B D P R T
Tudor Gothic mansion, designed for wealthy merchant Samuel Farmer, in the style later used at Windsor Castle. The service wing has been restored and includes dairy, kitchen, scullery, larders and laundry. Jeffrey Wyatt 1806. Entry: house, service wing.
Rail: Cheam; 213,151,408,726,293

Parity Projects House ●
78 Carshalton Grove SM1 4NB
→ Sat tours 10am, 11.30pm, 1.30pm, 3pm, pre-book ONLY by email to claire.elliot-square@parityprojects.com or 020 8643 6630. P G A E
An award-winning Victorian semi-detached home, the building is a 'work in progress' on a ground-breaking project to apply and test eco-principles for future reproduction. It aims to prove that energy and water use can be reduced to the lowest possible levels in any existing building. Sustainable features include hyper-efficient insulation and heating system, using renewable fuels. Parity Projects 2007.
Tube: Morden then 154; Rail: Carshalton; 154,407,X26,S3

Russettings
25 Worcester Road, Sutton SM2 6PR
→ Sun 10am-1pm. First come basis, queuing outside if necessary. Last entry 12.45pm. Max 25 at one time. d P T
A double-fronted red brick upper-middle class house, Russettings is one of a few Victorian villas to survive in Sutton. The well-preserved interior includes an entrance hall with a mosaic tiled floor and an oak galleried staircase. Frederick Wheeler 1899.
Rail: Sutton; 470,S4

St Mary's Beddington
Church Road, Beddington (in Beddington Park) SM6 7NL
→ Sat 11am-5pm/Sun 1pm-4.30pm. Last entry 4.30pm. B D R T
Grade II* listed 13C church, housing the historic Carew Chapel, a Morris-designed organ screen and several Nuttgens windows. Restoration by Joseph Clarke.
Rail: Hackbridge, Wallington; 407,410,463

The Phoenix Centre
Mollison Drive, Roundshaw, Wallington SM6 9NZ
→ Sat 9am-6pm. Tours between 9am-11am only. D P R T G
Built at the heart of the Roundshaw Estate, this centre is a 32,000sqm complex integrating a unique combination of 15 different community uses in a safe and accessible environment. Broadway Malyan 2004. Entry: library, café, sports hall, youth centre, fitness centre.
Tube: Morden; Rail: Wallington; 154,455,54

Upper Mill, The Grove Park
The Grove Park – entry via Mill Lane or North Street SM5 2TH
→ Sat 2pm-4pm. d
An alpine-style wooden building (1887) which housed a private water-driven electricity generating plant. The building rests on the remains of a flour mill designed by John Smeaton in the 1770s. Entry: ground floor.
Tube: Morden, then 157; Rail: Carshalton; 127,157,407,X26,53

Whitehall
1 Malden Road, Cheam SM3 8QD
→ Sat 10am-5pm/Sun 2pm-5pm. Sat bookstall. B d R T
Originally a farmer's house dating to 1500, with jettied upper storey. Later additions through the centuries reflect the changing lifestyles of the owners, including the Killicks for over 2 centuries. Restored by John West & Partners 1974-76.
Rail: Cheam; X26,151,213

WALKS/TOURS

Tour of Two Estates
→ Meet: Sat 10.30am outside Water Tower, West Street, Carshalton SM5 3PS
A tour of the landscape creations of two famous bankers and their families at the beginning of the 18C.
Tube: Morden then 157; Rail: Carshalton; 127,157,407,X26,S3

Supported by

Sutton

Tower Hamlets

Christ Church Spitalfields
Commercial Street/Fournier Street E1 6LY
→ Sat 10am-3.30pm/Sun 1pm-4pm. Regular tours. B D T
Grade I listed masterpiece of English Baroque, restored to its 18C splendour. Refurbished and restored by Whitfield Partners 1978-2002 and Purcell Miller Tritton from 2002. RIBA Award Winner 2006. Nicholas Hawksmoor 1714-1729. Entry: nave, vestibule, galleries, old vestry room.
Tube: Aldgate East; Tube/Rail: Liverpool Street; 67,8,149,78,26

Four Corners
121 Roman Road, Bethnal Green E2 0QN
→ Sat/Sun 10am-5pm. Regular tours every half hour and presentations on the history of the project. D T G
Refurbished building with new extension and sedum roof, with a clear circulation route forming the spine of building. A central courtyard or integrated 'hub' allows light and air to filter through. JaK Studio (refurb) 2007. Entry: gallery, darkrooms, offices, garden, green roof.
Tube/Rail: Bethnal Green; 106,8,277

George Green Building (National Skills Academy for Financial Services)
155 East India Dock Road E14 6DA
→ Sat/Sun architect-led tours 1pm, 2.15pm, 3.30pm. D T G A
A highly innovative refurbishment of a Grade II listed Victorian grammar school (1884) to create a flexible, technologically enabled working environment for this new academy. The main hall, the 'jewel in the crown', with an upper gallery space has been beautifully restored. Tooley & Foster Partnership (refurb) 2007. Entry: all except roof and service areas.
Tube/DLR: Canary Wharf; Rail: Limehouse; DLR: Poplar, All Saints; 15,115,D6,D7,D8

Hermitage Community Moorings
16 Wapping High Street E1W 1NG
→ Sat/Sun 10am-4pm. First come basis. Last entry 3pm. Information regarding history of the vessels. D N R T
An exciting new development of residential and recreational moorings for historic vessels on the Thames. The architectural scheme has been designed as a model for river dwelling that takes into account its tidal location. The unique Pier House, built to a high specification, provides a floating community centre just downstream from Tower Bridge. Anna Versteeg & Ollie Price 2009. Entry: The Pier House, possibly some historic vessels.
Tube: Tower Hill; 100,RV1

Kingsley Hall
Powis Road, off Bruce Road E3 3HJ
→ Sat 11am-5pm. Hourly tours from 11.30am. Last entry 4.30pm. Max 18 per tour. Exhibition of history and archives. C d P R T
Grade II listed, Pioneer East End community centre founded by peace campaigners Muriel and Doris Lester. Design included main hall and 5 rooftop cells for community volunteers. Links with Gandhi, George Lansbury, R D Laing's Philadelphia Association 1965-1970. Charles Cowles Voysey 1928. Entry: Gandhi's cell, Children's house, Peace garden.
Tube: Bromley by Bow; DLR: Bow Church; 8,25,108,S2

Limehouse Accumulator Tower
Limehouse Basin, Mill Place E14 7HZ
→ Sat/Sun 1pm-5pm. Regular guided tours by Greater London Industrial Archaeology Society.
Octagonal tower (1869) for regulating one of the first hydraulic power systems. Fine views over canal dock and beyond. Entry: spiral stair up to open balcony.
DLR/Rail: Limehouse; 5,15,115

Mulberry School for Girls ●
Richard Street, Commercial Road E1 2JP
→ Sat 10am-5pm. Tours every half hour, first come basis. Last entry 4.30pm. Max 30 per tour. C D T G
Landmark PFI building development, giving its users quality facilities in which to teach, learn, work and relax, and that has enabled teachers to develop new and innovative approaches to teaching. Awarded national accreditation for environmental management systems. Miller Construction 2004.
Tube: Whitechapel; DLR: Shadwell; 15,115

Museum of London Docklands
No. 1 Warehouse, West India Quay (off Hertsmere Road) E14 4AL
→ Sat/Sun 10am-6pm. No.1 Warehouse tours 1.30pm, 3.15pm, pre-book tours ONLY on 020 7001 9844. Duration 1 1/4 hours. Free entrance all other times for OHL visitors. B D R T
Grade I listed, late Georgian (1802) sugar warehouse now housing the Museum of London Docklands. Sensitively restored, the new multi-media displays coexist with the massive timber and stone structures of the original building. Purcell Miller Tritton (conversion) 2002.
DLR: West India Quay; DLR/Tube: Canary Wharf; Boat: Canary Wharf Pier; 277,D3,D7,D8

New Heart for Bow Project at St Paul's Old Ford
St Paul's Church, St Stephen's Road E3 5JL
→ Sat/Sun 1pm-4pm. Half hourly tours. Last entry 5pm. D N P R T
Victorian church, rehabilitated to include art gallery and gym in 'a building within a building' – a stunning Ark or Pod of tulipwood situated in the nave. "Stylish...thrilling..." Jay Merrick in The Independent. Winner of RICS Community Benefit Award 2005. Matthew Lloyd Architects LLP 2004.
Tube: Bow Church, Bethnal Green; 8 to Roman Road Market

One Bishops Square ● ●
One Bishops Square E1 6AD
→ Sun 10am-5pm. Last entry 4.30pm. Max 150 at a time. D R T G
An efficient, flexible, user-friendly and supportive working environment. 'Intelligent' building with many sustainable features including London's largest office-based solar installation and inbuilt computer system aimed at efficiency and energy conservation. Triple glazing and blinds reduce solar gain on all south-facing windows. Foster and Partners 2006. Entry: 6th floor coffee bar, office area, terrace, lobby.
Tube/Rail: Liverpool Street; 8,11,26,35,42

Queen Mary College, Institute of Cell & Molecular Science – Blizard Building
4 Newark Street E1 2AT
→ Sun 10am-4pm. First come basis, queuing if necessary. Last entry 4pm. Max 20 at a time. D Q T
Landmark building providing cutting-edge innovative research laboratory facilities. Glass-walled structure with applied Bruce McLean art, with dramatic interior including irregular range of pods such as the spectacular orange molecular pod. New Centre of the Cell also open. RIBA Award Winner 2006. Alsop Architects/Amec 2005. Entry: specified areas only.
Tube: Whitechapel; 25,339,106,205,254,746

Hermitage Community Moorings

Raven Row
56 Artillery Lane E1 7LS
→ Sat/Sun 11am-6pm. Architect-led tours Sat/Sun 12noon-4pm. Last entry 5.30pm. d N T A
Grade I listed former Huguenot silk merchants' shops now restored and transformed into a contemporary art centre. Baroque panels, sold to an American museum in the 1920s, have now been recovered and returned to the first floor of no.58. 6a Architects (refurb) 2008. Entry: galleries, baroque panelled room usually closed to public.
Tube/Rail: Liverpool Street; 8,48,149,242,26

Society for the Protection of Ancient Buildings
37 Spital Square E1 6DY
→ Sat 10am-5pm. Last entry 4.45pm. Advice on historic buildings and demonstrations of building crafts/skills. B R T
Richly panelled 1740s former Huguenot silk merchant's house, on the site of the Medieval hospital of St Mary Spital. Now HQ of SPAB. Entry: offices, rear courtyard.
Tube/Rail: Liverpool Street, Moorgate; 8,26,35,47,48,78

Spitalfields Charnel House
1 Bishops Square E1 6AD
→ Sat 10am-5pm. Last entry 4.45pm. Max 15 at one time. Archaeologists on site to explain history.
The Charnel House was used to store bones and was built c1310 in the heart of the Priory of St Mary Spital. It formerly had a chapel above, demolished c1700. It was rediscovered a few years ago and is now preserved.
Tube/Rail: Liverpool Street; 8,11,26,35,42

St Dunstan and All Saints Church
Stepney High Street E1 0NR
→ Sat 10am-5.30pm/Sun 12noon-5.30pm. d P R T
Grade I listed Medieval parish church (952AD) pre-dating the Tower of London. Fine interior with good memorials, stained glass and brasses. Many of the founders of Trinity House were buried here. Entry: nave and parish room.
Tube: Stepney Green; Rail/DLR: Limehouse; 15,25,115,309,339

St George's German Lutheran Church
55 Alie Street E1 8EB
→ Sat 10am-4pm. Exhibition about Dietrich Bonhoeffer who was involved with the work of the church. B D R T
The oldest surviving German church in England from 1763 with unaltered Georgian interior. Joel Johnson 1763.
Tube: Aldgate East, Aldgate; Tube/Rail: Liverpool Street; 15,25,42,78,100

One Bishops Square

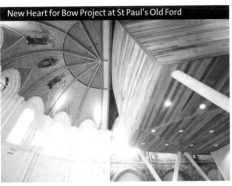
New Heart for Bow Project at St Paul's Old Ford

St John on Bethnal Green
200 Cambridge Heath Road E2 9PA
→ Sat/Sun 10am-5pm. Tours on the hour. Last entry 4.45pm. Film installation 'Gateway' in belfry. d T
Grade I 'Waterloo Church', interior remodelled by William Mundy after 1870 fire. Stations of the Cross by Chris Gollon. Sir John Soane 1826. Entry: church, galleries, crypt, belfry. NB. Parish mass Sun 10am.
Tube/Rail: Bethnal Green; 8,106,254,309,388,D3

St Mary's – 'Bow Church'
Bow Road E3 3AH
→ Sat 10am-5pm/Sun 12noon-5pm. Last entry 5pm. Max 100 at one time. Display on the history of the church. D N R T
Medieval village church, restored in late 19C and after bomb damage in WWII. 15C font and memorials from five centuries. Elegantly restored tower. Grade II* listed. Soon to be undergoing refurbishment in time for 700th anniversary in 2011 and for London 2012 Olympics. H S Goodhart-Rendel (restoration) C20. Entry: church, parish room, vestry.
Tube: Bow Road; Rail/DLR: Stratford: DLR: Bow Church; 25,8,D8,425

St Matthias Old Church – Community Centre
113 Poplar High Street E14 0AE
→ Sun 10am-6pm. Regular tours, first come basis. D P R T
Oldest building in Docklands built in the Gothic and Classical styles, with original 17C stonework and fine mosaics. One of only three churches built during the Civil War, it was originally the East India Company Chapel. John Tanner 1649.
DLR: Poplar, All Saints; 15,115,D6,D7,D8

Thames River Police
98 Wapping High Street E1W 2NE
→ Sat/Sun 10am-5pm. Regular tours, first come basis. Last entry 4pm. Max 25 at one time.
A unique ex-carpenters' workshop (1910), contained within a working police station. The workshop space now displays a history of Thames River Police. Entry: museum.
Bus: 100

The Rich Mix
35-47 Bethnal Green Road, London E1 6LA
→ Sat/Sun 9am-6pm. Regular tours, first come basis. Max 20 at one time. d N R T
An exciting new arts centre for cultural and creative diversity. To create a home for this innovative project, Penoyre & Prasad transformed a derelict factory building. Penoyre & Prasad 2006. Entry: café and possible entrance to screening areas.
Tube/Rail: Liverpool Street; 8,388

Three Mills Lock
Prescott Channel, Three Mills Island, Bromley-by-Bow E3 3DU
→ Sat/Sun 10am-5pm. Regular tours, first come basis. G
This state-of-the-art structure by VolkerStevin is the first lock to be built in London for over 20 years. Positioned at the mouth of the Olympic site, the mechanism offers a sustainable transport link for the 2012 games and beyond. Entry: lockkeeper's tower, lock surrounds.
Tube: Bromley-by-Bow; DLR: Bow Church; 488,D8,108

Tower Bridge Exhibition
Tower Bridge Road SE1 2UP
→ Sat/Sun 10am-4pm, tours on the hour, last tour 4pm. Pre-book ONLY through Open House, see p15 for details. Max 30 per tour. B d R T
Completed in 1894 after eight years of construction, two massive piers were sunk into the river bed to support the construction and over 11,000 tonnes of steel provided the framework of the towers and the walkways. These were then clad in Cornish granite and Portland stone to give the bridge a more pleasing appearance. Magnificent views from the high-level walkways. Sir Horace Jones 1881-94. Entry: walkways, steam engine rooms.
Tube: Tower Hill; Tube/Rail: London Bridge; DLR: Tower Gateway; 15,25,42,78,100,RV1

Tower of London
Tower Hill EC3N 4AB
→ Sat/Sun 11am-5pm. Tours every hour. Pre-book ONLY on toweropenhouse@hrp.org.uk. Last tour 4pm. Max 10 per tour.
The White Tower is the best preserved example of a Norman fortress and is currently being cleaned and repaired. See conservation techniques and explore the Norman's advanced design skills. NB. Most of the visit up on scaffolding: sensible footwear and clothing must be worn. Hard hats provided. No children under 12.
Tube: Tower Hill; Tube/Rail: Cannon Street, London Bridge; Rail: Fenchurch Street; DLR: Tower Gateway; 15,25,42,78,100,B1,RV1

Trinity Buoy Wharf/Container City ●
64 Orchard Place Leamouth (from Leamouth Road roundabout take Lower Lea Crossing, immediately take slip road on left, turn right onto Orchard Place) E14 0JW
→ Sat/Sun 11am-5pm. Tours at 12noon, 2pm, first come basis. Last entry 4.30pm. Free workshop for all ages 'Create your own wearable building', Sat/Sun 11am-4pm. C D N P R T A
Home to London's only lighthouse, a range of fine stock brick buildings and 3 examples of the innovative Container City Scheme that has converted shipping containers into arts studio spaces. Amazing views of Canary Wharf, the O2 and the Thames as well as sculptures, arts activities, workshops and performances. Nicholas Lacey Architects & Eric Reynolds/Buschow Henley/Eric Reynolds & ABK Arc 1950s-2002. Entry: Container Cities, lighthouse, historic buildings, pier.
DLR: East India; DLR/Rail: Canning Town; 277

Whitechapel Gallery
77-82 Whitechapel High Street E1 7QX
→ Sat 11am-6pm. Architect-led tours at 11am, 12noon, 2pm, 3pm, pre-book tours ONLY through Open House, see p15 for details. Max 20 per tour. B D N P R T A
Re-opened in April 2009 following a major expansion project, uniting two paired landmarks, the Gallery and former Library. With transformed galleries, education spaces and collection displays, the century-old institution continues its reputation as the artists' gallery for everyone. Robbrecht en Daem 1901/Witherford Watson Mann 2009. Entry: entire gallery including Clore Creative Studio, Study Studio.
Tube: Aldgate East; 250,135,254,115,25

WALKS/TOURS

Tower Hamlets Cemetery Park
Meet: Tower Hamlets Cemetery Park, Southern Grove E3 4PX
→ Sat 10am-5pm. History walks on the hour from 11am, except at 2pm for nature walk. Last walk 4pm. B D N P R T G
Last of the "magnificent seven" cemeteries, opened 1841. Burials ceased 1966, now 30 acres of mature woodland and glades managed as a nature park, with Soanes Centre educational facility (Robson Kelly 1993). Sustainable features: Soanes Centre was the first green roof in Tower Hamlets. Not constructed properly it provides an arid eco system which amongst other things supports spiders normally found in the Sahara. Thomas Wyatt & David Brandon.
Tube: Mile End; DLR: Bow Church; DLR/Rail: Limehouse; 25,277,D6,D7

Supported by

TOWER HAMLETS

Waltham Forest

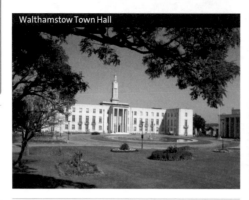

Walthamstow Town Hall

Hatherley Mews Offices

Assembly Hall
Forest Road E17 4JF
→ Sat/Sun 9am-11am. Regular tours, first come basis. Max 15-20 at one time. D P T
Grade II listed subsidiary building of the Town Hall built in a restrained style in Portland stone. P D Hepworth 1942. Entry: main hall, foyer.
Tube: Walthamstow Central; Rail: Wood Street; 123,275

Forest School
College Place E17 3PY
→ Sat 10am-2.30pm. Regular tours, first come basis. Last entry 2pm. Max 10 at one time. P T
Campus buildings include chapel in early picturesque Gothic style, partly designed by White, a pupil of Sir George Gilbert Scott, and dining hall with internal timber panelling and friezes from Jesus College, Oxford. William White 1875/ Richard Creed 1887/Ove Arup & Partners 1967/Tooley & Foster 2007. Entry: chapel, dining hall, theatre.
Tube: Snaresbrook; Rail: Wood Street; 20,34,357

Hatherley Mews Offices
Hatherley Mews E17 4QP
→ Sat 10am-4pm. Regular tours, first come basis. Max 8 at one time. R T
Striking multimedia office complementing the existing Victorian buildings that make up the Hiltongrove Business Centre. Modern design and construction techniques have created a spilt level interior flooded by natural light. Warm natural wooden floors are mirrored on the street frontage by the bold exterior cladding creating a new focus for the mews. Winner of London Borough of Waltham Forest's Best New Building Award 2004. Blackwell Friend Architects 2003.
Tube: Walthamstow

Queen Elizabeth's Hunting Lodge
Rangers Road, Chingford E4 7QH
→ Sat/Sun 12noon-5pm. Tours at 2pm, 3pm, 4pm. Last entry 4.45pm. C d P T
Unique Grade II listed atmospheric timber-framed hunt-standing (1543), commissioned by Henry VIII, set amongst ancient pollards of Epping Forest. 1589 fireplace and Tudor food displays in kitchen. (Owned by the City of London Corporation.) Entry: three floors.
Rail: Chingford; 97,179,212,313,379,444

St Mary's Parish Church
Church Hill E17 3BD
→ Sat 10am-5pm/Sun 1.30pm-5pm. NB. Sat closed between 11.45am-2pm. Restricted access to bell tower, max 6 per tour, no under 5s, weather permitting. Bell ringing demonstration Sat afternoon. B C D P R T
Grade II* listed church dating from 12C with medieval and Tudor features.
Tube: Walthamstow Central; W12,212,W16

St Mary with St Edward and St Luke, Leyton
35 Church Road E10 5JP
→ Sat 10am-4pm. B D P R T
A church has occupied the site since 700AD. Present building dates from 17C, with cupola salvaged from Leyton Great House in 1806, and has been fully restored after major arson damage in 1995.
Tube: Leyton; Rail: Leyton Midland Road; 58,69,97,158

The Pump House Steam & Transport Museum
10 South Access Road E17 8AX
→ Sat/Sun 11am-4pm. Last entry 3.30pm. B D P R T E
Grade II listed Victorian engine house remodelled in 1897 to take a pair of Marshall steam engines, still in working order. Entry: pump house, fire station.
Tube/Rail: Blackhorse Road; Rail: St James Street; 58,158,230,W19

Vestry House Museum
Vestry Road E17 9NH
→ Sat/Sun 10am-5pm. Regular tours, first come basis. B d N T
Built as a workhouse in 1730, the date plaque warns 'if any should not work neither should he eat'. From 1840-1870 it was a police station, then a private house, and from 1931 the Museum for Waltham Forest. Interior contains early C17 panelling and over-mantel from nearby demolished Essex Hall.
Tube/Rail: Walthamstow Central; W12,W16

Waltham Forest City Learning Centre ●
144 Billet Road E17 5DP
→ Sat 10am-1pm. Regular tours, first come basis. Last entry 12.30pm. Max 10 per tour. D P R T C
Distinctive building encompassing public/private spaces radiating around 2 raised drums. Energy efficiency and sustainability were an important part of the design concept. LBWF/Austin Smith Lord 2001.
Tube/Rail: Blackhorse Road, Walthamstow Central; 158,W11,W15

Walthamstow Town Hall
Forest Road E17 4JF
→ Sat/Sun 9am-12noon. Regular tours. Last entry 12noon. Max 15-20 per tour. D P T A
Impressive civic centre, built in Portland stone with a classical layout in Swedish influenced popular inter-war style. PD Hepworth 1937-42. Entry: committee rooms, chamber, basement.
Tube: Walthamstow Central; Rail: Wood Street; 123,275

William Morris Gallery
Lloyd Park, Forest Road E17 4PP
→ Sat/Sun 10am-5pm. Last entry 4.30pm. Max 150 at one time. NB. Georgian Walthamstow walk Sat 11am. B d N P T
Handsome 1740s Georgian former Water House with original features including oak-panelled and marble-flagged entrance hall with fine plasterwork. Formerly the home of the designer, craftsman, poet and socialist William Morris (1834-1896), now a museum of his work and that of his followers in the Arts and Crafts Movement. Entry: all public areas.
Tube/Rail: Walthamstow Central (then bus 34,97,215,275,357 to Bell Corner); Blackhorse Road (123 bus to Lloyd Park)

Woodford Green United Free Church
High Elms, Woodford Green IG8 0UP
→ Sat/Sun 1pm-5pm. Regular tours, first come basis. D P R T
Designed by a distinguished architect of the Arts and Crafts Movement. Charles Harrison Townsend 1904. Entry: church, adjoining room.
Tube: Woodford; Rail: Highams Park; 20,179,275,W13

WALKS/TOURS

Georgian Walthamstow
→ Meet: Sat 11am at William Morris Gallery, Lloyd Park, Forest Road E17 4PP. First come basis.
A tour around Georgian Walthamstow which retains more 18C houses than any of its neighbours. Ending in the rural backwater that is Walthamstow Village containing Ancient House – a notable 15C timber-framed hall house.
Tube/Rail: Walthamstow Central (then bus 34,97,215,275,357 to Bell Corner); Blackhorse Road (123 bus to Lloyd Park)

Supported by

Waltham Forest

Wandsworth

All Saints Church, Putney
Putney Common SW15 1HN
→ Sat/Sun 2pm-5pm. d P R T N
Grade II* listed, a collaboration between architect George
Street and the designers Edward Burne Jones and William
Morris. Exquisite example of late Victorian Arts & Crafts
church. Largest number of Burne Jones windows in London.
G E Street 1874. Entry: all areas.
Tube: Putney Bridge; Rail: Putney, Barnes; 22,265

Brandlehow Primary School ●
Brandlehow Road, Putney SW15 2ED
→ Sat 10am-4pm. First come basis, queuing outside if
necessary. Last entry 3.30pm. Max 25 at one time. G
Extension to a listed modern school building formed from
prefabricated timber elements clad with cedar panels. A
glazed corridor acts as a joint between the main building and
the extension. Franziska Wagner/team51.5° architects 2006.
Entry: new classroom.
Tube: East Putney; Rail: Putney; 270,220,337,14,74

Emanuel School
Battersea Rise SW11 1HS
→ Sat 2pm-4pm. Regular tours every 30 mins. Last tour and
entry 3.30pm. Access to school's archives. P T
Former Royal Patriotic orphanage, converted to school 1883,
with 1896 additions. High Victorian style with much stained
glass by Moira Forsyth. Set in 12 acres. Henry Saxon Snell 1871.
Entry: main building inc chapel, library, concert hall.
Tube: Clapham South; Rail: Clapham Junction; 77,219,319,337

Foster + Partners Studio
Riverside, 22 Hester Road SW11 4AN
→ Sat 10am-5pm. Regular tours. Last entry 4.45pm. R T A
Single-space, double-height purpose-built architects' studio
60 metres long – part of a larger river-side building that has
30 apartments and the Foster-designed Albion complex next
door. Foster + Partners 1990. Entry: entrance and mezzanine
(with view over whole studio).
Tube: Sloane Square; Rail: Clapham Junction; 19,49,239,319,345

Gala Bingo Hall (former Granada Cinema)
Mitcham Road SW17 9NA
→ Sun 9am-11am. Last entry 11am. P R T
Exceptional example of the "super cinema style" of the 1930s
with outstanding Gothic interior by Theodore Komisarjevsky.
The first Grade I listed cinema. Cecil Masey 1931. Entry: auditorium.
Tube: Tooting Broadway; Rail: Tooting, Earlsfield; 44,57,77,127,133

National Tennis Centre
100 Priory Lane, Roehampton SW15 5JQ
→ Sat/Sun 10am-3pm. Tours at 10am and 1pm. Max 15 per tour. d T
A new centre for young British players for world class
competition. Three-dimensional grid shell, dome-like roofs
form the largest volumes covering six in-door courts for year-
round use. The gyms and training areas on one side and the
residential areas, carefully articulated with balconies and
windows, on the other, give scale and richness to the façade.
Offices are joined by a courtyard. Hopkins Architects 2008.
Tube: Hammersmith, Putney Bridge; Rail: Barnes; 72,33,337,493

Pump House Gallery
Battersea Park SW11 4NJ
→ Sat/Sun 11am-5pm. Last entry 4.30pm. Max 50 at one time. d N
Beautiful Grade II listed Victorian ex-water tower overlooking
Battersea Park lake. Now houses a contemporary art gallery.
James and William Simpson 1861.
*Tube: Sloane Square; Rail: Battersea Park, Queenstown Road;
137,19,44,49,239,344,345,452*

Quaker Meeting House
59 Wandsworth High Street SW18 2PT
→ Sat 12noon-4pm. Max 25 at one time. D T
Grade II listed, this is the oldest Quaker meeting house in
Greater London (1778), with original panelling and a ministers'
gallery. Secluded burial ground and garden. Entry: ground
floor & garden, display of local Quaker history.
Tube: East Putney; Rail: Wandsworth Town; 28,39,87,156,337

Royal Victoria Patriotic Building
John Archer Way, Trinity Road SW18 3SX
→ Sat/Sun 10am-5pm. Last entry 4.45pm. Slide shows Sat/
Sun 11am, 3pm introduced by local historian Simon
McNeill-Ritchie. d P T
Imposing, Grade II listed Scottish Baronial-styled Victorian
institution, Crimean War orphanage, WWI military hospital
and WWII M15 interrogation centre. Restored and now a
thriving community of workshops, restaurant, studios and
flats. Decorated central hall a feature. Rohde Hawkins 1857/
John Dickenson (refurb). Entry: public areas, hall.
*Rail: Wandsworth Common, Wandsworth Town, Clapham
Junction; 77,219*

St Mary's Church
Battersea Church Road SW11 3NA
→ Sat 12noon-5pm/Sun 1pm-6pm. Regular tours. Fair in
churchyard. D R T
Classic Grade I listed Georgian church with outstanding
interior and monuments. New engraved glass doors by Sally
Scott. Joseph Dixon 1775-7.
*Tube: South Kensington, Sloane Square; Rail: Clapham Junction;
19,49,170,319,345*

St Mary's Church, Balham
Balham High Road SW12 9BS
→ Sat 10am-4pm. d R T
Grade II listed. Originally proprietary chapel. Parish church
since 1855. Victorian apsed chancel with mosaics. Wren-style
clock-tower and domed baptistery (now chapel). Modern
gallery rooms. F Hurblatt/Arthur Cawston/William Newton
Dunn/Brown Matthews Partnership (refurb) 1806 onwards.
Tube/Rail: Balham; 155,249,315,355

Thomas's London Day Schools Clapham: Reception Block ● A
Broomwood Road SW11 6JZ
→ Sat 10am-1pm. First come basis. Architect will be on site. D
G P T A
A new stand-alone classroom block including new specialist
classrooms, four outdoor semi-enclosed teaching spaces and
to the rear reception and support block. The main classrooms
are seen as a rolling form with inside and outside space
merging into one to create ever-changing teaching zones.
Sustainable features include compressed recycled timber
panel units. Claridge Architects 2008.
Tube: Clapham South; Rail: Wandsworth Common; G1

National Tennis Centre

Pump House Gallery

Supported by

Wandsworth

Westminster

Foreign Office & India Office

16 New Burlington Place
16 New Burlington Place W1S 2HX
→ Sat/Sun 10am-5pm. First come basis, queuing outside if necessary. Last entry 4.30pm. D T G A

Behind a retained Regent Street façade, The Crown Estate's new headquarters draws inspiration from this context with an architecture that is contemporary and dramatic whilst simultaneously addressing sensitive environmental issues. Hard landscaping and public art help to enhance a previously unwelcome urban space – Michael Bleyenberg's sculpture 'New Burlington Flare – Three Prisms' stands by the building. Sustainable features include photovoltaic cells, chilled ceilings and surface water drainage system harvesting up to 100,000 litres of grey water per year. Trehearne Architects 2006. Entry: part of open-plan office floor, 6th floor including board room, meeting rooms, restaurant, roof terrace.
Tube: Oxford Circus; Tube/Rail: Charing Cross; 3,6,15,23,88

26 Whitehall (former Admiralty Buildings)
26 Whitehall SW1A 2WH
→ Sat/Sun 10am-4.30pm. Tours 12noon and 2pm, first come basis, queuing outside if necessary. Last entry 4pm. d Q

Grade I listed Old Admiralty Building, behind Robert Adam's Admiralty Screen on Whitehall. Now owned by Cabinet Office; works of art and antiques from MOD Art Collection. Thomas Ripley (former Admiralty offices) 1725/Samuel Pepys Cockerell (former Admiralty House) 1785. Entry: Old Admiralty boardroom, state rooms in Admiralty House.
Tube: Embankment; Tube/Rail: Charing Cross; 24,11,12,159,3

Apsley House ●
Hyde Park Corner W1J 7NT
→ Sat/Sun 11am-5pm. Last entry 4.30pm. Talks at 11am, 12noon, 2pm and 3pm in the Waterloo Gallery about the Gallery, its paintings and its architect Benjamin Dean Wyatt. Max 40 per talk, first come basis. B d T

London palace of the first Duke of Wellington. Regency interiors restored 1992-5, collection of war trophies and magnificent art collection. Robert Adam 1771-8/Benjamin Dean Wyatt 1828-9.
Tube: Hyde Park Corner (exit 1); Tube/Rail: Victoria; 2,10,16,73,74

Argentine Ambassador's Residence
49 Belgrave Square SW1X 8QZ
→ Sat/Sun 12noon-5pm. First come basis, queuing if necessary. d Q

Known as the 'Independent North Mansion' and christened by Sydney Herbert as 'Belgrave Villa' and then simply 'The Villa' by his successor the 6th Duke of Richmond. Owned by Argentina since 1936 and with sumptuous interiors still intact. Thomas Cubitt 1851. Entry: all main rooms.
Tube: Hyde Park Corner; Tube/Rail: Victoria; 19,22,14,38,10,8

Arts Council England National Office ● ●
14 Great Peter Street SW1P 3NQ
→ Sat 10am-5pm. Last entry 4pm. Max 10 at one time. Exhibition of works from Arts Council Collection. d Q R T

A collaboration between Caruso St John Architects and artist Lothar Goetz has provided a stunning refurbishment of the National Office of Arts Council England. RIBA Award Winner 2009. Caruso St John Architects (refurbishment) 2008. Entry: reception/gallery space, meeting room, breakout spaces, some workspace and team areas.
Tube: Westminster, St James's Park; Tube/Rail: Victoria; 87,3,507,C10

BBC Bush House ●
Aldwych WC2B 4PH
→ Sat 10am-4pm. Last entry 4pm. Tours every 10-20 mins. NB. Studios not included. Security checks will take place before each tour. Max 15 per tour. Sat 3.30pm VocalEyes tour for blind and partially sighted people, contact Toby Davey toby@vocaleyes.co.uk/020 7375 1043 for more info and how to book. d Q

Built by American businessman Irving T Bush as a trade centre, Bush House has been the home of BBC World Service since 1940. Helmle and Corbett 1925-35.
Tube: Holborn, Temple; Tube/Rail: Waterloo, Charing Cross; 1,9,13,15,176,188

Benjamin Franklin House
36 Craven Street WC2N 5NF
→ Sat/Sun 10am-5pm. Last entry 4.30pm.

A Grade I listed Georgian house (1732), the only surviving home and workshop of Benjamin Franklin, retaining most of the original features including central staircase, lathing, 18C panelling; stoves, windows, fittings and beams. Patrick Dillon Architect (refurb) 2006.
Tube: Embankment; Tube/Rail: Charing Cross; 6,9,11,13,15,23,87

Channel Four Television
124 Horseferry Road SW1P 2TX
→ Sat 10am-5pm. Max 50 at one time. Last entry 4.30pm. D R T

Transmission centre with curving high glass and steel entry atrium. RIBA Award Winner. Richard Rogers Partnership 1994. Entry: reception, walkway, restaurant, drum.
Tube: St James's Park; Tube/Rail: Victoria; 11,24,211

Chelsea College of Art & Design (former Royal Army Medical College)
16 John Islip Street SW1P 4JU
→ Sat 10am-4pm. Regular tours, first come basis, queuing if necessary. Last entry 3.45pm. D R T G

By the Thames, a stimulating combination of listed Edwardian army buildings (1898-1907) sensitively combined with recently completed contemporary additional space to create a 21C art and design college, designed by award-winning architects. Sustainability features include grass roofs on several buildings. Allies and Morrison (refurb) 2005.
Tube: Pimlico; Tube/Rail: Vauxhall, Victoria; 2,36,88,185,436

16 New Burlington Place

Dover House, Office of the Secretary of State for Scotland
66 Whitehall SW1A 2AU
→ Sat 10am-4pm. Pre-book ONLY on 020 7270 6762. Last entry 3.15pm. Max 20 at one time. D T A
Elegant Whitehall façade and domed entrance commissioned by the Duke of York. Interesting original interiors. J Paine & H Holland 1754-8/1787. Entry: Ministerial rooms only.
Tube: Embankment, Westminster; Tube/Rail: Charing Cross;
3,11,12,24,53,87,88,159

Eco House Monmouth Road (Gap House) ● A
28D Monmouth Road W2 4UT
→ Sat 1pm-5pm. Architect-led tours every 30 mins. Pre-book ONLY through Open House, see p15 for details. Max 10 per tour. Last tour 4.30pm. G A
New family home with a minimal carbon footprint on a very narrow site (8ft wide), once the side alley and garden of adjacent house. Each room has good natural light whilst fitting in between two listed buildings in conservation area. Cost effective design methods achieved an environmentally friendly house, utilising amongst many eco-friendly devices ground source heat pump heating and rainwater harvesting. RIBA Award Winner 2009. Pitman Tozer Architects 2007.
Tube: Bayswater, Queensway; 70,23,7,27,52

Foreign Office & India Office ●
King Charles Street SW1A 2AH
→ Sat/Sun 10am-5pm. Last entry 4.30pm. Sun 9.30am VocalEyes tour for blind and partially sighted people, contact Toby Davey toby@vocaleyes.co.uk/020 7375 1043 for more info and how to book. B C D R T
Grade I listed Victorian government office buildings. Former India Office includes the magnificently decorated Durbar Court. Sir George Gilbert Scott & Matthew Digby Wyatt 1861-1868. Entry: Durbar court, India Office council chamber, Locarno suite and Foreign Office grand staircase.
Tube: Westminster; Tube/Rail: Charing Cross, Victoria;
3,11,12,24,53,87,88,159,453

former Conservative Club (HSBC offices)
78 St James's Street SW1A 1JB
→ Sat 10am-3pm. Timed entry every half hour, pre-book ONLY on 020 7024 0103 or 020 7024 0102. Last entry 2.30pm. Max 40 per tour. d T
Grand and monumental building with rich carvings and spectacular decorated saloon at its heart. Conserved and refurbished to replace 2 wings and provide new glazing to atrium at junction of new and old sites. Grade II* listed. Sidney Smirke & George Basevi 1844/Squire & Partners (refurb) 2004. Entry: Grade II* listed areas.
Tube: Green Park; Tube/Rail: Charing Cross, Victoria

Grosvenor House ●
Park Lane W1K 7TN
→ Sun 10am, 11.30am, 1.30pm, 3pm, 4.30pm architectural tours with Howard Hartley, pre-book ONLY on 020 7290 7170 (Mon-Fri 9.30am-5.30pm). Tours approx 60 mins. Max 15 per tour. See p12 for details of Rose Tea offer and overnight stay competition.
London's largest five-star hotel, after a four-year, multimillion pound restoration the Hotel re-launched in September 2009 as the European flagship property for Marriott. Where the hotel stands today was originally the London residence of the Grosvenor family. Opened to the public in May 1929 and quickly established itself as the glamorous home of the society set and wealthy Americans, attracting a fashionable crowd from Edward VIII and Mrs Simpson to Ella Fitzgerald and Jacqueline Onassis. Wimperis, Simpson & Guthrie 1926-9.
Tube: Marble Arch, Hyde Park Corner; 414,73,10,74,36,148

Holy Trinity Church
Prince Consort Road SW7 2BA
→ Sat/Sun 1pm-5pm. First come basis. D T
Bodley's last realised design with bright lofty interior, fine reredos, pulpit, chandeliers and stained glass. Grade I listed. GF Bodley 1901-6.
Tube: South Kensington; 9,10,52,70,360

Honourable Company of Master Mariners
HQS Wellington, Temple Stairs, Victoria Embankment WC2R 2PN
→ Sat/Sun 10.30am-4.30pm. Regular tours, first come basis. Last entry 4pm. Max 15 per tour. R T
Bought by the Master Mariners in 1947, HQS Wellington is the City's only floating livery hall. Gangway steep at low tide. Entry: court room, model room, main deck, quarter deck. NB. Unsuitable for the infirm.
Tube: Temple; Tube/Rail: Charing Cross

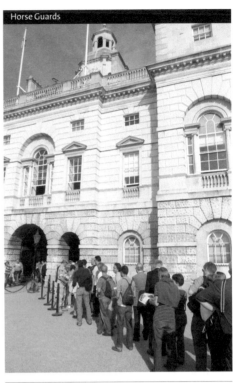
Horse Guards

Hopkins Architects' Office
27 Broadley Terrace NW1 6LG
→ Sat 1pm-3pm. D T A
The practice expanded its office campus in 1993, with a second building using its own Patera system, followed by a glass reception area in 1995. The buildings are linked by a covered walkway. Current work on display. Hopkins Architects 1982.
Tube/Rail: Marylebone; 139,189

Horse Guards
Whitehall SW1A 2AX
→ Sat/Sun 10am-3.30pm. Half hourly tours. Duration 45 mins. Approx waiting time for tour 1 1/2 hrs. Last tour 3.30pm. Max 40 at one time. B Q
Grade I listed beautifully-detailed Palladian composition at the heart of Whitehall, for a hundred years HQ of the British Army. Duke of Wellington's office as it was c1842. William Kent 1745-55. Entry: Horse Guards Arch, south side.
Tube/Rail: Charing Cross; 3,11,12,24,53,87,88,91,139,159

House of St Barnabas-in-Soho & Chapel
1 Greek Street, Soho Square W1D 4NQ
→ Sat/Sun 10.30am-5pm. Tours approx hourly. Last tour 4pm. R T
Soho's grandest Grade I listed Georgian townhouse. Fine Roccoco plasterwork commissioned 1754. Victorian Oxford Movement Chapel built 1862 by Joseph Clarke. Owned by the House of St Barnabas, a charity assisting vulnerable people back to independent living. Joseph Pearce 1746. Entry: house, chapel, gardens.
Tube: Tottenham Court Road, Leicester Square; Tube/Rail: Charing Cross; 14,19,24,29,38,176

IET London, Savoy Place
2 Savoy Place WC2R 0BL

→ Sun 10am-5pm. Hourly tours, first come basis. Last tour 4pm. Small historical exhibition. D R T

Originally built as a joint Examination Hall for the Royal College of Physicians and the Royal College of Surgeons, the building was renovated in 1909 for the Institution creating a spectacular 20C interior. Stephen Salter and H Percy Adams 1886.
Tube: Embankment; Tube/Rail: Charing Cross; 6,9,13,87,139

Iyengar Yoga Institute
223a Randolph Avenue W9 1NL

→ Sat 9am-2pm/Sun 10.30am-5.30pm. Last entry 15 mins before close. Max 6 at one time. D T

The first purpose-built yoga centre in Europe. Yoga's philosophy is translated into the crisp simplicity of the design, with light pouring in through a grid of square light wells in ceiling. Two yoga studios with underfloor heating. Shiva Design 1994.
Tube: Maida Vale, Kilburn Park; Rail: Kilburn; 6,16,46,98,187

Jewel Tower ●
Abingdon Street SW1P 3JX

→ Sat 10am-5pm. Talks at 11am, 12noon, 2pm and 3pm about the exterior of the Tower showing the remains of the Medieval Palace of Westminster and Dock. Max 30 per talk, first come basis. B R

Built c1365 to house the treasures of Edward III and one of two surviving buildings of the original Palace of Westminster.
Tube: Westminster; Tube/Rail: Charing Cross, Victoria, Waterloo; 3,11,12,24,53,87,88,159,211

King's College Chapel, London
Strand WC2R 2LS

→ Sun 1pm-4pm. N D T

The Strand Chapel has recently been restored including the replacement of the windows with figurative stained glass. George Gilbert Scott 1864. Entry: quadrangle, main entrance hall & stairs, chapel.
Tube: Temple; Tube/Rail: Charing Cross, Waterloo; 168,171,15,11,26

Linnean Society of London
Burlington House, Piccadilly W1J 0BF

→ Sat 10am-5pm. Last entry 4.45pm. T

Part of the extension to Burlington House to provide accommodation for learned societies. Banks & Barry 1873. Entry: meeting room, 'double cube' library, entrance hall.
Tube: Piccadilly, Green Park; 9,14,19,22,38

Mark Masons' Hall
86 St James's Street SW1A 1PL

→ Sun 10am-5pm. First come basis, queuing outside if necessary. Last entry 4pm. Max 50 at one time. D R T

Fronted in stone, the style is 'Grosvenor Hotel' Italianate. Coarse foliage ornament fronts the building, the grand interiors adapted for Masonic use in the 1970s. James Knowles Jr 1866. Entry: Entrance Hall, Brazil Temple, Grand Temple, 1st floor all rooms & restaurant, 2nd floor bar only.
Tube: Green Park; Tube/Rail: Charing Cross, Victoria; 8,9,12,13,14

Eco House Monmouth Road (Gap House)

Marlborough House
Pall Mall SW1Y 5HX

→ Sat 10am-5pm. Last entry 4.30pm. Max 150 at one time. D R T

Originally home of the Dukes of Marlborough, and later of Edward VII and Queen Mary. Now HQ of the Commonwealth Secretariat and Commonwealth Foundation. Sir Christopher Wren 1709-11 & Sir James Pennethorne 1861-3. Entry: all fine rooms on ground floor, gardens.
Tube: St James's Park, Green Park, Piccadilly; Tube/Rail: Victoria, Charing Cross; 23,12,9,15,159,88,6,38,14,24

Methodist Central Hall Westminster
Storey's Gate SW1H 9NH

→ Sun 1pm-5.30pm. Great Hall dome open 1pm-5pm. B D R T E

A masterpiece of Edwardian neo-baroque on a prominent site. Great Hall was the venue for the Inaugural General Assembly of the United Nations in 1946. Lanchester & Rickards 1906-1912. Entry: Great Hall, Great Hall dome, café.
Tube: St James's Park, Westminster; Tube/Rail: Victoria, Waterloo; 11,24,88,159,87,453,148

Park Lane Hotel
Piccadilly W1J 7BX

→ Sat/Sun 10am-4.30pm. Pre-book ONLY on 020 7290 7170 (Mon-Fri 9.30am-5.30pm). Max 10 per tour. D T

London's finest monument to Art Deco features original marble bathrooms, fireplaces and recently restored Grade I listed Ballroom. Henry Tanner 1927. Entry: rooms selected on day.
Tube: Green Park, Hyde Park Corner; Tube/Rail: Victoria; 14,19,9,22,38,8,10

RIBA

Portcullis House
Victoria Embankment SW1A 0AA

→ Sat 10am-5pm. Last entry 4.30pm. Max 300 at one time. C D Q R T A

Portcullis House contrasts its imposing façade with a generous light-filled courtyard. RIBA Award Winner. Michael Hopkins and Partners 2001. Entry: ground floor courtyard and 1st floor. Entry to Portcullis House only via main entrance on Victoria Embankment.
Tube: Westminster; Tube/Rail: Charing Cross; 3,11,12,24,53,87,88

Reform Club
104 Pall Mall SW1Y 5EW

→ Sat 10am-5pm/Sun 10am-3pm. Pre-book ONLY by email to generaloffice@reformclub.com. NB. Regret no children under 12 admitted. Max 15 per tour.

Built as a Whig gentleman's club and inspired by Italian Renaissance palaces. Lobby leads to an enclosed colonnaded courtyard with 'complementary' glazed roof and tessellated floor. Tunnelled staircase leads to upper floor. Sir Charles Barry 1841. Entry: ground & 1st floor principal public rooms.
Tube: Piccadilly Circus; Tube/Rail: Charing Cross

RIBA
66 Portland Place W1B 1AD

→ Sat 10am-3.30pm. Tours at 11.30am, 12.30pm, 2pm, including areas not normally open to the public. Max 20 per tour. Exhibition in Library. B d R T

Fine example of Grade II listed 1930s architecture with many original features and fittings. Grey Wornum 1932-4. Entry: council chamber, Aston Webb room, Jarvis hall, Lutyens room and all public areas.
Tube: Great Portland Street, Oxford Circus, Regent's Park; 88,C2,453

Royal Academy of Arts
Piccadilly W1J 0BD
→ Sat/Sun 10am-6pm. Tours of 'The John Madejski Fine Rooms', RA Schools Casts Corridor, the Library and Print Room at 11am, 2pm, 4pm. Max 25 per tour. B d R T
Burlington's 18C Palladian town house with remodelling by Colen Campbell, William Kent and Samuel Ware. Ingeniously inserted glass stairs and lift between Smirke's 19C main galleries and Foster and Partners' 1991 Sackler Wing galleries. RIBA Award Winner (Sackler Galleries). Entry: entrance, Sackler Wing and Sculpture Gallery, De Grey Court, John Madejski Fine Rooms.
Tube: Green Park, Piccadilly; Tube/Rail: Victoria; 9,14,19,22,38

Royal Albert Hall
Kensington Gore SW7 2AP
→ Sun 10am-4pm. Regular half-hourly tours from the Box Office at Door 12. Pre-book ONLY on 0845 401 5029 (dedicated line) or via the website. Last tour 3pm. Max 20 per tour. Visitors with special access needs should advise when booking. B D R T
Built in 1871, the Royal Albert Hall is one of the world's leading entertainment venues. Grade I listed, it recently underwent a £69m redevelopment. Captain Fowkes and General Scott 1871. Entry: auditorium, Queen's Box, gallery, sub arena.
Tube: South Kensington, High St Kensington; Tube/Rail: Victoria; 9,10,52,380,452

Royal Astronomical Society
Burlington House, Piccadilly W1J 0BQ
→ Sat 10am-5pm. Tours at 10am, 11.30am, 2pm & 4.30pm. Pre-book ONLY on 020 7734 4582/3307. Tours include Society's library and archives with books dating back to 1480. Max 25 per tour. d T A
Part of the extension to Burlington House to provide accommodation for learned societies, the home of the Royal Astronomical Society since 1874 with recent refurbishment. Banks & Barry 1874/Peregrine Bryant Associates 2007.
Tube: Piccadilly, Green Park; Tube/Rail: Victoria; 9,14,19,22,38

Royal Ballet School: Bridge of Aspiration
46 Floral Street WC2E 9DA
→ Sat 10am-5pm. Regular tours on the hour, first come basis. Max 20 per tour. D T
Purpose-built facilities for the Royal Ballet lower school with the 'Bridge of Aspiration' linking the school to the Grade I listed Royal Opera House. From street level the bridge evokes the fluidity and grace of dance. Wilkinson Eyre Architects 2003. Entry: studios, Bridge of Aspiration
Tube: Covent Garden; Tube/Rail: Charing Cross; 14,6,9,11,13,15,23

Royal College of Pathologists
2 Carlton House Terrace SW1Y 5AF
→ Sat 10am-5pm. Last entry 4.45pm. Max 50 at one time. d R T
A light and spacious modern interior which maintains the spirit of the original Nash shape. Recent refurbishment includes new education centre in a previously under-used basement. No. 2 has great views of St James's Park. John Nash 1828/Bennetts Associates (refurb) 2008. Entry: lower ground, ground and 1st floors.
Tube: Piccadilly Circus; Tube/Rail: Charing Cross; 3,9,12,13,15,19,23,139,159,453

Royal Courts of Justice
Strand WC2A 2LL
→ Sat 10am-4pm. d N Q R T
Street's masterpiece and one of Victorian London's great public buildings. 13C Gothic given a Victorian interpretation. G E Street 1874-82. Entry: main hall, selected courts and areas of interest. Partial disabled access only – contact prior to attendance.
Tube: Temple, Holborn, Chancery Lane; Tube/Rail: Waterloo, Charing Cross; 4,11,15,23,26,76,172,341

Royal Geographical Society with IBG
1 Kensington Gore (Exhibition Road entrance) SW7 2AR
→ Sat 10am-5pm. 'Show and Tell' from Collections in Foyle Reading Room 10am, 12.30pm, 3pm, max 25 per group. Exhibition in pavilion: Images of Ethiopia – photographs by Nick Danziger. d R T
Originally a private home in R Norman Shaw's Queen Anne style, with later additions for the Society. Richard Norman Shaw 1874/Kennedy and Nightingale 1930/Studio Downie 2001-4. Entry: pavilion, Foyle reading room, Ondaatje theatre, council room, map room, education room, Lowther room, terrace and garden.
Tube: South Kensington; Tube/Rail: Paddington, Victoria; 9,10,52,452

Royal Institution of Great Britain
21 Albemarle Street W1S 4BS
→ Sun 10am-6pm. Regular tours and scientific demonstrations throughout the day. Special events will be taking place. D R T
Grade I listed building (beautiful Adam style 18C interior, 1838/1930s Vulliamy/Guthrie façade), reinterpreted by Terry Farrell & Partners forming an iconic series of spaces for listening, thinking and talking about science. Lewis Vulliamy (façade) 1838/ Rome Guthrie 1930s.
Tube: Green Park, Piccadilly Circus; Tube/Rail: Charing Cross, Victoria; 9,14,19,22,38

Royal Society of Chemistry
New Burlington House, Piccadilly W1J 0BA
→ Sat/Sun 10am-4pm. Last entry 3.30pm. D T
Part of the quadrangle building extension to Burlington House, purpose built for the learned societies. Rooms recently restored in conjunction with English Heritage. Banks & Barry 1873. Entry: reception, ground floor rooms, council chamber, meeting room, library.
Tube: Green Park, Piccadilly Circus; Tube/Rail: Victoria; 9,14,22,19,38

RSA
Royal Society for the Encouragement of Arts, Manufactures & Commerce, 8 John Adam Street WC2N 6EZ
→ Sun 12noon-5pm. Last entry 4.30pm. D R T
Purpose designed as part of the massive Adelphi development, this amazing complex includes the Great Room (with its famous painting series by J Barry), a suite of Adam rooms, cavernous brick vaults and theatre, and Modernist interventions. Adam Brothers 1774. Entry: Great room, Vaults, Benjamin Franklin room, Library, Shipley room, Durham St auditorium, Romney & Adelphi rooms.
Tube/Rail: Charing Cross; 6,9,87,91,176

Rudolf Steiner House
35 Park Road NW1 6XT
→ Sun 2pm-5pm. Tours every 15 mins. Last entry 4.30pm. B d N P R T
Unique example of Expressionist architecture in London with sculptural staircase based on organic plant forms. Grade II listed. New café area and renovations in 2008. Montague Wheeler 1926-37/Nic Pople 2008. Entry: all areas except offices.
Tube: Baker Street; Tube/Rail: Marylebone; 2,13,18,27,30,74,82,11

Seaford House
37 Belgrave Square SW1X 8NS
→ Sat/Sun 9am-5pm. T
Grade II* listed stucco fronted town house for Earl of Sefton. Remodelled in 1902 with a unique marble staircase, friezes and panelling for Lord Howard de Walden. Philip Hardwick 1842. Entry: 1st and ground floor.
Tube: Hyde Park Corner; Tube/Rail: Victoria; 2,8,16,36,38,52,73,82

Serpentine Gallery Pavilion 2009
Kensington Gardens W2 3XA
→ Sat/Sun 10am-10pm. First come basis, queuing outside if necessary. D N R T
This year's Pavilion is by Kazuyo Sejima and Ryue Nishizawa of SANAA who have, in a short time, developed from a relatively little-known Japanese partnership to an internationally esteemed firm responsible for high-profile projects including the 21C Museum of Contemporary Art in Kanazawa, the Glass Pavilion at the Toledo Museum of Art in Ohio, and the New Museum in New York. Entry: pavilion and gallery.
Tube: Knightsbridge, South Kensington, Lancaster Gate; 9,10,52,94,148

Society of Antiquaries of London
Burlington House, Piccadilly W1J 0BE
→ Sat 1pm-5pm. Regular tours, first come basis. Last entry 4.45pm. d T
Part of New Burlington House, purpose built in 1875 for learned societies. Imposing top-lit library with double galleries and marbled columns. Ground floor now authentically restored. Banks & Barry 1875. Entry: main stairs, library, meeting room, council room.
Tube: Piccadilly Circus, Green Park; Tube/Rail: Victoria; 9,14,19,22,38

St Anne's Tower
St Anne's Churchyard, Wardour Street W1D 6AF
→ Sat 10am-5pm. Regular tours, first come basis. Last entry 4.30pm. Max 25 at one time. R T
Extraordinary brick, stone and copper Grade II listed church tower with bulbous lead spire. Clock by Gillett and Johnston 1884. S P Cockerell 1803. Entry: tower, clockroom, church, community centre.
Tube: Piccadilly Circus, Leicester Square; Tube/Rail: Charing Cross; 14,19,38,24

St Augustine's Church, Kilburn Park Road
Kilburn Park Road NW6 5XB
→ Sat 10am-5pm. Tours 11am, 3pm, 4pm. B D N R T
Pearson's grand masterpiece, with its lofty and atmospheric interior with brick vaulting, rich wall paintings and a profusion of stone sculptures in the chancel. J L Pearson 1871-1898.
Tube: Kilburn Park; Rail: Kilburn High Road; 16,31,32,98,206,316

St Barnabas Church
St Barnabas Street SW1W 8PF
→ Sat 10am-5pm/Sun 2pm-5pm. Regular tours, first come basis. Last entry 4.45pm. d R T
Church in Early English style, full of Pre-Raphaelite decoration. Important works by Bodley, Comper and Cundy and windows by Kempe and Tower. First Oxford Movement church. Thomas Cundy 1850. Entry: church, crypt.
Tube: Sloane Square; Tube/Rail: Victoria; 11,211,170,C10

St Martin-in-the-Fields
Trafalgar Square WC2N 4JJ
→ Sat 10am-5pm. Tours of the church and crypt pre-book ONLY on 020 7766 1100, otherwise general access. Max 25 on tours. B d N R T
One of Britain's finest churches, built in the Italian Baroque tradition. Following a £36m renewal programme new spaces including the St Martin's Hall and the Sir Neville Marriner room will be open for activities throughout the day. James Gibbs 1726/Eric Parry Architects (modernisation) 2008. Entry: church, crypt, lower crypt, foyer.
Tube: Leicester Square; Tube/Rail: Charing Cross; 11,24,29,774,91

St Mary Magdalene-in-Paddington Parish Church
Rowington Close W2 5TF
→ Sat 9am-5pm. Half hourly tours of the crypt. Music at 5pm. N P R T
Church by the architect of Royal Courts of Justice. Painted ceiling by Daniel Bell; glass by Holiday and Comper; magnificent Comper crypt chapel. Decorated in gilt, it literally glows and is considered one of Comper's masterpieces. G E Street 1867-72. Entry: church and crypt.
Tube: Warwick Ave, Royal Oak; Rail: Paddington; 6,187,414,18,36

St Marylebone CE School Performing Arts Centre ● A
64 Marylebone High Street W1U 5BA
→ Sat 10am-5pm. Half-hourly tours, pre-book ONLY through Open House, see p15 for details. Architects on site. Max 20 per tour. D T G A
School in the heart of the Marylebone Conservation area with new underground gymnasium and classroom block providing much needed improved facilities and access. At street level the clock tower and cor-ten finish link the school to the street but there is little to announce the new lower-courtyard and light-filled vast underground gymnasium. Sustainable design. RIBA National Award Winner 2008 and shortlisted for the Prime Minister's Better Public Building Awards. Gumuchdjian architects 2007. Entry: performing arts centre.
Tube: Baker Street; Tube/Rail: Marylebone; 189,139,113,82,13

talkbackTHAMES ●
20-21 Newman Street W1T 1PG
→ Sat 11am-5pm. Regular architect-led tours. Last entry 4.30pm. T A
TV company HQ designed to foster a calm atmosphere and community environment. Offices organised around multi-storey cloistered courtyard, with gardens, terraces and bridges. RIBA Award Winner. Buschow Henley Architects 2001. Entry: main entrance, lower courtyard, 1st floor lobby, 1st & 2nd floor decks, herb area.
Tube: Tottenham Court Road, Goodge Street, Oxford Circus; 55,73,98,176,390

The College of Optometrists
42 Craven Street WC2N 5NG
→ Sun 1pm-5pm. Last entry 4.45pm. Max 20 at one time. B d T
HQ of professional and examining body for UK optometrists occupying two terraced houses, no. 41 (Flitcroft c1730 with later additions) and no. 42 (rebuilt by Tarmac plc, c1989). Entry: Council room, Panelled room, Sutcliffe room, Print room, Giles room, Library.
Tube: Embankment; Tube/Rail: Charing Cross; 3,11,12,24,53

The Dorchester ●
Park Lane W1K 1QA
→ Pre-book ONLY: Behind-the-scenes tour Sun, email diary@ thedorchester.com to enter ballot for draw on Monday 14 September; successful applications notified by email. Max only 2 tickets per booking. Give names of all attendees in application. Max 20 on tour. Martin Hulbert of Fox Linton Associates on site to discuss new spa design.
One of London's most iconic luxury hotels, built in 1931. Prince Philip hosted his bachelor's party on the eve of his wedding to Queen Elizabeth II in the hotel's Park Suite, while General Eisenhower planned the Normandy Invasion from his suite. Interiors by the best of the century's designers from Oliver Ford to Oliver Messel and most recently Fox Linton Associates. Owen Williams & Curtis Green 1931/Fox Linton Associates (spa refurb) 2009.
Tube: Hyde Park Corner; Tube/Rail: Victoria 2,10,16,36,73,74,82

The Hub – Regent's Park Sports Pavilion ●
Regent's Park, Outer Circle NW1 5HA (postcode for tube station)
→ Sat/Sun 9am-6pm. D N R T G
A delicate glass and steel circular tea room and terrace with 360 degree views of the park. Beneath the tea room are the clustered changing and multi-function spaces that are covered by a gently sloping grass mound. Highly sustainable design with nearly 90% of building submerged with consequent thermal properties. David Morley Architects 2005.
Tube: Regent's Park, Great Portland Street, Baker Street, Camden Town; Tube/Rail: Euston, Marylebone; 2,13,18,27,30,C2,5

The Lansdowne Club
9 Fitzmaurice Place, Berkeley Square W1J 5JD
→ Sun 1pm-5pm. Tours approx every 15 mins, first come basis, queuing outside if necessary. Last entry 4.30pm. Max 20 per tour. Q T
Robert Adam house, partly demolished in 1931 and reconstructed as a club house in the Art Deco style, retaining 5 original rooms. Restoration work ongoing. Robert Adam 1768/ Holloway & White 1934-35.
Tube: Green Park; Tube/Rail: Victoria; 9,14,19,22,38

The Naval Club
38 Hill Street W1J 5NS
→ Sat 11am-5pm/Sun 1pm-5pm. Regular half hourly tours. Pre-book ONLY on 020 7493 7672 or cdr@navalclub.co.uk (Commander John Prichard). Last tour 4.15pm. Max 12 per tour. D R T
Grade II listed Georgian town house c1748-1750 reputed to have been 18C residence of William Pitt the Younger. First floor decorated in ornate white and gold 'Louis XVI' style. Dark stock brick building with Ionic porch and moulded architraves to sash windows. Entry: ground, 1st, 2nd floors and public rooms.
Tube: Green Park, Bond Street; Tube/Rail: Victoria; 2,3,14,74,159

The Royal Society

Royal Ballet School: Bridge of Aspiration

Arts Council England National Office

The Royal Society
6-9 Carlton House Terrace SW1Y 5AG
→ Sat 10am-5pm. Tours every 20 mins, first come basis. Max 20 per tour. Exhibition on Victorian science, displays of portraiture. d T

Grade I listed Nash-designed town houses, refurbished in the 1890s before conversion into the German Embassy. 2004 refurbishment provided additional facilities for the home of the UK's national science academy. Nash/Speer/William Holford & Partners/Burrell Foley Fischer 1828/2004. Entry: lecture theatres, reception rooms, library.
Tube: Piccadilly Circus; Tube/Rail: Charing Cross; 29,91,24,9,6,13

University of Westminster
309 Regent Street W1B 2UW
→ Sat tours at 10am, 11.30pm, 2pm, 3.30pm, pre-book ONLY on 020 7911 5789. Max 25 per tour. T

309 Regent Street has been an educational establishment since 1838 when it opened as the Royal Polytechnic Institution. Its history boasts one of London's first public swimming pools and the premiere of the Lumiere brothers moving film. The oak-panelled Fyvie Hall features paintings by Delmar Banner and the Old Cinema is home to a Compton organ that gave sound to silent pictures. George Mitchell 1911.
Tube: Oxford Circus; 25,88,139,189,C2

Wellington Arch
Hyde Park Corner, Apsley Way W1J 7JZ
→ Sun 10am-5pm. Last entry 4.30pm. Tours at 11am, 12noon, 2pm, 3pm of the war memorials around Wellington Arch including the 2006 New Zealand war memorial. Max 30 on tours, first come basis. B D R

Splendid London landmark. Recently restored by English Heritage, it now offers access to rooms previously used as a police station. Hosts exhibitions and has amazing views. Decimus Burton 1826-30.
Tube: Hyde Park Corner; Tube/Rail: Victoria; 2,8,9,10,14,16

Westminster Academy ● ●
255 Harrow Road W2 5EZ
→ Sat 10am-4pm. Architect-led tours every half hour. Max 100 at one time. Special childrens activity. C D R T G A

A colourful and dynamic academy for 1175 students including a dramatic glazed atrium, integrated supergraphics, separate sports hall and extensive landscaped playground. Sustainable features include, externally: green roof, large glazed atrium for natural light, projecting balconies for sun-shading, natural terracotta cladding panels, storm water attenuation. Internally: wood-wool acoustic panels, recycled carpet. RIBA London Building of the Year 2008. BSCE Award Inspiring Design: Secondary School. Allford Hall Monaghan Morris 2007.
Tube: Warwick Avenue, Royal Oak; Tube/Rail: Paddington; 18,36

Westminster Archives Centre
10 St Ann's Street SW1P 2DE
→ Sat 10am-5pm. Tours every hour on the hour. Last tour 4pm. Max 15 per tour. B D N R T

Modern red brick building purpose-built to house Westminster City's historic records. Opportunity to see the conservator at work and the hidden treasures in the strongrooms. Tim Drewitt 1995.
Tube: St James's Park; Tube/Rail: Victoria; 11,24,88,211,148

Westminster Hall
House of Commons (Cromwell Green entrance) SW1A 0AA
→ Sun 10am-5pm. Last entry 4.30pm. Max 300 at one time. D Q R T

One of the finest and largest Medieval halls in Europe with a magnificent hammerbeam ceiling. Work began in 1097 and the architect for the 14C rebuilding was Henry Yevele with Hugh Herland the designer of the roof.
Tube: Westminster; Rail: Victoria; 11,77A,12,53,24,109,159

Wigmore Hall
36 Wigmore Street W1U 2BP
→ Sat 11.30am-3pm. Last entry 2.30pm. 15 minute performances at 12pm, 1pm and 2pm in auditorium by members of Ignite ensemble. Short creative music workshops at 12.30pm, 1.30pm and 2.30pm in Bechstein room. D R T

Refurbished in 2004, sumptuous auditorium with famous Art Nouveau mural. Thomas E Collcutt 1901. Entry: auditorium, stage, green room, Bechstein room, Gerald Moore room.
Tube: Bond Street, Oxford Circus; all buses to Oxford Street

WALKS/TOURS

Architectural Highlights of Paddington
→ Meet: Sat 2pm/Sun 12noon, 2pm at Brunel Statue, Platform 1, Paddington Station W2 1FT. Pre-book by Friday 18 September ONLY on 020 3145 1200 or email walks@inpaddington.com or online at www.inpaddington.com.

A walking tour of Paddington's architectural treasures, ranging from graceful 19C buildings to stunning contemporary work by notable architects including Carmine (Michel Mossessian and Partners), Sheldon Square (Sidell Gibson) and Waterside (Richard Rogers Partnership).
Tube/Rail: Paddington; Tube: Edgware Road; 23,15,36,27,436,46

Big Changes in Paddington and Heatherwick's Rolling Bridge
→ Meet: Sun 1pm outside Hilton London Metropole, 225 Edgware Road W2 1JU. Pre-book by Friday 18 September ONLY on 020 3145 1200 or email walks@inpaddington.com or online at www.inpaddington.com.

An overview of the massive regeneration of the Paddington Waterside area including Paddington Basin and PaddingtonCentral. See Thomas Heatherwick's renowned Rolling Bridge in action.
Tube/Rail: Paddington; Tube: Edgware Road; 23,15,36,27,436,46

Brunel – Designer, Engineer, Legend
→ Meet: Sat 11am, 1pm, 3pm at Brunel Statue, Platform 1, Paddington Station W2 1FT. Pre-book by Friday 18 September ONLY on 020 3145 1200 or email walks@inpaddington.com or online at www.inpaddington.com.

Meet Isambard Kingdom Brunel, renowned engineer of the 19C, known widely for his design of Paddington Station and the Great Western Railways. Listen to chronicles of his extraordinary life and experience his passion for Paddington.
Tube/Rail: Paddington; Tube: Edgware Road; 23,15,36,27,436,46

Westminster Academy

Sponge Trail of Eco-Buildings ●
→ Meet: The Hub – Regent's Park Sports Pavilion, Regent's Park, Outer Circle NW1 5HA. For days and times and full details see spongenet.org, or to download trail routes visit Sponge entry on openhouse.org.uk. G

Sponge, the network of young professionals with an interest in sustainability and the built environment, is highlighting buildings in the Regent's Park and Portobello area in the Open House programme with sustainability features or those that are fully fledged eco-buildings! Some have specialised eco-tours for those in the eco-know, and some are good for a more informal visit. Look out for those that are pre-book only.
Tube: Regent's Park, Great Portland Street, Baker Street, Camden Town; Tube/Rail: Euston, Marylebone; 2,13,18,27,30,C2,5

Vibrant Victoria
→ Meet: Sat/Sun 10.30am, 1.30pm, location given with booking. Pre-book ONLY by email to info@victoria-partnership.co.uk. Max 40 per tour.

An exploration of the history and development of this fascinating area from swampy fields to 21C regeneration. Including delightful squares, a prison site, canal, brewery, the Victoria stations and a variety of architectural styles.
Tube/Rail: Victoria; 8,16,38,44,52

Supported by

City of Westminster

Westminster Property Association
WPA is an association of property owners and their advisers in the City of Westminster formed in 1988 and which presses Westminster City Council for a user friendly planning framework encouraging a built environment which supports Westminster's unique diversity and contains better public realm, good and innovative building design and environmentally sustainable development.

Programme index

Listed here are special events, and buildings by type. The website search facility at openhouse.org.uk/london enables you to use different criteria such as location, architect and period, and pull out additional special activities taking place.

Special Events

Competitions/Special Offers/Publications

Talks

Other special events are indicated throughout the Buildings by Type index:

- ● Spotlight Event
- A Architect on site
- C Children's event

Buildings by Type

The following issues and themes are also indicated throughout

- ● Art in the Public Realm
- ● Green Exemplar
- ● Housing
- ● Office Exemplar
- ● School Exemplar

Architectural Practice

Art Studio

Cemetery

Cinema

Civic

Club

Community/Cultural

(Community/Cultural continued)

Education

Image copyright credits

front cover left: Foreign Office & India Office – Nick Woodford, middle: 85 Swains Lane - Lyndon Douglas, right: City Hall - Hiroki Matsuuchi; inside front cover London skyline at dusk – Dennis Gilbert/VIEW; p2 London 2012 Olympic Park – Olympic Delivery Authority; p4 top right: 'The Dalston Mill', by EXYZT, 15 July 2009 – 6 August 2009, Dalston – Eliot Wyman, bottom left: My City Too! responding to 'Poured Lines: Southwark Street', by Ian Davenport, Southwark, top left: 'Gill Sans', by Ron Haselden with architects Robert Ian Barnes and Taeko Matsumoto, Southwark – Ron Haselden; p5 top left: Capital City Academy – Foster and Partners, bottom left: Castle Green – Bouygues UK, top right: Junior Open House; p6 top left: Eco House Monmouth Road (Gap House) – Luke Tozer, bottom left: Green Sky Thinking – Hanne Lund, bottom right: Junior Open House; p7 Lloyd's of London – Mark Charrington; p8 top left: Victoria Thornton; p9 top right: Robert Elms; p10 top right: Adelaide Wharf – Tim Soar , bottom left: 'Kiosk by Office of Experiments', from 'Limitations Permitted', by Manu Luksch and Neal White in collaboration with FLIX – John Clare, bottom right: King's Cross Construction Skills Centre – Morley Von Sternberg; p11 bottom left: Eco House Sherland Road; p12 top right: inspired children, bottom left: City of a 1000 Architects, bottom right: Box Architecture; p13 left: London Night Hike, right: 120 Fleet Street (ex Daily Express) – Alexander Somerville; p16 Northbury Junior School Extension – Charlotte Wood; p17 Townley Grammar School for Girls – © Kilian O'Sullivan/VIEW, Danson House – Bexley Heritage Trust; p18 St Mary Magdalen's Catholic Junior School – Redshift Photography 2009, Sattavis Patidar Centre – Raffaele Damiano; p19 The Berresford House – Ivor Berresford; p20 Lumen United Reformed Church and Community Centre – Nick Kane, 85 Swains Lane – Lyndon Douglas; p22 London School of Economics, New Academic Building – Jens Willebrand; p23 Roundhouse – Gareth Gardner; p24 International Headquarters of the Salvation Army – Richard Waite; p25 Bart's Hospital Great Hall – Hanne Lund, Guildhall Art Gallery – Diane Wilbraham; p26 Bank of England – Ken Allinson, Lloyd's of London – M. Huelin; p27 10 Queen Street Place – © Peter Cook/VIEW; p28 No. 1 Croydon (formerly NLA Tower) – James Hartcup; p29 2 Castlebar Road – David Grandorge, Northala Fields: A Recycled New Park – LDA Design; p30 Gunpowder Park – LDA Design; p31 Queen's House – National Maritime Museum; p32 Greenwich Peninsula as seen from Trinity Buoy Wharf – P Krobot; p33 The Bridge Academy – Martine Hamilton Knight; p34 Eds Shed/Sunken House – © Ed Reeve/VIEW, Hackney Empire Theatre – Ken Allinson; p35 Latymer Upper School: Performing Arts Centre – Nick Kane; p36 Maggie's Centre – Zamri Arip; p38 Former Grosvenor Cinema – Jane Dean; p40 Stockley Academy – Aedas, Indoor Athletics Centre, Brunel University – Morley Von Sternberg; p42 Bennetts Associates Architects – © Peter Cook/Bennetts Associates/VIEW; p43 Kings Place – Keith Paisley; p44 The Octagon – Alexander James; p45 The Yellow Building – Monsoon Accessorize HQ – Timothy Soar, St Thomas' C of E Primary School – © Fisher Hart/VIEW; p46 The Michael Tippett School – Tim Soar; p47 National Theatre – Tim Soar; p48 Crossways Sixth Form – Nick White; P49 Baitul Futuh Mosque – Mary J Carpenter; p50 London 2012 Olympic Park – Olympic Delivery Authority; p51 Valentines Mansion – © Paul Riddle/VIEW; p53 Heathfield Children's Centre and Nursery – Mark Hadden, Royal Botanic Gardens: Jodrell Laboratory – RBG Kew ; p55 Quay House – © Anthony Coleman/VIEW, City Hall – Linus Lim; p57 BedZED – Peabody Trust; p59 One Bishops Square – Jean-Remi Baudot; p61 National Tennis Centre – © Anthony Weller/VIEW, Pump House Gallery – Pump House Gallery; p62 Foreign Office & India Office – Grant Smith; p63 16 New Burlington Place – The Crown Estate, Horse Guards – Grant Smith; p64 Eco House Monmouth Road (Gap House) – Nick Kane, RIBA – Shane Browne; p66 The Royal Society – The Royal Society, Royal Ballet School: Bridge of Aspiration – Patrick Baldwin, Arts Council England National Office – Hélène Binet; p67 Westminster Academy – Tim Soar

Several of the images used were entries into last year's photography competition. Many thanks to all that submitted.

Take part in our survey

1. How many buildings did you visit during Open House London?

2. This year, did you choose to visit part(s) of London that you hadn't visited before?
Yes / No
If yes, where?

3. Does Open House London make you think differently about London?
Yes / No
If yes, how?

4. Of the following issues concerning the built environment, which is the most important for London? Please circle one:
Making buildings greener   Building well designed schools
Providing more high quality housing   Improving the design of public spaces
Making it easier to walk and cycle around the city

5. Which building(s) and places in London do you think would benefit from being renewed or regenerated for the future?

6. Do you think contemporary architecture makes a positive difference to London?
Yes / No

7. Which recent London building do you think will stand the test of time?

8. What do you think is the most important factor in making well designed housing?
(eg public space, materials, quality standards, size and number of rooms, private outside space)

9. 'The quality of the design of new schools and/or early years facilities in general is better nowadays compared to 10 years ago' (please circle one):
Strongly agree   Agree   Neither agree nor disagree
Disagree   Strongly disagree

10. What is your favourite artwork in London's public spaces?

Resources and publications

I would like to order the following: Cost

1 **Annual Open House London Event Programme**
18 & 19 September 2010 Event (published August 2010).   £6.50 (incl p&p)
EARLY BIRD OFFER: Order before 31 December 2009   £4.50 (incl p&p)

2 **Mapguide to Contemporary Architecture** (2007 edition)
A map of 150 London buildings with details of address, architect & year.   £3.95 (incl p&p)

3 **The Architects and Architecture of London**
Ken Allinson – brand new architectural guide explaining why London is the way it is.   £22.95 (incl p&p)

4 **London's Contemporary Architecture: A Visitor's Guide**
Ken Allinson – full colour, 5th edition, 2009. Map-based walking tour guide to London's contemporary buildings.   £22.95 (incl p&p)

Sub Total   £

Donation to support Open House – architecture education charity   £

TOTAL   £

GIFT AID Please tick here ☐   Signature_____
(Gift Aid is a simple scheme that enables charities to reclaim the tax you pay on your donations and subscription, at no extra cost to you. Please provide address below left and sign above. You must pay tax at least equal to the tax that we will reclaim on your donation.)

Visit....
openhouse.org.uk/shop for more books and products
openhouse.org.uk/tours for architecture tours year-round

You can also fill in the survey online at openhouse.org.uk/poll

---

DETAILS (please complete for both survey and/or purchases):

Name:

Address:

London Borough or County: Postcode:

E-mail: Tel:

IT WOULD ALSO BE USEFUL IF YOU COULD LET US KNOW THE FOLLOWING:

Nationality: Age:

Occupation:

What newspaper do you most often read?

Are you new to the Open House London event?   Yes / No

Where did you see or hear about Open House London this year? Please circle as many as apply
other websites/newsletters   local library   word of mouth   BBC London   transport advertising
leaflet/poster   Twitter   Facebook   newspaper/magazine (which one)

METHOD OF PAYMENT (if making a purchase above):

Cheque: £_____   (made payable to Open House)

Credit card details:
I authorise Open House to charge £_____ to my *VISA/MASTERCARD/SWITCH/DELTA (*delete as appropriate) SORRY NO AMEX

No. ☐☐☐☐ ☐☐☐☐ ☐☐☐☐ ☐☐☐☐ ☐☐☐☐

Expiry date_____ Issue date_____

Issue Number (Switch/Delta only) _____

Date: _____

Do you want to receive our free enewsletter. If yes please tick here ☐

* The charity's education initiatives are funded solely through trusts and donations
Registered Charity No.1072104

Tear out page and send to: FREEPOST RRXR-UBCB-ZKYC, Open House, 44-46 Scrutton Street, London EC2A 4HH

Support us to open eyes, minds and doors for everyone

openhouse.org.uk/support

Jane Priestman OBE Hon FRIBA
Chair of Trustees, Open House
"Open House highlights the value of good design and aims to open eyes and minds to the city's wealth of architecture. Through our programmes we hope to challenge perceptions, break down barriers and inspire people to demand better design for current and future generations."

London voices
"Buildings are a large part of society and I think it is wonderful that it is possible to share them in more ways than just photos or on the internet. Open House illustrates far more than an image, and shows to everyone how important good design is, and what an impact it can make."

"We should have more pride in the beautiful built environment in London. This is only fostered by greater knowledge of and exposure to the buildings themselves."

Follow Us on twitter

Find us on Facebook

The Open House London 2009 event is only possible through the support of the following organisations

Media Partners

Westminster Sponsor

Event Sponsors

London authorities supporting the event: Barking & Dagenham, Bexley, Brent, Bromley, Camden, City of London Corporation, City of Westminster, Croydon, Ealing, Enfield, Greenwich, Hackney, Hammersmith & Fulham, Haringey, Harrow, Havering, Hillingdon, Hounslow, Islington, Lambeth, Lewisham, Merton, Newham, Redbridge, Richmond, Royal Borough of Kensington & Chelsea, Southwark, Sutton, Tower Hamlets, Waltham Forest, Wandsworth

Family Events Sponsors

The London String of Pearls

London Night Hike Partner

Property owner supporters

Thanks to 700 property owners, representatives and organisers for their incredible goodwill and energy.

Volunteer support

Thanks to the architectural profession and the 6000 volunteers giving up their free time.

Talk & Exhibition Sponsor

Supporters & Partners

Charity

Sponsors & Supporters

Art in the Open Sponsors & Supporters

My City Too Sponsors & Supporters

Green Sky Thinking Initiative Partners/Supporters

Architecture Education Programmes Sponsors & Supporters

About Open House

Trustees – Jane Priestman OBE Hon FRIBA (Chair), Edwin Heathcote, Eva Jiricna CBE RIBA, Fred Manson Hon OBE, The Rt Hon Nick Raynsford MP
Supporters at Large Board – The Rt Hon Nick Raynsford MP (Chair), Keith Clarke, David Curley, Nick Forwood, John Smith, Prof Rick Trainor, Baroness Valentine
Art in the Open Advisory Board – Elliot Lipton (Chair), Peter Bishop, Achim Borchardt-Hume, Tania Kovats, Fred Manson, Jason Prior, Cllr Guy Nicholson, Victoria Stark
Founding Director – Victoria Thornton Hon FRIBA
Open House London Team – Jeni Hoskin (Project Manager), Hiromi Sasaki
Open House Team – Education: Suzie Zuber (Head of Architecture Education), Ros Croker, Elise Le Clerc, Dimitrios Tourountsis
Design Advocacy: Daisy Froud, Sarah Yates
Art in the Open: Louise Trodden (Head), Rachel Fleming-Mulford
Development: Julie Leonard, Mary Loxley
Assistant to Director: Anna Cassidy
Volunteers – Rosa Appleby Alis, Matt Ayling, Alice Badjan, Helen Baehr, Alasdair Bethley, Katy Binks, Adrianna Carroll-Battaglino, Rosa Couloute, Gregory Cowan, John Cunningham, Mark English, Jo Fells, Jean Fisker, Catherine Foster, Sarah Givans, Bill Green, Joseph Henry, Rob Hurn, Alan Jacobs, Robin Key, Hilary Kidd, Imran Maqbool, Richard Morgan, Bina Naran, Elizabeth Nokes, Gonca Ozer, Richard Purver, Rosemary Read, Alicia Rendle, Leonora Robinson, Stuart Rock, Melissa Smith, Harriet Stone, Miriam Sullivan, Suzanne Tarlin, Paul Thornton, Natalie Traynor, Bonny Tydeman, Louise Yeung, Jessica Yorke

ISBN 978-0-9546902-8-1

Special thanks also to: Greater London Authority, East Potential, Lendlease, Barbican Art Centre, Queen Mary University of London, Design Museum, Golden Lane Campus, 3D Reid, Sheppard Robson, Design London, Whitechapel Gallery, Royal Institution of Great Britain, Allen and Overy, Camden Unlimited, LB Bexley, LB Camden, Imperial College, Gleeds, Jeroboams, Kirin, AHMM Architects, UBS, Ken Allinson, D4 Display, David Littlefield, Hanne Lund, Grant Smith, Morley von Sternberg, Marissa Keating, Ken Worpole, Keith Ashton

£6.50 where sold

OPEN HOUSE LONDON is part of Open House, the architecture education charity.

Registered charity no. 1072104
openhouse.org.uk